# Motivation, Agency, and Public Policy

*Of Knights and Knaves, Pawns and Queens*

JULIAN LE GRAND

 **OXFORD**
UNIVERSITY PRESS

# OXFORD

UNIVERSITY PRESS

Great Clarendon Street, Oxford OX2 6DP

Oxford University Press is a department of the University of Oxford.
It furthers the University's objective of excellence in research, scholarship,
and education by publishing worldwide in

Oxford New York

Auckland Cape Town Dar es Salaam Hong Kong Karachi
Kuala Lumpur Madrid Melbourne Mexico City Nairobi
New Delhi Shanghai Taipei Toronto

With offices in

Argentina Austria Brazil Chile Czech Republic France Greece
Guatemala Hungary Italy Japan Poland Portugal Singapore
South Korea Switzerland Thailand Turkey Ukraine Vietnam

Oxford is a registered trade mark of Oxford University Press
in the UK and in certain other countries

Published in the United States
by Oxford University Press Inc., New York

© Julian Le Grand 2003

The moral rights of the author have been asserted
Database right Oxford University Press (maker)

First published 2003
First published in paperback 2006

British Library Cataloguing in Publication Data

Data available

Library of Congress Cataloging in Publication Data

Data available

Typeset by Newgen Imaging Systems (P) Ltd., Chennai, India
Printed in Great Britain
on acid-free paper by
Biddles Ltd., King's Lynn

ISBN 0–19–926699–9   978–0–19–926699–9
ISBN 0–19–929891–2 (Pbk.)   978–0–19–929891–4 (Pbk.)

1 3 5 7 9 10 8 6 4 2

*For Zoe and Polly*

In contriving any system of government, and fixing the several checks and controls of the constitution, every man ought to be supposed a knave and to have no other end, in all his actions, than private interest. By this interest, we must govern him and, by means of it, notwithstanding his insatiable avarice and ambition, co-operate to the public good.

(David Hume, 'On the Independency of Parliament')

I wouldn't mind being a Pawn, if only I might join—though of course I should *like* to be a Queen best.

(Lewis Carroll, *Alice Through the Looking Glass*)

Fancy what a game of chess would be if all the chessmen had passions and intellects, more or less small and cunning; if you were not only uncertain about your adversary's men, but a little uncertain about your own; if your Knight could shuffle himself on to a new square on the sly; if your bishop in disgust at your Castling, could wheedle your pawns out of their places; and if your pawns, hating you because they are Pawns, could make away from their appointed posts that you might get checkmate on a sudden. You might be the longest-headed of deductive reasoners, and yet you might be beaten by your own Pawns. You would be especially likely to be beaten, if you depended arrogantly on your mathematical imagination, and regarded your passionate pieces with contempt.

(George Eliot, *Felix Holt: The Radical*)

# Preface to Paperback Edition

The first edition of this book was published in September 2003. Two things then happened, one predictable and one less so. The book was picked up and discussed by the quality press, and—somewhat later—in academic journals; and I entered No 10 Downing St on a two-year secondment as a senior policy adviser to the Prime Minister.

The reviews were mostly favourable, some embarrassingly so. A few of the pieces in academic journals took the form of longer review articles, sometimes linking the book to those by other authors, especially Richard Titmuss: one of my predecessors in the chair that I now hold and that is actually named after him. These made serious points about the book's arguments; and the publishers and I considered that they ought to have a wider airing than was possible if they remained within the confines of an academic journal. Accordingly, we have taken the opportunity of the production of a paperback edition of the book to reprint three of the articles here. This has been done with the kind permission of the papers' authors, and the editors and publishers of the journals involved, and we are very grateful to them. I have also added an Afterword that tries to respond to some of the points they make.

My time in Downing St had a rather different impact. The Government of Prime Minister Tony Blair was busy implementing what I have called quasi-market reforms in health, education and social services. I had been intimately involved in formulating the analyses that underlay these reforms, and in initiating and developing some of the specific policy ideas that flowed from them. Even outside the immediate confines of public services, ideas such as the Child Trust Fund to which I had a strong paternity claim were being implemented—in that case by HM Treasury. Basically, as Mathias Risse comments in the review article reprinted here, I was in the unusual position for an academic of having to put my money where my mouth was.

So did this experience of being involved in the actual implementation of 'my' policy ideas actually change my mind about the ideas themselves or, more importantly, about the analyses that underlie them? No, it did not. Indeed, if anything, it reinforced my view that an understanding of the fundamentals concerning the motivation of service professionals and the agency of service users is essential if policy towards public services, and more generally towards the welfare state, is to be properly designed and implemented. It is towards promoting that understanding that this book is addressed: a task that is as important now as it was in 2003.

*London School of Economics*
*March 2006*

# *Preface*

I first encountered the quotation from David Hume with which this book opens when preparing for my inaugural lecture as a newly appointed professor at the London School of Economics. University 'inaugurals' are rather daunting events when new professors deliver a formal lecture to an audience that includes not only their own department's colleagues and students but also staff and students from other parts of the university together with friends and relatives. Most of these know nothing about the area in which the lecturer is working or indeed his or her specialist discipline. So lecturers are supposed to lay out their wares in a non-specialised fashion that both informs and entertains—and that convinces the listeners that the university has made an excellent appointment.

The lecture was somewhat anaemically titled 'New Visions of Welfare', and my preparations for it were not going well. It was supposed to reflect upon the dramatic changes that at the time (the mid-1990s) had just transformed the welfare state. These included the break-up of the old state monopolies providing public services such as health care and education, and their replacement by so-called 'internal' or 'quasi' markets. In those parts of the welfare state concerned with cash benefits, such as social security and income support, there seemed also to be a desire to look outside the old ways of doing things, to question the usefulness of cash benefits as a means of achieving redistribution, and to find different ways of reducing poverty and inequality. It was apparent that all these changes represented some kind of cosmic shift in thinking about public services and the welfare state. But it was far from clear exactly what the nature of this shift was and where it had come from. The welfare state had been in existence for fifty years or so, and, despite numerous political and economic crises during that time, its basic form and structure had remained virtually intact during all that time. What was it that had led to these dramatic changes? Why were policy-makers now engaging in radical reforms? Was there a consistent pattern here, one that might give some insight into what really was going on?

The passage from Hume gave me a clue to part of the puzzle. In it, Hume appears to be recommending that public policy-makers ought to assume that all those involved with governmental organisations were fundamentally self-interested—knaves—and to design policies accordingly. Yet it was apparent from looking at the history of that prime example of a governmental organisation, the welfare state, that the architects who originally designed it had not followed Hume's dictum at all. So far from assuming that everyone was a knave, they seem to have believed that public service professionals and other workers were in fact public-spirited altruists: not knaves but knights. More-over, the people whom the welfare state was supposed to benefit were assumed to be neither knights nor knaves but something closer to pawns: pas-sive recipients of services and benefits, supposed to accept what they were offered by the public service knights without demur.

What seemed to have happened in the 1980s and 1990s was a shift in both these sets of beliefs. Policy-makers now seemed to hold that public sector workers were more like knaves than knights. Moreover, perhaps in part because of subliminal fears of the sort to which the quotation from George Eliot alludes, they believed that the beneficiaries of the welfare state ought to be treated, not like pawns, the least powerful pieces on the chess board, but more like queens, the most powerful. Put another way, there were changes in policy-makers' beliefs about *motivation*—what motivated those working in the public sector—and *agency*—the capacity of individuals, especially the bene-ficiaries of welfare, to engage in independent or autonomous actions. And these changes led to profound shifts in policy-makers' views about the way that pub-lic services in particular and the welfare state in general ought to be designed.

With these insights, I rapidly revamped the lecture; and both it and a sub-sequent article based upon the subject seemed to go over quite well (Le Grand 1997*b*). But I felt unsatisfied. There were many questions left unanswered. These were not so much empirical or historical (what had actually happened?) but normative or policy-oriented (what should have happened, and what should happen now?). Were these changes in beliefs about motivation and agency well-founded? Should service users be pawns or queens? What does actually motivate those who work in the public sector? Are they really simply knights or knaves, or—as seems much more plausible—are they really both, with the balance of motivation depending on the context in which they are exercised? How should policies be designed that make appropriate use of that balance of motivation—and that turn pawns into queens, if that were indeed desirable?

My attempts to answer at least some of these questions have resulted in this book. It should, I hope, be of interest to academics and students in most areas of social science, including economics, public policy, social policy, politics, sociology, social psychology, and political philosophy. However, it should also interest those outside academia concerned about public policy and public services, including politicians, civil servants, public sector professionals, opinion formers in the media and elsewhere, and the interested lay public. To this end it is written in what I hope is a reasonably accessible style. Jargon is rarely used, and explained when it is. There is an annex to Chapter Four that uses demand and supply diagrams to illustrate some of the chapter's argu-ments. But those unfamiliar with graphical techniques need not worry: the arguments are explained verbally in the chapter's main text. References use the author-date abbreviated style, with full details of the reference concerned to be found in the bibliography at the end of the book.

Two points about the metaphor of knights and knaves should be made here. First, the *Shorter Oxford English Dictionary* gives as the main sense of the word 'knave' 'an unprincipled man: a base and crafty rogue'. (Interestingly, it explicitly says that an earlier meaning of the word—a boy or lad employed as a servant—is frequently opposed to knight.) As I explain later, the way I use the term follows David Hume and other political philosophers in having a slightly broader interpretation: as simply one who follows his or her self-interest. Whether the individuals concerned are base or crafty in their pursuit of self-interest is not of direct concern.

The second point concerns gender. 'Knave' and 'knight' sound masculine; not surprisingly, given the *OED* definition above. But, in using them as metaphors, I do not intend to imply that the arguments concerned refer only to men. In fact, as we shall see in Chapter Four, significant gender issues arise in any discussion of altruism versus self-interest. Hence, as used here, each term is supposed to encompass both men and women.

As always in enterprises of this kind, my debts to colleagues, friends, and family are legion. Among colleagues and friends, three stand out. Nicola Lacey read the whole manuscript through several times. Her perspective as an intelligent and perceptive outsider was quite invaluable and made me rethink large parts of the book. Nicholas Barr and Geoffrey Brennan also read the manuscript. Nick Barr made some crucial suggestions concerning a reordering of the material, as well as making very useful detailed points. Geoff Brennan, irritatingly but quite correctly, pointed out a critical theoretical omission in an earlier draft, and suggested that another chapter be written to cover it—which it duly was. I am deeply grateful to all of them.

I am also grateful to Phil Agulnik, Dan Hausman, and David Nissan, each of whom has allowed me to use parts of the works that I originally wrote jointly with them, and from whom I have benefited from many conversations about the material. In addition, I owe particular debts to Howard Glennerster, John Hills, Martin Knapp, Elias Mossialos, Carol Propper, Ray Robinson, and other colleagues at the Economic and Social Research Council's Centre for Analysis of Social Exclusion (CASE) and LSE Health and Social Care, both at the London School of Economics. They have not only provided me with helpful comments, useful references, and psychological support when needed, but have had to put up with hearing endless repeats of, and variations on, metaphors involving knights and knaves, pawns and queens—which they have done with amazing grace.

During part of the period of writing the book, I was a member of the Fabian Society's Commission on Taxation and Citizenship and the Institute of Public Policy Research's Commission on Public/Private Partnerships. This had the cost of delaying the book but the benefit of significantly improving some key parts of it. The hypothecation chapter has particularly benefited from the contributions to the Fabian Commission of its Secretary, Michael Jacobs (who is also the General Secretary of the Fabian Society), and its Chairman, Raymond

Plant. Discussions with other members of the Commission, including Fran Bennett and Nicholas Monk, were also very helpful, although they will not agree with my conclusions. The Fabian Society also kindly gave me permission to reproduce material from a pamphlet of which I was co-author (Nissan and Le Grand 2000). The debates in the IPPR Commission about the provision of public services were also very helpful, discussions with its Secretary, Gavin Kelly, and the Director of IPPR, Matthew Taylor, being especially useful.

I am also very grateful to the following for comments, either on the chapters themselves or on earlier versions of the material in them, and for supplying useful references: Ros Altmann, Kate Baxter, Tessa Crilly, Bleddyn Davies, Alain Enthoven, Bruno Frey, Victor Fuchs, Robert Goodin, Andrew Healey, Gervas Huxley, Iona Heath, Jeremy Kendall, Amanda Killoran, Rudolf Klein, Stephan Leibfried, Penny Leonard, Rodney Lowe, Manos Matsaganis, Susannah Morris, Jenny Roberts, Claire Ungerson, Anne West, and Karen Wright. Financial support came from LSE Health and Social Care, and from the Economic and Social Research Council's grant to CASE under number RES-558-28-5001.

I owe a great deal to my editors at Oxford University Press. Andrew Schuller oversaw the whole process and provided some helpful comments on the text. Matthew Derbyshire looked after the production process and made crucial suggestions concerning presentation. And Michael James's excellent copy-editing saved me from many verbal infelicities and reference errors.

Last, but far from least, I must thank my family. This is not only for their patience in putting up with a book-obsessed husband and father but for the positive help that they have provided. In particular, my daughter Zoe assisted with the references, and her sister Polly helped me sort out the economics behind some of the ideas. So it is not just for the usual reasons that this book is dedicated to them.

Somebody—I believe it was Iris Murdoch, but I have been unable to track down the exact source—once said that you never finish a work of philosophy, only abandon it. As I regularly tell my Ph.D. students, this is a maxim that applies to all academic work, not just to philosophy. And it certainly applies to this book, which, although it has gestated for over six years, I have had to abandon well before it is finished. Some of the issues it addresses are of such a scale that I have had neither the time nor the energy to develop them to the extent that ideally they would need. I can only lay the baton down at this point and hope that some of those reading the book will be motivated to pick it up and take it further.

*Julian Le Grand*
*London School of Economics*
*March 2003*

# Contents

List of Figures                                                                                                xvi

1.  Introduction: Motivation, Agency, and Public Policy                           1

### PART I.   THEORY: OF KNIGHTS AND KNAVES

2.  Knights and Knaves in the Public Sector:
    What Do We Mean and What Do We Know?                                    23

3.  Motivation and the Policy Context                                                        39

4.  A Theory of Public Service Motivation                                                  51

### PART II.   THEORY: OF PAWNS AND QUEENS

5.  Agency and Public Services                                                                   73

6.  Agency and Public Finance                                                                    85

### PART III.   POLICY

7.  Health Care                                                                                            95

8.  School Education                                                                                   107

9.  A Demogrant                                                                                         120

10.  Partnership Savings                                                                              137

11.  Hypothecation                                                                                       147

Epilogue: *Doux Commerce Publique*                                                      163

*Postscript*                                                                                                169
*References*                                                                                               209
*Index*                                                                                                       225

# List of Figures

| | | |
|---|---|---:|
| 1.1 | Motivation, agency, and ideology | 16 |
| 4.1 | Knavish supply | 68 |
| 4.2 | Knightly supply | 68 |
| 4.3 | Knightly supply and low demand | 69 |
| 4.4 | Knightly supply and high demand | 69 |
| 4.5 | Knightly supply and moderate demand | 70 |
| 4.6 | Knightly and knavish supply and demand | 70 |

# 1

# Introduction: Motivation, Agency, and Public Policy

It is not from the benevolence of the butcher, the brewer or the baker that we expect our dinner but their regard to their own interest. We address ourselves not to their humanity but to their self-love, and never talk to them of our own necessities but of their advantages.

(Adam Smith, *The Wealth of Nations*)

The private market . . . narrows the choices for all men—whatever freedom it may bestow, for a time, on some men to live as they like. It is the responsibility of the state, acting sometimes through the processes we call 'social policy', to reduce or eliminate or control the forces of market coercions which place men in situations in which they have less freedom or little freedom to make moral choices, and to behave altruistically if they so will.

(Richard Titmuss, *The Gift Relationship*)

Should we leave the education of our children to the professionals on the grounds that teacher knows best? When ill, should we be patient and simply trust the doctor to make us well again? Should we have the right to choose the hospital where our illness is to be treated, or to choose the school where our children are educated? Or would such choice lead to destructive competition between schools and hospitals, competition that would damage not only the people making the choices but also those who work within those institutions and indeed the wider social interest? Would greater patient or parental power undermine professional and other forms of altruistic motivation? More generally, would empowering the users of public services destroy the so-called public service ethos, and would society be both materially and morally impoverished as a result?

Resolving these questions for public services such as health care or education is of crucial importance. But similar issues arise elsewhere in that collection of public policies often termed the welfare state, including those that more directly concern our personal incomes and expenditures. Should government compel us to save more in order to pay for our pensions? Should we be required to take out insurance against the possibility that we might need long-term care?

Or are there other ways in which savings might be encouraged? Is the best way to promote equality of opportunity for young adults through higher education, or should there be publicly funded schemes, such as stakeholder or capital grants to young people, that offer a wider range of choices? More generally, should we trust government to spend wisely on our behalf, or should we have a greater say over how our tax moneys are spent?

It is to these questions that this book is addressed. In fact, they are all among even broader issues concerning the design of public policy, issues that form the underlying theme of the book. These concern the roles of *motivation* and *agency*. Assumptions concerning human motivation—the internal desires or preferences that incite action—and agency—the capacity to undertake that action—are key to both the design and the implementation of public policy. Policy-makers fashion their policies on the assumption that both those who implement the policies and those who are expected to benefit from them will behave in certain ways, and that they will do so because they have certain kinds of motivation and certain levels of agency. Sometimes the assumptions concerning motivation and agency are explicit; more often they are implicit, reflecting the unconscious values or unarticulated beliefs of the policy-makers concerned.

Conscious or not, the assumptions will determine the way that public policies are constructed. So, for instance, a policy instrument designed on the assumption that people are motivated primarily by their own self-interest— that they are, in the words of David Hume quoted at the beginning of this book, *knaves*—would be quite different from one constructed on the assumption that people are predominantly public-spirited or altruistic: that they are what we might term, in contrast to knaves, *knights*. Similarly, a policy that took no account of individuals' capacity for independent action—one that treated those working in the public sector or those who received its benefits as passive victims of circumstance, or *pawns*—would be different from one that treated workers or recipients as active agents, that is, not as the least powerful piece on the chess board, the pawn, but as the most powerful, the *queen*.

These assumptions—or, more precisely, the relationship between the assumptions and the realities of human motivation and agency—are crucial to the success or otherwise of public policy. Policies designed on the assumption that those who work in the public sector are basically knights are likely to have disastrous consequences if in fact most of those individuals are predominantly knaves. But the same may be true for policies fashioned on the basis of a belief that people are knaves if the consequence is to suppress their natural altruistic impulses and hence destroy part of their motivation to provide a quality public service. Similarly, policies that, consciously or unconsciously, treat people as pawns, may lead to demotivated workers and disgruntled beneficiaries, again causing adverse outcomes for the policies concerned; while policies that give too much power to either workers or beneficiaries may result in individuals making mistakes that damage their own or others' welfare.

I return to these conceptual distinctions at the end of the chapter. There too I shall provide a road map for the rest of the book so as to guide the reader through its principal arguments. But first I want to illustrate the importance of beliefs about human motivation and agency in policy design by providing a concrete example. This is one of the most important developments in the welfare states of Britain and several other countries to have taken place since their inception: what might be termed the 'quasi-market revolution' in public service delivery. As will be explained, this was a shift from an essentially statist method of providing key public services such as health care and education to a more market-oriented method of service delivery: a dramatic policy change and one from which there are many lessons for policy design to be learned. Moreover, since most public services are still struggling with the legacy of that revolution, it is also one of direct relevance to current questions concerning policy reform—including those in the opening paragraphs of this chapter.

## POLICY ASSUMPTIONS AND THE WELFARE STATE

In most countries, the state has historically played a major role in both the finance and the delivery of social services such as education, health care, housing, and social care. Often this role has taken the form of some kind of state bureaucracy actually providing the service, while simultaneously using state revenues to subsidise it such that it is free (or offered at highly subsidised prices) at the point of use. Thus in many countries governments—central, State, or local—run schools and colleges, usually providing school education free and college education either free or at a fee well below cost. Governments of countries with national health systems own and operate the principal medical facilities, and supply the health care offered by those facilities free or with low co-payments. Many governments also both finance and provide other social services, such as long-term care for elderly people, care for those with a physical or mental disability, and public housing for the less well-off.

During the 1980s and the early 1990s, there was something of a revolution in this kind of social policy. In several countries where a combination of state provision and state finance had been the norm, the state, while retaining control of finance, began to pull back from provision. Instead of providing the service through monolithic state bureaucracies, provision became competitive with independent providers competing for custom in market or 'quasi-market' settings.[1] These reforms were always controversial and in some countries there have been attempts to reverse them subsequently, although often more at the level of rhetoric than in reality.

---

[1] 'Quasi-markets' because, although they were markets in the sense that they involved competition, they differed from normal markets in a number of ways. On the demand side, the state not the consumer provided the finance, usually appointing a purchasing agent to act on behalf of the consumer; and on the supply side non-profit or even publicly owned agencies competed for custom instead of, or as well as, for-profit ones. See Le Grand and Bartlett (1993: 10).

The growth of these quasi-markets had a number of causes. A major factor was fiscal pressure leading governments to search for new ways of using increasingly scarce resources more efficiently.[2] However, underlying the whole movement was a fundamental shift in policy-makers' perceptions concerning motivation and agency. This I shall illustrate using the British case as a prime example, but referring to other countries as appropriate.

### Knights Rampant: The British Welfare State 1945–1979

The mood of Britain immediately after the Second World War has rightly been regarded as a triumph of collectivism. The fact that the country had not only survived the war but had emerged on the winning side was widely ascribed to a spirit of national unity and selfless dedication to the common cause. As the historian Peter Hennessy (1992: 44) has noted, there was a 'widespread, if not wholesale, usurpation of individual greed by collective good'. He quotes a senior civil servant saying, 'It seems to me that the most remarkable of the many remarkable things about the Second World War is that it really was our "Finest Hour". There were, of course, some who were "private-spirited" . . . but they were never a large number . . . There was a sense of comradeship that spread right across the old class distinctions.'[3]

This spirit, of the importance of collective endeavour and the relative insignificance of individual self-interest, profoundly affected the shape of the post-war welfare state. As Corelli Barnett (1986: 11) put it in his anti-welfare-state polemic *The Audit of War*, as far back as 1940–1, 'members of the British cultural elite had begun to busy themselves with design studies for a "New Jerusalem" to be built in Britain after the war was won. Selfish greed, the moral legacy of Victorian capitalism would give way to Christian community, motivating men to work hard for the good of all.'

In fact, the social historian Rodney Lowe has argued that two types of collectivist approaches characterised the post-war welfare state.[4] There were the reluctant collectivists, pre-eminent among whom were William Beveridge and John Maynard Keynes. And then there were the more full-blooded collectivists or democratic socialists, as Lowe terms them, who included T. H. Marshall, Richard Titmuss, and Anthony Crosland. Of these, Lowe says, 'despite the predominant influence of Beveridge and Keynes in the early post-war years, it was the democratic socialists which gave the British welfare state its unique international reputation. At home these ideals also infused the

---

[2] See Glennerster and Le Grand (1995) for further discussion of this point.

[3] Dame Alix Meynell, senior civil servant, Board of Trade 1925–55, quoted in Hennessy (1992: 38).

[4] Amateur historians of British post-war social policy such as myself are fortunate that three excellent histories of the welfare state since 1945 have been published in the past decade—by Rodney Lowe (1993), Howard Glennerster (1995), and Nicholas Timmins (1995)—as has a third edition of Rudolf Klein's (1995) superb study of the development of the National Health Service. What follows draws heavily on all four.

welfare legislation of the 1945–51 Labour governments and provided the logic for further advances which the Conservative ministers struggled to refute.' And, Lowe argues, at the end of the day it was the social democratic approach, albeit tempered by that of the reluctant collectivists, which determined the evolution of the post-war welfare state: for 'social democracy had history on its side' (Lowe 1993: 18–20).

What then were the assumptions concerning human motivation and agency implicit in the social democratic welfare state? In answering this question, it is useful to distinguish three sets of actors. First, there were those who devised the welfare state and worked within it: the politicians and civil servants who devised its policies, the managers who administered it, and the professionals and others who delivered its services. Second, there were those who paid for welfare under the fiscal system: taxpayers. Third, there were those who received the benefits of the welfare state: social security recipients, doctors' patients, school pupils and their parents, council house tenants, and so on.

Taking up the collectivist legacy of the Second World War, and following ideas of the public service ethos developed in the late nineteenth and early twentieth centuries by thinkers such as Jowett, Toynbee, Tawney, and Temple,[5] the democratic socialists assumed that the state and its agents were both competent and benevolent (Lowe 1993: 23). It followed that the first group—those who operated the welfare state—could be trusted to work primarily in the public interest: they were knights, not knaves (Donnison 1982: 20–1). Professionals, such as doctors and teachers, were assumed to be motivated primarily by their professional ethic and hence to be concerned only with the interests of the people they were serving.[6] Similarly, politicians, civil servants, state bureaucrats, and managers were supposed accurately to divine social and individual needs in the areas concerned, to be motivated to meet those needs and hence to operate services that did the best possible job from the resources that were available.

The second group—the taxpayers—were also assumed to be at least partly knightly in their willingness to pay taxes. Part of the collective view that 'social justice would be guaranteed by a predominant altruism' (Lowe 1993: 19), they were supposed to accept a 'growing burden of progressive taxes . . . required

---

[5] Ideas that were in fact themselves rooted in Plato and Hegel. See Raymond Plant's (2001) illuminating paper on the public service ethic.

[6] It is useful here to follow Klein (1995: 243) and distinguish between attitudes towards professionals as individuals and professionals as a collectivity. Few of the politicians who had dealings with the collective organs of the medical profession, such as the British Medical Association, would have regarded them public spirited altruists: indeed, in all probability they would have agreed with Enoch Powell (1976: 14) when he wrote 'the unnerving discovery every Minister of Health makes at or near the outset of his term of office is that the only subject he is ever destined to discuss with the medical profession is money'. However, at the individual level the assumptions were different. For built into the concordat that provided the foundations of the NHS was the assumption of clinical freedom or autonomy whereby individual doctors could exercise their professional discretion in the way they used public resources (Klein 1995: 243).

to finance social services' (Donnison 1982: 20–1; see also Reisman 1977: 91). More specifically, it was assumed that the better-off would not only cooperate in collectivist enterprises such as national insurance and social services out of enlightened self-interest, but also willingly acquiesce in the payment of re-distributive taxation that helped the disadvantaged, either because they empathised with the latter's plight or because they saw it as part of their civic responsibility to do so.

The democratic socialists did not assume that the third group—individuals in receipt of the benefits of the welfare state—were active altruists or indeed active egoists. Rather they were considered to be essentially passive: pawns. Those who used social services were supposed to be content with a universal, often fairly basic, standard of service. So one of the principal ideological sup-porters of the welfare state, the London School of Economics academic Richard Titmuss, spoke of the desirability of 'one publicly approved standard of service' (Titmuss 1968: 195). In practice, with respect to the National Health Service for instance, this meant that patients were supposed to live up to their appellation and be patient. They were to wait patiently in queues at general practitioners' surgeries or at outpatient clinics; if they needed further treat-ment they had to be prepared to wait their turn on hospital waiting lists. When the time arrived for them actually to go to hospital, they were supposed cheerfully to accept being on a public ward, being served horrible food and, most significantly, being treated by doctors too busy, or too elevated, to have time to explain what was happening to them. As Rudolf Klein has put it, in the early model of the National Health Service (NHS), 'it would be the doctor's judgement which would determine who should get what . . . It was the experts who would determine the need for health care, frame the appropriate priorities and implement their policies universalistically throughout the NHS' (Klein 1995: 248; see also Glennerster 1995: 69).

Similarly, the parents of children in state schools were expected to trust the professionals and to accept that teachers knew what was best for their chil-dren. The period between 1944 and 1975 has been identified as the 'golden age of teacher control'.[7] Moreover, as with the NHS, especially following the comprehensive reforms of the mid-1960s, parents were supposed to concur that 'the overriding objective in [education policy] was equality' (Lowe 1993: 203) and hence to accept whatever degree of uniformity of educational provi-sion that attaining this objective required.

In housing, council house tenants were expected to be grateful for the privilege they had been accorded in being granted a tenancy (Dunleavy 1981: 28–33). Their accommodation was standardised, with heavy restrictions

---

[7] Chitty (1988), quoted in Lowe (1993: 227). This was not just because it was assumed that teach-ers knew best; there was also a fear of malign government influence. Nicholas Timmins (1995: 323) quotes the General Secretary of the National Union of Teachers arguing in 1954 that democracy was best safeguarded by 'the existence of a quarter of a million teachers who are free to decide what should be taught and how it should be taught'.

on their freedom of action over what could be done with it.[8] And again the experts were presumed to know best about the housing that people wanted.[9]

Similar views characterised the beliefs of at least some of the democratic socialists about social security recipients. As Alan Deacon (1993) has argued, Richard Titmuss, for instance, assumed that the beneficiaries of social security had very little choice at all; that the economic and social system was so all-powerful that they were simply its victims; that they had no freedom of action and hence were simply passive recipients of state largesse.[10]

However, it has to be acknowledged that this view does not seem to characterise the actual delivery of social security policy. The post-war history of this policy (and indeed its entire history) is peppered with the development of different forms of checks and balances to control the perceived problem of the people variously termed the work-shy, loafers, or scroungers (Deacon 1976; Bryson and Jacobs 1992; Jacobs 1994). Here there seems to have been a constant tension between the assumption that welfare recipients were basically passive—pawns—and the assumption that they had some capacity for agency and hence responded (in an essentially knavish) fashion to the incentives with which they were faced.

Social security, therefore, is perhaps a partial exception. But it is not implausible to describe the bundle of implicit assumptions concerning human behaviour that characterised the rest of the democratic socialist welfare state as one designed to be financed and operated by knights for the benefit of pawns.

### The Triumph of the Knaves: The British Welfare State After 1979

For much of the period following the Second World War, the democratic socialist welfare state reigned largely unchallenged. But, partly because of the fiscal crises of the early 1970s, in the latter part of that decade and in the 1980s there were serious assaults on almost all the assumptions that underpinned it, especially those concerned with motivation and agency.[11] The notion that, for the sake of the collectivity, everyone would passively accept standardised, relatively low levels of services was challenged by studies showing that in key areas of welfare the middle classes extracted at least as much as if not more

---

[8] See Anthony Crosland who, writing in the *Guardian* in 1971, said that the Council 'decides what repairs are to be done, what pets may be kept, what colour the doors will be painted, what play areas there should be, where a fence should be put up. The tenant is not consulted. He has no right of appeal.' Quoted in Timmins (1995: 366).

[9] Power (1993), especially chapter 19. Timmins (1995: 186) too illustrates the point with the story of Nicholas Taylor, an assistant editor at the *Architectural Review*. He 'proposed that some evidence should be sought on what people actually wanted, to go with an issue "on the best of current housing". He was scornfully dismissed by the proprietor with the words: "But we KNOW what should be done!".'

[10] Deacon (1993). For more on Titmuss's assumptions concerning motivation and behaviour, see Reisman (1977), including the preface by Robert Pinker.

[11] Glennerster (1995: 193–5); Lowe (1993: 23–7); Timmins (1995: Part V).

than the poor in terms of both the quantity and the quality of service (Le Grand 1982). More generally, it became increasingly apparent that many people—particularly, but not exclusively, the middle classes—wanted different kinds and different levels of service. Richard Titmuss (1974: 151) himself may have enjoyed being in a public ward; but many people did not. The length of waiting lists for medical treatment became a perennial political issue. Many of the better-off put their children in private schools and took out private health insurance; many more subscribed to private pensions. The consensus supporting comprehensive education began to break down, with influential voices encouraging an end to teacher control over the curriculum, a return to selection, traditional teaching methods, and a focus on excellence (Timmins 1995: 318–29). As council estates declined and tenants felt increasingly powerless, owner-occupation became overwhelmingly the preferred form of housing tenure.[12]

The assumption that knightly behaviour characterised those who worked within the institutions of the welfare state proved even more vulnerable. Fuelled in part by people's experience both of dealing with and of working within the welfare bureaucracies, many politicians and policy analysts grew increasingly sceptical of the view that bureaucrats and civil servants necessarily operated in the public interest, and that professionals were only concerned with the welfare of their clients (Glennerster 1995: 193). Instead there was an increasing acceptance of the argument of the public choice school of economists and political scientists that the behaviour of public officials and professionals could be better understood if they were assumed to be largely self-interested.[13]

The idea that knightly behaviour characterises those who pay for welfare was also challenged. Political scientists and theorists Robert Goodin and John Dryzek (Goodin and Dryzek 1987) and, more comprehensively, social historian Peter Baldwin (1990) argued that the growth of welfare states funded by taxation or social insurance in a wide variety of developed countries was not the outcome of altruistic gestures by the better-off; rather it was directly related to the self-interest of the middle classes. Econometric studies by economists and sociologists came to similar conclusions (Peltzman 1980; Pampel and Williamson 1989). A more micro-level study undertaken by David Winter and myself of changes in public expenditure and tax relief under the first Thatcher administration, based on the assumption that politicians were vote-maximising, found a pattern of change that unequivocally favoured the better-off (Le Grand and Winter 1987).

Taxpayer resistance to redistributive welfare became an accepted political fact on the left as well as the right. For instance, social policy analyst David Piachaud (1993: 3) argued in a Fabian pamphlet that 'there is now virtually no

---

[12]  Power (1993: 211–16). Tax incentives were also an important factor in the growth of owner-occupation; but the fact that these incentives were in place is itself an indication of the importance the political system attached to owner-occupation.

[13]  Plant (2001: 9–10); Lowe (1993: 22–3). For a useful review of public choice theory see Mueller (1989).

likelihood of further substantial redistribution of income through taxes and social security benefits'; a judgement he based not on technical impossibility or social undesirability but on political infeasibility. Frank Field (1995: 1–2), later to become briefly a Labour minister, went further, claiming that politicians who argue that the middle class will support redistribution to the poor are a 'public menace, distracting from the real task'.

The election of Mrs Thatcher's neo-liberal Conservative government in 1979 in Britain epitomised these changes in belief. The new government viewed the public sector in general, and public-sector professionals in particular, with great suspicion. It considered professionals and other workers in the public sector to be much more in the business of pursuing their own concerns than in pursuing the public interest: more knaves than knights. Moreover, because of the state monopoly in provision of social services, these knaves were able to exploit their monopoly position and treat the users of services as pawns. If users were dissatisfied with the service they received they had nowhere else to go; hence they could be treated as passive recipients with relative impunity. In the view of the new government, this situation was fundamentally undesirable: users ought to be queens or, to take a similar but more familiar metaphor, the consumer should be king.

Fundamentally, there were two changes in belief here. One was essentially empirical: a change in belief about the way the world worked, in particular about what actually motivated individuals, especially those who worked within the public sector. The other involved a shift in values: users of services ought not to be treated as passive recipients of welfare largesse but should have the lead role in determining the quantity and quality of the services they received.

These changes had a direct consequence for the view about the way in which public services ought to be delivered. As we shall discuss in more detail later, if it is believed that workers are primarily knaves and that consumers ought to be king, then the most obvious mechanism of service delivery is the market. For the market is the way in which the pursuit of self-interest by providers can be corralled to serve the interests of consumers. So the Thatcher government's instinct was to try to deal with what it perceived to be the major problems in the welfare state by injecting market mechanisms in one form or another into the delivery of public services.

Although that government flirted briefly with full privatisation of public services, it rapidly realised that there were both political and economic reasons why that would not be possible in the British context. These included the adverse consequences of private markets for equity: no British government could allow the distribution of, for instance, education and health to be left to be determined by the distribution of income. The government also became aware of economists' arguments concerning market failure in this area, especially those that derived from poor information on the part of users and the opportunities that this gave knavish providers to exploit their knowledge monopoly (Lawson 1992: 615).

Hence the chosen mechanism was the 'quasi-market'. In such a market the state retains control of financing the service. This divorces the distribution of the service concerned from the distribution of income and thus contributes to a more egalitarian distribution of the service. However, instead of also providing the service concerned, the state allows provision to be undertaken by independent providers competing with one another for custom. The state gives potential users a voucher to purchase the service concerned; alternatively, to overcome the problem of poor information for users, it appoints and funds an informed purchasing agent of some kind to purchase the service on behalf of the user.

Although they all had this basic structure, the quasi-markets actually put in place by the government took slightly different forms in different sectors. So the National Health Service had two kinds of state-funded purchasers: health authorities, which purchased on behalf of geographical districts, and GP fund-holders or primary-care practitioners who purchased secondary care on behalf of the patients on their lists. Providers were semi-independent non-profit units that provided hospital and other services.

In education, what was effectively a voucher scheme was set up. Parents were given free choice of school; schools were given budgetary independence and encouraged to compete for pupils through a funding formula that was based on the number of pupils they managed to attract. In social care, social workers were appointed as 'case-managers' and given a budget to purchase care on behalf of their clients from private, non-profit, or public providers. In housing, public housing tenants were given the option of changing their landlord to a non-profit housing association; they and private tenants were also eligible for a means-tested benefit to pay their rent: again, effectively a voucher.

These kinds of change were not unique to Britain. Mrs Thatcher's government was indeed an active agent in the process, but the shifts in attitude the changes represented were part of a much wider, more global movement. Fuelled by fiscal crises, disenchantment with large state bureaucracies and with their perceived inefficiency and unresponsiveness, and increasingly influenced by the public choice school of economists, many countries experimented with market or quasi-market mechanisms for delivering social services. Sweden introduced a quasi-market in health care in the Stockholm region, and the Netherlands planned a competitive scheme for public health insurers. Belgium has had a quasi-market in education for many years. Cleveland and Milwaukee and the State of Florida in the United States introduced fully-fledged voucher schemes in education. Many states in the US are introducing so-called charter schools: independent schools that receive a 'charter' from a state agency and, as in the British system, are funded on a per-pupil basis and so have to compete for pupils for economic survival.

New Zealand took some of the ideas even further. Health services were split into purchaser and provider in a similar fashion to the British and competition between providers encouraged. The providers became separate state-owned enterprises and were required to operate as efficient businesses while exhibiting a sense of social responsibility. In education, operating responsibility for schools was transferred from the Department of Education to each school's board of trustees and full parental choice of schools was introduced, setting up a quasi-market for the state system.

So the shifts in governmental beliefs and attitudes described here were not peculiar to Britain but were worldwide. Moreover, despite changes of government, they endure. To return to the British case, the Labour government of Tony Blair that replaced the Conservative administration in 1997 has espoused many of the same values as its predecessor, especially with respect to the importance of having a responsive system for users and, with one partial exception, has done little to reverse the quasi-market changes that the Conservatives introduced.

The partial exception concerns the National Health Service, where the quasi-market was allegedly abolished in 1997. However, even then key elements of the market remained, at least in England, including the purchaser–provider split, the possibility that purchasers could shift their purchasing between competing providers, and secondary-care purchasing being undertaken by primary-care organisations. More recent policy developments have heralded a shift back to other aspects of the internal market, including the use of private providers, financial flows based on prices, the setting up of independent 'foundation hospitals', and the re-introduction of competition for elective surgery (UK Department of Health 2002; Lewis 2002; Le Grand 2002).

## IDEOLOGY AND BELIEFS

This brief review of recent history suggests that there were at least two major ideological forces that have influenced the design of public policy, especially in the context of the British welfare state: what we might term social democracy and neo-liberalism.[14] These ideologies differed in their attachment to both ends and means. So far as ends are concerned, social democrats prioritised social justice and other egalitarian objectives, while neo-liberals emphasised the importance of individual liberty and freedom. And with respect to means, neo-liberals advocated the operations of the competitive market; social democrats relied upon the benign intervention of the state.

Now the differences between neo-liberals' and social democrats' views about means, and in particular about the respective roles of the market and the state, arose in part because of the differences between their views about ends. Neo-liberals viewed the state as the principal threat to individual liberty; hence they were deeply suspicious of any extension of state power even when

---

[14] Not everyone will agree with the way in which I use these labels. However, it is hoped that the rather stylised set of pictures that are painted here have enough accuracy so as not seriously to distort the scenes that they are trying to represent, however they are labelled.

it was apparently relatively benign. Social democrats, on the other hand, were appalled by the inegalitarian consequences of market outcomes, outcomes that they regarded as fundamentally unjust. Hence they were reluctant to rely on market mechanisms to allocate resources. This was especially so in areas that social democrats regarded as fundamental to social welfare, such as health and education, where they generally preferred to suspend the market completely.

However, their differences over means did not stem only from different views about ends. For even where they agreed on a social objective, such as the general importance of improving average levels of education and heath care, they still differed over the relative merits of the market and the state as a means of achieving those ends. And, as our example of the recent history of the welfare state has illustrated, this in turn arose from another fundamental divergence: their different beliefs about motivation and agency.

First, motivation. Neo-liberals believed, and indeed still believe, that all human beings are fundamentally self-interested. For them, the safest assumption to make when constructing government institutions and formulating government policy is David Hume's maxim that everyone is a knave.[15] Inevitably, therefore, they endorse the competitive market as the principal means for organising economic and social production; for, as we know from the works of David Hume's near contemporary, Adam Smith, the market is the method by which self-interest can be harnessed to serve the common good. Economic agents operating in a competitive market will find it in their self-interest to provide goods and services of high quality and at low prices; for, if they do not, they will lose business and therefore income and ultimately their livelihood. As Smith put it in the well-known passage from *The Wealth of Nations*:

He, generally, indeed, neither intends to promote the public interest, nor knows how much he is promoting it . . . he intends only his own gain, and he is in this . . . led by an invisible hand to promote an end which was not part of his intention. Nor is it always the worse for society that it was no part of it. By pursuing his own interest he frequently promotes that of society more effectively than when he really intends to promote it.[16]

---

[15]  In fact it was the philosopher and satirist Bernard Mandeville (1731: 332) who was the first to draw attention to the necessity of designing policies that 'remain unshaken though most men should prove knaves'. Mandeville was actually less cautious than Hume, although Hume is the one usually quoted in this context. For Hume (1875: 117–18) went on to muse that it 'appears somewhat strange that a maxim should be true in *politics* which is false in *fact*'. Hume's view is extended by James Madison (Hamilton, Madison, and Jay 1970: Nos. 10 and 51), and in recent years it has been defended at length by James Buchanan (1987). See also Brennan and Buchanan (1985: 45–61).

[16]  Smith (1776/1964: Book IV, ch. II, p. 400). Adam Smith himself would not necessarily have endorsed the self-interest view of human motivation. In fact one of his earlier works, *The Theory of Moral Sentiments* (Smith 1759/1976), shows a more complex understanding of human nature; see for instance the quotation at the beginning of Chapter Two of this book. Falkner (1997) has a more detailed discussion of Smith's views.

Not only does their belief about the fundamental self-centredness of human nature lead neo-liberals to endorse the competitive market, it fuels a parallel distrust of collective institutions, including—indeed especially—those of government. For, if the pursuit of self-interest promotes the common good in a market context, it is highly destructive in a collective one. In an environment where production is organised collectively, selfish individuals will try to 'free-ride' on the activities of others. That is, they will sit back and wait until others do all the hard work of production and only then come forward to consume its fruits. If everyone behaves this way—and, by assumption, everyone will, because they are all equally self-interested—then nothing will be produced; or, at best, only things that can be of direct benefit to the producer himself or herself will be produced.

The nursery story *The Little Red Hen* provides the perfect neo-liberal parable about the evils of collectivism. In the story the eponymous hen asks all the farmyard animals in turn whether they will help her bake a cake. In turn each of them refuses, pleading tiredness or other commitments. So she bakes the cake herself, and then asks the other animals if they will help her eat it. They all rush eagerly to the table, casting aside their alleged fatigue and salivating in eager anticipation. But she then refuses to give them any, saying she will eat it entirely by herself. And she does.

Many of those on the left, from socialists to social democrats, have a greater faith in human (and perhaps even farmyard animal) public-spiritedness. They would argue that individuals have a greater capacity than is acknowledged by neo-liberals for acting in ways that further others' interests as well as, or indeed even instead of, their own: that they can act as 'knights' as well as knaves. Hence collective, or more generally non-market, institutions can work. Moreover, in many circumstances, especially those associated with poor information or where social benefits and costs exceed private ones, collaboration will out-perform competition.

Indeed, for the social democrat it is not government that is to be distrusted, it is the market. For the market can be socially destructive, 'narrowing the choices for all men' as Richard Titmuss argued in the quotation at the head of this chapter. He went on: 'If it is accepted that man has a sociological and biological need to help then to deny him opportunities to express this need is to deny him the freedom to enter into gift relationships' (Titmuss 1970/1997: 310–11).

So their different views as to what motivates human beings—altruism or egoism—lead neo-liberals and social democrats to opposing views about the respective roles of the market and the state. But it is not only with respect to beliefs about motivation that the two ideologies of social democracy and neo-liberalism differ. There is also a divide concerning beliefs about agency: that is, about human beings' capacity for autonomous action. And this divide also contributes to their views about the appropriate use of market and state forms of resource allocation.

On much of the social democratic left it is believed that individuals are largely or wholly the product of their environment; indeed even the individual as a concept is a social construct. Hence individual behaviour is best understood by focusing on the constraints under which individuals operate; in consequence, policy should focus on these. So the poor, for instance, are viewed as victims of the system: 'pawns' at the mercy of structural forces over which they have no control.

That the social democrats tended to regard individuals as inactive victims is a point well made by Alan Deacon and Kirk Mann (1999: 417), who point out its relevance to academic debates concerning public and specifically social policy: 'It is important to stress that the question of agency was not merely neglected in academic studies of social policy, but was consciously dismissed. For much of the post-war period it was not considered to be a proper subject for concern and enquiry.'[17]

They ascribed the predominance of this attitude to, again, Richard Titmuss. Reacting in part to the judgemental individualism that characterised much nineteenth-century policy towards the poor, Titmuss and his followers did not believe that the autonomous behaviour of individuals was relevant to social policy. As Deacon and Mann (1999: 418) put it: 'Above all [Titmuss] was resolutely opposed to anything that might appear to reopen the debate about personal responsibility for social pathology. Arguments about problem families or cycles of deprivation were an irrelevance or worse. Anyone who either could not or would not understand that was simply beyond the pale.'

Although rather more difficult to document, there also seems to have been an implicit belief on much of the social democratic left that, when recipients of public services or social security were not acting as pawns (that is, not acting at all), they would behave more like knights than knaves. So, if individuals or families were confronted with an incentive structure such as a means test that it would be in their self-interest to evade or avoid, they simply would not do so—even if they had the capacity and there was little risk of their getting caught. The belief in the essential goodness of human nature that characterised social democratic views of those who worked in the public sector carried over in large part to their views about the beneficiaries of the welfare state.

In contrast, policy analysts further to the right viewed individuals not as victims of unavoidable circumstance but as autonomous beings who did have a measure of control over, and responsibility for, their own lives. In other words, they were not pawns but queens.[18] Such neo-liberal thinkers strongly rejected the determinism of the left. Thus Deacon and Mann quoted Lawrence Mead (1992: 129–30) castigating what he terms 'sociologism', which 'construes the personality as essentially passive' and where

The poor are seen as inert, not active. They are spoken of in the passive voice. They are people who are or have been disadvantaged in multiple ways. They do not do things

---

[17]  See also Deacon (1993) and Williams (1999).

[18]  Williams (1999: 669) uses the terms 'active welfare subject' and 'passive welfare subject' to make the same distinction.

but rather have things done to them. They are the objects, not the subjects of action. They are not to blame for conditions such as dropping out of school, AIDS, or drug addiction but rather 'at risk' for them. They 'experience' behaviours such as crime or illegitimacy rather than commit them.

It is important to note that this belief in the autonomy of the individual appeared to be both empirical (individuals, even poor ones, in reality *do* have choices) and normative (individuals *should* have choices and should be held responsible for the choices they make). So policy-makers should not treat the people their policies are trying to help as pawns. This was partly because that would be empirically incorrect (welfare recipients are not pawns, but active agents who respond to incentive structures, probably in a self-interested way) and may lead to the policies concerned having perverse consequences. But it was also because it was the morally incorrect thing to do. It is simply wrong to treat people like pawns.

It is worth noting that, in the latter part of the period we reviewed above, there were several attempts to reconcile social democratic and neo-liberal views of the world, or even to replace them altogether by attempting to construct viable alternatives. One of these was market socialism: economic and social policies designed to achieve social democratic ends, such as greater equality and social justice, by neo-liberal means, such as a greater reliance on the market (Le Grand and Estrin 1989). Although the market socialists' beliefs about agency and motivation were not made explicit, the emphasis was on the effectiveness of market mechanisms and the relative failure of collectivist ones even to achieve social democratic ends. And this in turn derived in large part from a view of the world that incorporated the key actors as both self-interested and active agents.

More recently, there was an attempt to construct an ideological foundation for the centre-left governments of Tony Blair in the United Kingdom and Bill Clinton in the United States: a foundation that was to be neither neo-liberal nor social democratic (at least as the latter was conventionally understood). As part of this attempt, the sociologist and then Director of the London School of Economics, Anthony Giddens, and others developed the so-called third way. This had a number of differences from both social democracy and neo-liberalism with respect to the ends that it set out to achieve.[19] The beliefs about means were less clear; hence it is more difficult to infer the implicit views about agency and motivation. But, as with market socialism, these seemed to be nearer the neo-liberal position than the social democratic one. The welfare state was described as an instrument not for redistribution but for 'pooling risk', and relabelled the 'social investment state' whereby the incentives were for the individual to build up the stock of human capital and to develop their capacity for entrepreneurial

---

[19]  I have argued that the ends that seemed to be implicit in the Blair Government's interpretation of the third way included commitments to community, opportunity, responsibility, and accountability (Le Grand 1998). Giddens has a slightly different list (1998: 66).

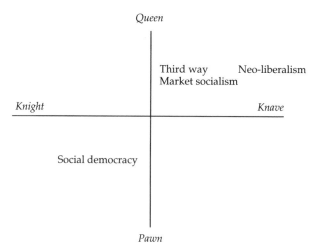

**Figure 1.1.** *Motivation, agency, and ideology*

activity and risk-taking (Giddens 1998: 116–18). And, although there was advocacy of community organisations, the voluntary sector, and the re-invigoration of civil society, there was also an explicit recognition of the overall desirability of markets, albeit social ones (Giddens 1998: 99–100).

## AXES OF MOTIVATION AND AGENCY

It may be helpful to summarise some of these arguments in Fig. 1.1. This has two axes at right angles to one another. The horizontal axis represents the spectrum of views about what motivates human beings, from extreme altruism (the pure knight) on the far left to pure self-interest (the complete knave) on the far right.[20] The vertical axis refers to the spectrum of human agency, from passive individual (pawn) at the bottom to active, autonomous agent (queen) at the top. The axes bound four quadrants, knight/pawn, knight/queen, knave/pawn, knave/queen. The axes can refer to those who work within the public sector, or to recipients of public services, or both.

The changes in policy-makers' beliefs that we have been discussing can be illustrated in the figure. Suppose the horizontal axis refers to policy-makers' beliefs concerning the motivations of those who work in the public sector, and the vertical one to their beliefs concerning the capacity for agency of the recipients of public sector services. Then policy-makers established in the social democratic tradition are located in the bottom left-hand quadrant (knight/pawn).

---

[20]  For the record, I should note that, in the article based on my inaugural lecture that introduced the terminology of knights, knaves, and pawns, I suggested that being a pawn was in contrast to being a knight or a knave (Le Grand 1997b). However, I now think that was incorrect. The true opposite of being a pawn is being a queen, not a knight or a knave.

Neo-liberal policy-makers on the other hand would be most comfortable in the top right-hand quadrant (knave/queen). So the shift that gave rise to the quasi-market revolution can be represented as a movement from the bottom left-hand quadrant to the top right-hand one. Market socialism and the third way can each be represented by a slight shift back along the horizontal axis, while remaining firmly in the top right-hand quadrant.

Many people could react to this figure, and indeed to the analyses underlying the whole chapter, by accusing them of being far too simplistic. The realities of human motivation and agency, they might contend, are far too complex to be adequately summarised by this kind of approach. There are many kinds of knights, lots of different types of knave. In fact, most human beings are in all probability some combination of both knight and knave, with different aspects coming to the fore in different circumstances. Also, individuals are not simply either pawns or queens. Although many people like to make their own choices much of the time, there are occasions (as when very ill, for instance) when it is a great relief to them to put their fate in the hands of trusted others: times when it is preferable to be a pawn rather than a queen.

But such a reaction would miss the point. The concern here is not with trying to represent reality; that discussion comes later in the book. Rather the aim is to capture *policy-makers' perceptions* of reality and to show how this has affected policy design. More precisely, it is to illustrate how the assumptions concerning motivation and agency, implicit or explicit, that are held by policy-makers and other policy analysts affect policy development and reform. These assumptions may indeed be simplistic or even simple-minded; but, as we have seen in our discussion of the developments in the welfare state, they can be very powerful.

## THE REST OF THE BOOK

The remainder of the book is divided into three parts and an epilogue. Part I—'Theory: Of Knights and Knaves'—is, as its title suggests, intended to provide the book's theoretical underpinnings concerning motivation. This is not to say that the discussion is entirely theoretical in the pejorative sense of having nothing to do with empirical reality; indeed far from it, for it includes a large amount of empirical material. Rather it is intended to provide the book's conceptual framework and to justify the fundamental analytical and philosophical stance concerning motivation that underlies the policy discussions that follow later in the book.

Chapters Two, Three, and Four are concerned primarily with motivation and public services. Chapter Two formulates more precisely what is meant by 'knights' and 'knaves' and examines the empirical evidence concerning the existence of different kinds of motivation in the public sector. It concludes that both self-interested and altruistic motivations exist and, more interestingly, that altruistic motivations often require that the individual himself or herself performs the relevant act. Chapter Three considers the impact of the policy context on motivation, asking whether individuals' motivations are independent of the context in which they operate or whether they are in fact deeply affected by that context. Do market-oriented policies corrupt—turn knights into knaves? Alternatively, does government corrupt—or lead to moral atrophy? The answers are somewhat surprising, with both markets and governments devaluing knightly motivations on occasion but at other times rewarding or revaluing it. Chapter Four uses the material from the two previous chapters to develop what I believe to be a largely new theory of public service motivation. This allocates a key role to the sacrifice involved in performing altruistic acts. The chapter goes on to discuss some of the theory's implications for policy design and also its morality.

Part II—'Theory: Of Pawns and Queens'—is intended to provide the analytic and philosophical framework for considerations of agency. It is more normative in nature. Chapter Five discusses the fundamental question as the relative balance of power between individual users and professionals with respect to public services such as health care and education, while Chapter Six examines whether individuals should be left to make their own decisions with respect to other areas of welfare, such as saving for their pension or long-term care.

Part III—'Policy'—deals with some specific policies or proposals designed to address motivation and agency issues. They are discussed in some detail because, as the well-known phrase has it, therein the devil often lurks. Indeed, there is a broader point here. Academics too often get away with the enunciation of broad principles, leaving the hard choices involved in policy formulation and implementation to be made by someone else. But it is these hard choices that test and illuminate the underlying principles; choices that sometimes require the revisiting and revision of the latter. Certainly that has happened in this case: the policy analyses of Part III have not simply followed from the economic and philosophical analyses of Parts I and II, but have materially influenced them.

Chapters Seven and Eight review the experience of two market-oriented policies that have been tried in British health care and education: the holding of budgets for hospital care by organisations of primary-care physicians (General Practitioner practices and, more recently, Primary Care Trusts); and parental choice and competition in primary school education. They conclude that these schemes have been broadly effective, and, where the schemes have problems, offer some ideas for improvement.

The next three chapters look at policies outside the arena of public services but still within the general area of public policy and the welfare state. Each concerns a specific proposal that would turn pawns into queens, or that, when compared with alternatives, would affect positively individuals' capacity for agency. They are all proposals in which I have been heavily involved, as initiator, or advocate, or both. Chapters Nine and Ten discuss ideas for which I was an initiator: the idea of a universal stakeholder or demogrant to every young adult in Chapter Nine, and 'partnership' matching grants to encourage savings for pensions and long-term care in Chapter Ten. Chapter Eleven considers increasing individual citizens' control over the fiscal system through hypothecation or the earmarking of particular tax revenues for specific uses, an old idea but one that needs reviving, as I have advocated in a variety of different contexts.

The Epilogue is a reflective piece on the theme of the book as a whole. It considers the effect of using markets in the public sector on society, and argues that they need not corrupt and can be beneficial for agency. In short, it is not necessary to turn knights into knaves for pawns to become queens. What are needed are appropriately designed public policies, ones that employ market-type mechanisms but that do not allow unfettered self-interest to dominate altruistic motivations: a form of 'doux commerce publique'.

# PART I

# THEORY: OF KNIGHTS AND KNAVES

# 2

## Knights and Knaves in the Public Sector: What Do We Mean and What Do We Know?

No man giveth but with intention of Good to himselfe, because Gift is Voluntary; and, of all voluntary acts, the Object is to every man his own Good.

(Thomas Hobbes, *Leviathan*)

How selfish soever man may be supposed, there are evidently some principles in his nature, which interest him in the fortune of others, and render their happiness necessary to him, though he derives nothing from it except the pleasure of seeing it. Of this kind is pity or compassion, the emotion which we feel for the misery of others, when we either see it, or are made to conceive it in a very lively manner.

(Adam Smith, *The Theory of Moral Sentiments*)

You might not see one in a hundred with *gentleman* so plainly written as in Mr Knightley.

(Jane Austen, *Emma*)

The previous chapter spelt out how, in the closing years of the twentieth century, several countries, including Britain, saw some significant changes in policy-makers' perceptions about motivation and agency: changes that in turn led to radical reforms in the way in which public services were delivered. In particular, a belief that those who worked in a public service had as their principal aim not the satisfaction of their own desires but meeting the needs of the essentially passive beneficiaries of the service was replaced by a conviction that public service workers were motivated largely by self-interest and that users of services were (or should be) active consumers. This led to a policy drive to replace state-based delivery systems by market-based ones, which were viewed as better placed to harness the forces of self-interest to serve the (newly discovered) consumers of public services. Systems run by knights for the benefits of pawns were to be replaced by ones run by knaves in the service of queens. Subsequently, although there has been a partial move away from market incentives in some areas such as health care, the essence has remained in others, such as education and social services.

But how soundly based were these policy shifts? Should we rely on knavish motivations to deliver our public services? Or, as Richard Titmuss has argued, are we thereby ignoring or damaging what is often termed the public service ethos, and hence actually damaging the services concerned? Should our health systems, our education systems, our social services incorporate incentive structures that reward (or penalise) the knave, or ones that encourage (or discourage) the knight?

It might seem that there is a ready answer to these questions and indeed a ready solution to the policy-makers' dilemma over which assumptions to make about human motivation: namely, to find out what actually does motivate people in the public sector. Surely, in a world of advanced scientific inquiry, we can establish whether those who implement public policy are in fact knights or knaves, self-interested egoists or public-spirited altruists? If so, once that is established, then we can design our policies accordingly, relying on self-interested incentive structures if individuals turn out to be knaves and on altruistic ones if they turn out to be knights.

Sadly, the world is not that simple. Philosophers, social psychologists, economists, evolutionary psychologists, and scholars from a wide range of other disciplines have all tackled the issue of motivation without achieving much by way of consensus. There is controversy over the meaning of terms such as self-interest and altruism, and over the extent to which either phenomenon can be found in the real world.

So this chapter explores the question of what kind of motivation is meant when we use terms such as 'knights' and 'knaves', 'altruism' or 'self-interest', and what evidence there is for the existence of such motivations in the public sector. The literature is large and I can review it only relatively briefly.[1]

Two general points before I look at knaves and knights separately. First, the terms are used here as a shorthand for describing individuals' motivations, not necessarily individuals themselves. So, in describing individuals as knights, for instance, I do not mean to imply that they are always motivated to perform knightly acts or that they will always behave in a knightly fashion. Rather, I mean that on occasion their acts have knightly motivations. It is perfectly possible for someone to be both a knight and a knave: that is, to have altruistic motivations for some of his or her activities or behaviour and self-interested ones for others.

---

[1] Useful reviews of the literature on altruism in general from a variety of disciplines can be found in Batson (1991: ch. 2) and Page (1996: ch. 1). Rogers (1997) provides an anthology of philosophical writings on self-interest and altruism from Plato to the present day. More recent philosophical contributions can be found in Paul, Miller, and Paul (1993). The arguments concerning the possibility of altruism from the evolutionary psychologists'/biologists' perspective can be found in R. Wright (1994) and Ridley (1996).

The reference to 'behaviour' brings us to the second point. It is important to distinguish between motivation and behaviour. I use the term 'behaviour' to describe a set of actions or activities undertaken by an individual. Motivation is a psychological state that is one, but only one, of the factors that may determine behaviour. Other factors include the outside constraints that people face, including the availability of time and of financial resources, and their intrinsic skills and abilities. So an individual may wish to become a doctor in order to help patients, and may have the ability to pass the necessary exams, but cannot pay for the training from his or her own resources. So he or she borrows to finance it. The behaviour is the activity of borrowing to finance medical education. The motivation is the (knightly) one of wishing to help patients, the constraints are ability and financial resources. Behaviour is the product of an interaction between motivation and constraints.[2]

## WHAT WE MEAN: THE KNAVE

For the purposes of this book, the term 'knave' is used to mean simply an individual whose principal concern is to further his or her self-interest. Defining knaves this way follows the usage of David Hume in the quotation that opened this book, but also that of more modern political philosophers (see for instance Pettit 1996 and Hausman 1998). As noted in the Preface, this is a little broader than the common usage of the term, where it can mean individuals who indeed pursue their self-interest but whose activities in furthering that end take them to the borders of legality: people who bend the rules or who are in other ways slightly shady. But, although such individuals are certainly part of our canvas here, they are not its sole focus. Rather, the emphasis in this book is on individuals who pursue their own interest by any means, legal or illegal.

However, simply defining knaves in terms of the pursuit of self-interest is not sufficient. For, as many writers have noted, the concept of self-interest itself is not uncomplicated (see for instance Kavka 1986 and Hill 1993). Perhaps the simplest interpretation is that underlying the conception of so-called economic man or *homo economicus*. This is a genus of individuals whose self-interest is defined solely in terms of their own consumption: that is, such individuals are motivated entirely by the desire to acquire material wealth that they consume themselves for their own benefit. The clause 'that they consume themselves for their own benefit' is important because this excludes two categories of people who would be better described as knights: those who want to acquire material wealth primarily in order to benefit others (for instance, through giving the money away), and those who might consume

---

[2] In this sense I am using the term 'motivation' in a fashion that comes close to economists' terminology of preferences. I use motivation partly because it is probably more recognisable in the context of this book to both economists and non-economists and partly because the term has associations with activity (one is motivated to *do* something) in a way that the term 'preferences' does not.

something they do not wish to in order to benefit others (for instance, wearing clothes that are not to one's own taste in order to please one's partner).

*Homo economicus* is the model that non-economists often believe—wrongly—underlies all economic analysis. It is true that many, perhaps most, economists would defend it as a helpful abstraction that under a wide variety of circumstances can yield useful predictions. However, there are few who would consider it an adequate representation of the complexity of human motivation, not even of that part which is purely self-interested; and several distinguished economists have developed models that incorporate much more sophisticated conceptions of motivation.[3]

In fact, as many authors have pointed out, self-interest has a wide variety of elements that contribute to it. These include material wealth certainly, but also such important considerations as security, autonomy, status, and power. A full list might be even broader than this, including these but also pleasure, the avoidance of pain, liberty, glory, the possession of certain objects, fame, health, longevity, self-respect, self-development, self-assertion, reputation, honour, and affection (Kavka 1986: 42, quoted in Hill 1993: 1). It is this broader conception of self-interest that will underlie the way in which the term is used in this book. Again the rider needs to be added that some of these elements qualify as factors promoting self-interest only when they are used for personal benefit; some of them, such as power or high status, could be desired solely for the purpose of being in a position to confer benefits on others—in which case they become a knightly rather than a knavish motivation. This is a point to which I shall return.

## WHAT WE MEAN: THE KNIGHT

The terms 'knight' or 'knightly motivation' will not be found in the relevant literature, which uses instead an eclectic bundle of nouns and adjectives to describe the individuals or the motivations concerned. Of these the most common are 'altruism' and 'altruistic behaviour'; but, as Janet Finch (1989: 223) has observed, 'altruism . . . can be used merely as a way of referring to behaviour whose nature we do not really understand, but of which we vaguely approve'. References can also often be found to 'moral', 'collectivist', 'public-spirited', or 'pro-social' behaviours. These terms are either left irritatingly undefined or defined in such a way that is too narrow for our purposes. So Robert Goodin (1993: 66) notes that, particularly, social psychologists use terms such as 'altruistic', 'moral', or 'pro-social' virtually interchangeably, much 'to a philosopher's chagrin'.

So how should knights be defined? It might seem as if we can simply do so as individuals who are motivated to help others. However, this immediately

---

[3] The pioneer was Gary Becker (1976; 1981). More detailed discussion of some of the wider theories of motivation now being developed by economists can be found in Rabin (1997) and Frey (1999: ch. 1).

raises the question as to the exact nature of this motivation to help others. Is it not itself an expression of self-interest? Famously, in the quotation with which this chapter opened, Thomas Hobbes (1651/1985) argued that everyone was fundamentally selfish even when engaged in apparently charitable actions. Other philosophers of the period agreed. So La Rochefoucauld (1678/1964, maxim 82): 'the most disinterested love is, after all, but a kind of bargain in which the dear love of our own selves always proposes to be the gainer in one way or another.' And Bernard Mandeville (1714/1989: 92): 'the humblest Man alive must confess that the Reward of a Virtuous Action, which is the Satisfaction that ensues upon it, consists in a certain Pleasure he procures to himself by Contemplating his own Worth.' So, in a Hobbesian/Rochefoucauldian/Mandevillian world, there are no knights—only knaves.

Actually, there seem to be two distinct versions of the Hobbesian view concerning the non-existence of altruism. One allows for the possibility of unselfish acts, but makes the empirical claim that they rarely, if ever, occur in practice: that when people profess unselfish motives for their actions they are generally being hypocritical and covering up a fundamentally selfish motive. The other is the more sweeping assertion that unselfish behaviour is logically impossible: that any freely chosen act, including an apparently selfless one, must have been motivated by the desire to undertake that act; and meeting one's desires is the definition of self-interest.

The first claim can be readily refuted by empirical investigation, as we shall see shortly. The second is harder to argue against (although some philosophers have tried, including David Hume, Adam Smith, and John Stuart Mill);[4] but it is not always necessary to do so. In fact, for the purposes of this book, the debate is relatively easy to resolve. The resolution is that proposed by another enlightenment philosopher, Joseph Butler (1997: 122–3), who argued 'But this is not the language of mankind . . . There is . . . a distinction between the cool principle of self-love, or general desire for our happiness, as one part of our nature, and one principle of action; and the particular affections towards particular external objects, as another part of our nature and another principle of action.'

In our terminology, knaves can be defined as self-interested individuals who are motivated to help others only if by so doing they will serve their private interests; whereas knights are individuals who are motivated to help others for no private reward, and indeed who may undertake such activities to the detriment of their own private interests. Put another way, the distinction is between, on the one hand, those who are motivated to perform only those activities that are of direct benefit to their own material welfare, such as their own personal consumption of material goods, and, on the other hand, those that are motivated to engage in 'other-directed' activities, that is, activities which benefit others and which do not positively affect their own material

---

[4] See Batson (1991: ch. 2) and Page (1996: ch. 1) for reviews of their contributions and a more general discussion of the issues involved.

welfare. The fact that both kinds of individual may be 'selfish', in the sense that they both derive satisfaction or some other kind of positive feeling from their activities, is irrelevant for our purposes.

So a philosophical distinction between knights and knaves can be drawn. However, a rather different kind of challenge to the existence of altruistic motivations has come from evolutionary psychology. This relatively new area of scientific endeavour applies Darwinian principles to social behaviour, and argues that much, perhaps even most, such behaviour is ultimately determined by genetic factors. If this is accepted, then one possible implication is that, since genes are in Richard Dawkins's (1989) terms ultimately 'selfish', so must be the behaviour that is determined by them. Genes are intrinsically knaves; they cannot be knights.

However, most evolutionary psychologists would argue that such an implication would be too simplistic. It is perfectly possible for genes to be selfish but for the organism that embodies them to be altruistic. For altruistic behaviour by an organism may well serve the interest of the genes, that is, their long-term propagation and survival. So, for instance, the genetic pattern that causes parents to make sacrifices for their children is likely to dominate a genetic pattern that does not; for, other things being equal, more children of the sacrificial parents will survive than of the non-sacrificial ones. It is more difficult for the neo-Darwinians to explain altruistic acts to non-relatives. However, some have tried, arguing that, under many of the circumstances that human beings find themselves, genes that promote trust and cooperation with strangers are more likely to survive than ones that promote competition (for a full discussion, see Ridley 1996).

So both philosophy and evolutionary psychology allow for the existence of altruistic motivation. That is as well, because such motivation undoubtedly does exist.

This assertion is based not only on common sense but also on a large body of research undertaken by social psychologists, economists, and other social scientists. This I examine shortly. But before I do so there are three other areas of potentially confusing terminology that need clearing up.

First, the relationship between self-interest, altruism, and rationality. Self-interest is often identified with rationality, with the implication that only self-interested individuals are truly rational. Thus rational, self-interested individuals are often described as *homo economicus* on the grounds that the analysis of the behaviour of such individuals underlies contemporary analyses of economists.[5] However, as indeed many economists themselves have pointed out, rationality does not imply self-interested motivations or vice versa. There seems no reason why an individual engaging in a rational calculus of the costs and benefits of a particular activity should confine the analysis only to those costs and benefits that impact directly on the individual himself or herself. A knight who includes the costs and benefits to others as part of his or her calculations as to

[5] See, for instance, Fukuyama (1995: 17–20), and Pettit (1996: 62–3).

whether or not to undertake the activity is being as rational as a knave who includes only those that affect him or her personally. Both knights and knaves can be rational; both, of course, can also be irrational.[6]

The second point concerns the relationship between altruism and collectivism or cooperation. Unselfishness is often linked with a belief in the importance of cooperation or of engaging in collective action; selfishness with individualistic or competitive actions. However, the link is not automatic. For self-interested individuals could believe that the best way to promote their self-interest is to work with others in a cooperative way; this, after all, is often the rationale behind joining a trade union. Results from game theory, including the well-known Prisoner's Dilemma, show on many occasions that self-interest can best be served by cooperation.

So not all collectivists are knights. But are all knights collectivists? Is a belief in collectivism a necessary condition for being a knight? At first sight, there may seem to be something odd about an altruist, say, deliberately engaging in competitive actions or supporting the operations of a competitive market, especially those which involve someone else's welfare diminishing (such as a small corner shop going out of business due to the competition with an out-of-town supermarket and thereby depriving a local community of elderly people of ready access to shopping). However, it is far from impossible. For an altruist may believe the operation of competitive markets will in the long run do more to further the interests of those whom he or she cares about than the operation of more collectivist systems (for instance, the supermarket could provide a delivery service for the elderly with goods at lower prices). And, as we shall see in subsequent chapters, in this the altruist who believes in competition may be right, even in the context of public services. To be a knight does not necessarily imply being a collectivist.

The final point concerns the currently fashionable issue of trust. Sometimes altruism and trust seem to be confused. Put another way, the pursuit of self-interest by an individual is taken to exclude the placing of trust in either him or her or in other individuals similarly motivated (see for instance Fukuyama 1995: ch. 2). But neither a trusting individual (one who places trust in others) nor a trustworthy individual (one in whom trust is placed) is necessarily a knight. I might know you to be a knave, but nonetheless trust you to pursue my self-interest in a particular situation simply because it is a situation in which both our self-interests coincide (bailing out a leaky lifeboat, for instance). In that case we can trust each other, even though we both are acting as knaves. Of course it may be easier on occasion to trust someone to pursue your interests if you think they genuinely have your welfare at heart; but feelings of altruism between two individuals are not essential to a relationship

---

[6] I am defining rationality here in terms of the consistent assessment of the costs and benefits of different actions. Andreoni and Miller (2002) have demonstrated that subjects behaving altruistically can conform in that behaviour to more general revealed preference rationality axioms.

of trust existing between them or vice versa. As with collectivism, there is no automatic link between knightly and trusting behaviour.

## WHAT WE KNOW

In the eighteenth century Bernard Mandeville ran into a great deal of trouble for his contention that most men were knaves. For John Brown, Hobbes and Mandeville were 'detested names, yet sentenc'd never to die; snatched from oblivion's grave by infamy!' John Wesley wrote 'til now I imagined that there never appeared in the world such a book as the works of Machiavel. But de Mandeville goes far beyond it.'[7] But, in a more modern, possibly less idealistic, world, it is difficult to see what the fuss was about. That all individuals are to a great extent knaves—that is, motivated in large part by material self-interest— is almost uncontroversial. The issue is rather the reverse: do people engage in knightly acts in non-trivial ways? Or, put in a way of direct relevance to the concerns of this book, is the assumption of altruistic motivation fulfilled in enough instances to make it safe to construct public policies on that assumption?

That altruistic behaviour towards immediate family or other kin exists is so obvious that it needs little demonstration. What is of more interest is evidence of the existence of apparently altruistic behaviour that is directed towards non-related individuals, including in many cases complete strangers, and, more significantly, evidence of the motivation that lies behind that behaviour. This comes from a wide variety of sources, including interviews with those who have engaged in apparently altruistic behaviour, laboratory experiments, and empirical tests using observed behaviour. The range of such studies is vast.[8] But the conclusions drawn from them are unequivocal. As Matthew Rabin (1997: 13), an economist reviewing both the psychological and the economic literature, says:

> It has been experimentally verified that people contribute to public goods more than can be explained by pure self-interest, that those free to allocate money as they choose do not universally grab all the money and that people sacrifice money to retaliate against unfair treatment . . . there is no debate among behavioural researchers about whether underlying preferences depart non-trivially from self-interest.

Of particular interest to this book is evidence concerning the altruistic (or self-interested) motivation of individuals involved in the provision of public services. This we should look at in a little more detail.

---

[7] Quoted in Harth (1989). Actually much of the critics' venom was stimulated by Mandeville's proposition that not only were most men knaves, but that it was actually better for the economy and indeed civil society that they were so instead of being virtuous moralists. This point is discussed further below.

[8] For reviews of the psychological and sociological literature, see Krebs (1970), Pialavin and Charng (1990), and Monroe (1994). A comprehensive literature review of the psychology and economics literature can be found in Rabin (1997: 13–26); see also Rose-Ackerman (1996) and, for earlier references, Phelps (1975). For some more recent references, see Andreoni and Vesterlund (2001) and Andreoni and Miller (2002).

## MOTIVATION AND PUBLIC SERVICES

We begin with Richard Titmuss's reports in *The Gift Relationship* on interviews with apparent altruists in an area close to our public policy concerns: that of blood donation. The knights in this case were a sample of 3,800 people who had given blood to the British National Blood Transfusion Service. These individuals gave blood with no expectation of financial or other material reward (except for a cup of tea and a biscuit after they had made their donation); they gave anonymously; and they did not know the potential recipients of their donation. Of these, over a quarter gave compassion as a reason for their act. These included (reproduced as written):

'Knowing I mite be saving somebody's life.' 'I came forword in hope to help somebody who needs blood.' 'I felt it was a small contribution I could make to the welfare of humanity.' (Titmuss 1970/1997: 293)

Feelings of duty were also apparent among the Titmuss donors:

'My conscience—having served five years on active service in the war (1939–45), helping to destroy life, and during this period my wife was receiving blood to save her life, it occurred to me, after demobilisation, that I could at least ease my conscience.' 'Feeling of guilt at receiving so much in life and giving so little.' 'Sense of duty and community and duty to the nation as a whole.'

As were more personal factors:

'I felt this was a wonderful service I wanted to be a part of.' 'I wanted to do something to convince myself I was 18 and I always wanted to be blood donor—snob appeal.' 'Primarily to conform with teenage contemporaries.' (Titmuss 1970/1997: 297)

Two conclusions can be drawn immediately from these interviews. The first is that, undeniably, altruistic motivations exist. The second is that they in turn seem to take a variety of forms, including compassion, duty, and a desire to conform.

But it could be objected that these kinds of interviews are not immediately relevant to our concerns. Blood donors are not strictly workers in the public sector, although that did not stop Titmuss from drawing inferences from these interviews about motivations in the public services (or more widely). But there is also a range of evidence of more direct relevance.

A recent survey of the values of public and private sector managers was undertaken by Jane Steele (1999) of the Public Management Foundation. This involved in-depth interviews with seventeen top managers from the public, private, and non-profit sectors, followed by detailed telephone interviews with 400 more. The study found considerable evidence both that knightly motivations existed in the public sector and that they were much more pronounced than in the private sector. Out of sixteen possible personal goals, the most frequently named goal of public sector managers was to provide a service to the community, whereas this did not even appear among the top ten goals for private sector managers. In contrast, for private sector managers the two (equally) most important goals were improving the financial performance of the organisation and achieving organisational goals or targets.[9] The first of these did not appear among the top ten goals for public sector managers, whereas the second appeared sixth. Moreover, these differences did not fade with age or experience; they were not a feature of only the older generations. In a later piece, Steele complemented this work by exploring the motivation of managers and doctors within the British National Health Service, together with Alison Graham (Graham and Steele 2001). This involved a survey of 125 NHS staff: 65 managers, 24 hospital doctors, 20 medical managers, and 16 GPs. Again, the researchers found a strong commitment to altruistic concerns. Among thirteen possible motivating factors, the 'desire to provide a good quality service to users' was ranked the highest by all groups, except GPs.[10] None of the groups was especially motivated by prospect of personal gain; 'the amount I earn', 'my status in the community', and 'my career development prospects' all ranked near the bottom. This is consistent with previous research concerning the motivation of hospital consultants (Shaw, Mitchell, and Dawson 1995).

The motivations of doctors working in the public sector are of particular interest, since the practice of medicine has traditionally been heavily constrained by norms other than direct self-interest, in both the public and the private sectors.[11] These include both general moral principles of honesty, charity, and mutual respect and norms that are peculiar to the medical profession, to many of which its members swear solemn oaths. The effectiveness of these norms in influencing how health care providers behave (like the effectiveness of all norms) is controversial, but no one would deny that they have some potency, at least in influencing the way in which doctors think about their profession. So, for instance, a British Medical Association survey of 600 doctors'

---

[9] These goals and targets were left undefined, so it is possible that some of them were other-directed and hence altruistic.

[10] GPs ranked 'working in a productive team', ' a desire to help the community', 'working with able, motivated colleagues', 'my reputation amongst my colleagues' above the desire to provide a good quality service. See Graham and Steele (2001: Table 2.1, p. 7). Interestingly, another review of the factors influencing GPs' behaviour concluded that 'the evidence for societal interests and reputation/status being [factors] is . . . weak . . . as is the evidence for patients' interests being [a factor]' (Scott 1997: 33).

[11] It is remarkable how little hard evidence actually exists concerning doctors' motivations with respect to the competing claims of self-interest and altruism, at least in the United Kingdom. A study by Nick Bosanquet and Brenda Leese (1989), promisingly titled *Family Doctors and Economic Incentives*, does not in fact deal directly with the issue of motivation, being more concerned with demonstrating the effect of area factors on GP behaviour. The British Medical Association has undertaken a number of surveys of doctors' core values (BMA 1995*a, b, c*) and has supported work by the Policy Studies Institute on the views of young doctors (Allen 1997). Although none of these directly addresses the question of self-interest versus more altruistic motivations, they do contain useful information. In an interesting recent contribution, Matthew Gothill (1998: S38) has argued that 'neither altruism nor egoistical self-interest adequately explain [General Practitioners'] motivation', arguing instead that 'process' satisfaction drives GPs in their behaviour, especially in the consulting room. However, he provides little evidence to support the assertion.

attitudes towards medicine as a career found only ten (2 per cent) who felt that medicine was 'a job like any other and that doctors have a right to work normal hours and forget about work when they get home' (BMA 1995a, part II: 11). On the other hand, the same survey indicated how difficult it was to find a balance between altruism and more self-interested concerns. Over half of the respondents (58 per cent) agreed with the statement that 'medicine is a major commitment, but doctors also deserve a decent family life and leisure time'; while a further 29 per cent felt that 'the practice of medicine must be organised in a way which allowed doctors to balance their career with family and other interests'. Only three considered that 'medicine is a vocation and only those who considered it their primary commitment should enter the profession' (BMA 1995a, part II: 5).

Tessa Crilly and I have explored the motivation and goals of NHS Trusts, using a survey of 1,500 hospital consultants and managers and a statistical analysis of the behaviour of 100 acute trusts over three years (Crilly and Le Grand 2004). The results showed that consultants considered service (quality and volume) goals to be more important than financial break-even. While a financial break-even target was found to be the primary goal of managers on average, they proved to be a heterogeneous group, with quality ranking as the main priority among those managers who were closest to service delivery. Although a commitment to service goals cannot be automatically attributed to knightly motivations (it could also derive from more knavish concerns such as a desire for professional approval), the striking aspect of these results was how relatively little commitment there was among consultants and a significant group of managers to maintaining the financial health of the institution.

Peter Taylor-Gooby and colleagues (2000) investigated the motives of British dentists deciding whether to treat patients privately or through the National Health Service. They found that dentists were led to leave the NHS because of both knavish and knightly motives. By going 'private', they wanted to have a higher income and to have more independence for their personal benefit. However, an important motivating factor was that they also believed that by so doing they could give more time and attention to their patients, and hence provide a higher quality of care. As Taylor-Gooby and colleagues comment, the interpretation they gave of their patients' interests was heavily conditioned by their professional culture (emphasising restorative rather than preventive work, for instance); however, the fact remains that patients' interests appeared to be a significant factor in their decision.

Outside the medical arena, Jeremy Kendall has investigated the motivations of independent providers (profit and non-profit) of residential care and domiciliary care for elderly people. In 1997 he and colleagues interviewed just over fifty providers of residential care, asking questions about their principal motives for being in business. Of these, the most widely cited motive was meeting the needs of elderly people (85 per cent), while 87.5 per cent cited one or both of two other knightly motivations: a feeling of duty and responsibility towards society as a whole, and similar feelings towards a particular section of society. This compares with the numbers citing apparently more knavish concerns of professional accomplishment (76 per cent), developing skills (67 per cent), a satisfactory level of personal income (58 per cent), independence and autonomy (40 per cent), and income or profit maximising (a mere 8 per cent) (Kendall 2001).[12] When interviewees were asked to rank these priorities, the one ranked highest most frequently was the needs of the elderly (41 per cent), followed by professional accomplishment (15 per cent) and income (14 per cent) (see also Forder *et al.* 1997).

In 1999 Kendall and colleagues (2003) asked similar questions of fifty-six providers of domiciliary care. Of the respondents nearly half gave as their most important motivation the knightly motives of meeting the needs of elderly people (29 per cent), duty/responsibility to society as a whole (11 per cent), and duty/responsibility to a particular section of society (9 per cent). In contrast, only 13 per cent gave priority to financial motives, while the remainder concentrated on professional accomplishment and creative achievement (21 per cent), independence and autonomy (11 per cent), and developing expertise (5 per cent).

Outside the UK, Gene Brewer and colleagues have reviewed some of the US studies on public service motivation (Brewer, Selden, and Facer II 2000: 255). Most of this is consonant with the UK evidence, and suggests that public employees report a greater concern for serving the community and helping others than private sector ones. However, one study of public, private, and non-profit sector employees did not find any significant difference between them in the commitment to service, helping, pay, or job security (Gabris and Simo 1995).

All the evidence quoted so far has been derived from interviews or responses to questionnaires. In these situations there may be what has been termed a 'halo' effect: people responding in the way they think they ought to respond rather than revealing their true motivations. Actual behaviour might be a more accurate guide to motivation than stated intentions. Julien Forder (2000) has examined such behaviour with respect to pricing of for-profit and non-profit providers of residential care for people with mental health problems. He found that both groups did not set prices as high as they could have done—or should have done if they were out to maximise their profits. Non-profit providers had lower mark-ups than for-profit ones; but even the latter did not fully exploit their market power.

Most of the other empirical studies of actual behaviour have concentrated on the effect of financial incentives in motivating public sector workers. A review of the evidence outside the health care sector by economists Simon

---

[12] Kendall regards the desire for greater independence and control as neither knavish nor knightly but (keeping up the medieval metaphor) as 'mercantile'. Hence he coins the term 'merchant' to set alongside the knights and knaves.

Burgess, Carol Propper, and Deborah Wilson (2002) concluded that public sector workers do work harder and produce more output when they have a financial incentive to do so; they also manipulate the quality and timing of what they do so as to maximise their financial rewards, often in ways that the organisation neither intended nor wanted. However, Burgess, Propper, and Wilson cite evidence that public sector workers can also behave altruistically. Caseworkers in a job-training scheme in the United States took on hard-to-place workers even though their narrow financial interest would have been better served by accepting more employable workers.

There have been two systematic reviews of the literature on the impact of financial payments on medical practice and behaviour.[13] One reported on studies of primary care physicians in the US, Canada, Denmark, and Scotland. The researchers found that those paid on a fee-for-service basis provided more services than those paid by salary or by capitation (that is, according to the number of patients on their list) (Gosden *et al.* 2001: 53). The other examined a large number of studies (eighty-nine) in a variety of countries on the impact of financial incentives on medical practice. It concluded that financial incentives had an impact on the use of health care resources, including admission rates to, and length of stay in, hospital, on compliance with clinical practice guidelines, and on achieving a general immunisation targets (Chaix-Couturier *et al.* 2000).

Peter Dolton and colleagues have examined the impact of both pecuniary and non-pecuniary rewards for teachers. They found that relative earnings in teaching compared with non-teaching alternatives have a marked effect on graduates' choice of occupation, on teachers' decisions to leave teaching, and on the decision by ex-teachers to return to teaching. However, non-pecuniary factors were also very important—especially for women. But the latter appears to be the result not so much of more public service motivations in women than in men, but to familial concerns about the compatibility between teaching and family responsibilities (this work is summarised in Dolton, McIntosh, and Chevalier 2002). Reviews of the labour supply of nurses have come to similar conclusions (Antonazzo *et al.* 2000).

Overall, it is hard to dispute the view that altruistic motivations are prevalent among the providers of public services. But we must be careful how we interpret the evidence. Altruism exists alongside more self-interested motivations, and is combined with them to affect behaviour in different ways.

But the research shows more than the mere existence of altruism in the public sector. It tells us something about the nature of altruistic motivations that will be important for our subsequent analysis. More specifically, there appear to be two rather different kinds of altruistic motivation, or, in terms of the metaphor underlying this book, two different kinds of knight: the 'act-irrelevant' and the 'act-relevant'.

---

[13] I am grateful to Elias Mossialos for drawing these to my attention.

First, the act-irrelevant knights. These are individuals who are motivated to help a person in distress solely because of their reactions to their perception of the situation in which the person finds himself or herself. This reaction could spring from compassion or pity for the individual concerned. Or it could arise because they consider the individual's situation to be unjust or unfair.[14] The concept of altruism implicit in the idea of this kind of knight probably corresponds closely to many common-sense interpretations of the term.

Now act-irrelevant knights would be content if the person who is the focus of their altruistic concern were helped by someone else; they do not necessarily have to provide the help themselves. They are prepared to free-ride on others' actions. Who actually performs the helping act is irrelevant: hence their title. They may be distinguished from 'act-relevant' knights: people who have concern for an individual in distress but who are motivated actually to provide the necessary help themselves. This could arise from a feeling of positive reward from undertaking the helping activity: what has been described as a 'warm glow' (Andreoni 1990). This satisfaction could in turn arise from a number of internal factors, such as the individual's perception of himself or herself as a caring person, or external ones such as social recognition or peer approval (for further discussion see Piliavin and Charng 1990 and Rose-Ackerman 1996: 713).

Alternatively, act-relevance could be motivated not so much by feelings of positive satisfaction from performing a helping act but by a sense of duty or obligation to the individual concerned and the desire to avoid a sense of guilt if the individual concerned does *not* perform the act. Or it could be motivated by a sense of reciprocity: a motivation to help those who have been kind or thoughtful in the past. This kind of motivation might appear actually to be a form of knavery; and indeed, if it takes the form of requiring others to be helpful towards you in return for your being nice to them, then it is a self-interested act and not a knightly one. But it need not necessarily take the form of a direct exchange in this way. You could decide to be nice to people simply because they have been nice to you in the past and you therefore have good feelings towards them, not because you are expecting good things from them in the future. Reciprocal act-relevant knights are different from knaves.[15]

This distinction between act-irrelevant and act-relevant altruism has also been described as a distinction between 'pure' and 'impure' altruism (Andreoni 1990). However, I prefer not to use these terms since they seem to imply some kind of moral judgement that one is better than the other: a judgement that, at least to me, has no obvious justification.[16] The only important question is whether both kinds exist and, if so, to what extent.

---

[14] Compassion and a sense of justice are often confused. However, they are quite different, one leading to generosity, the other to giving people their just deserts. The distinction is apparent in the proverb: be just before you are generous.

[15] This does not exhaust all the different kinds of knights. For discussions of other kinds of altruistic motivations see Margolis (1982), Collard (1978; 1983), and Sugden (1984; 1993).

[16] Nor to others: see for instance Rose-Ackerman (1996: 713).

Evidence concerning the extent of act-relevance and act-irrelevance comes from studies of charitable giving. Consider an individual giving £100 annually to charity who hears that a friend of hers is also about to start giving £100 a year to the same charity. If she were an act-irrelevant altruist, she would stop her charitable donation; for the beneficiaries of the charity would still be receiving the help that she thought was appropriate, albeit from the actions of her friend rather than herself. However, if she was an act-relevant altruist, she would not stop, since it would be the act itself that would be her motivating force, not—or not only—the situation of the people she was trying to help.

This argument has been developed in the context of the relationship between government spending and charitable donations. More specifically, it can be shown that, if individuals are concerned only with others' welfare—that is, if they are act-irrelevant knights—increases in government spending on those others should be matched dollar-for-dollar or pound-for-pound by falls in knightly help so that the total assistance given (public and private) will remain constant.[17] In other words, if individuals are act-irrelevant altruists, government spending on welfare should lead to a fall in charitable donations.

Casual observation of different countries' experiences might suggest that there was something in this view. Germany, Canada, and the United Kingdom all have much larger government welfare sectors than the US, but much lower levels of giving. The ratio of private giving to personal income in Britain fell by half between 1934 and 1975, a period of sustained growth in government (Clotfelder 1985: 96–8; Falush 1977).

However, there are other features of the real world that do not lend much comfort to the thesis. The US has consistently given an amount equivalent to around 2 per cent of its GNP, regardless of the growth of government. And roughly the same proportion of people give in both the US and the UK: 85 per cent give in the US, and 80 per cent in the UK (Pettipher and Halfpenny 1993).[18]

More systematic empirical investigations also tend not to support the view that government activity seriously 'crowds out' knightly behaviour in the form of charitable giving. Reviewing these studies in 1985, Charles Clotfelter (1985: 274–5) concluded that 'the econometric evidence on this question [whether increased government spending reduces private giving] shows little if any effect of this sort, in spite of the apparent relationship observed among nations in the size of government and the strength of private giving'.

Moreover, little supporting evidence for crowding out has emerged since Clotfelter's review. Bruce Kingma (1989) found slight crowding out with

---

[17] Sugden (1982), Warr (1982), Roberts (1984), Bernheim (1986).

[18] However, it is worth noting that the pattern of giving is very different. As Karen Wright has pointed out, in the US giving is 'heavily interlaced with self-interest, either directly through tax benefits, benefits from the supported charity or social status; or indirectly through the social goals one might desire', whereas in the UK 'the British expect giving should be altruistic, even self-sacrificing'. Wright goes on to describe the US as an illustration of 'generosity' to be contrasted with the UK's 'altruism'. See K. Wright (2002: 21–2).

respect to US public radio, with 15 cents of donations crowded out for every dollar of government grants. Julian Wolpert (1993) found in a study of US local communities that local public generosity moves in tandem with private generosity, not in the opposite directions, as the crowding-out hypothesis would predict. In Britain, Jyoti Khanna, John Posnett, and Todd Sandler (1995) studied a sample of 159 charities from 1983 to 1990 (the height of the Thatcher period) and found no crowding-out effect on charitable donations of government grants to the charities; indeed, if anything there was a slight crowding-in effect, with a £1 increase in government grants being associated with a 9.4 pence rise in charitable donations.

A possible exception is a more recent experiment by James Andreoni. In a controlled laboratory setting involving 108 economics undergraduates he found quite a lot of crowding out (71 per cent). But as he noted:

The controlled setting of the laboratory deliberately eliminates other factors such as sympathy, political or social commitment, peer pressure, institutional consideration or moral satisfaction associated with particular cases that may influence contributions to public goods in general. The fact that crowding out measured here is much higher than in econometric studies indicates that perhaps these factors may also be having an important effect on individual contributions (Andreoni 1993: 1326).

## CONCLUSION

What does this brief review of the literature tell us that would be useful for designing policy? There are three key conclusions. The first and most important—although perhaps the least surprising—is that altruistic behaviour exists. People can behave as knights, and indeed frequently do so, even in situations where their actions are diametrically opposed to those that would further their self-interest. Moreover, these motivations appear to be prevalent among providers in the public sector, although interacting in complex ways with more self-centred motivations.

Second, there are, at least in principle, different kinds of knights, motivated by different considerations. In particular, there are act-irrelevant knights, motivated by compassion or feelings of injustice but not necessarily by the need to perform knightly acts themselves. And there are act-relevant knights, individuals in part motivated by the same considerations as the act-irrelevant knights, but also motivated by the need to perform the helping acts themselves. This may in turn be motivated by 'warm-glow' feelings, by feelings involving the alleviation of guilt, or by feelings of duty.

Third, the evidence suggests that much altruistic behaviour is of the act-relevant kind. This is of great importance for policy design, as we shall see in subsequent chapters.

# 3

# Motivation and the Policy Context

> Today the key word . . . in economics is 'character' . . . [the reason] why
> individualist economists fear socialism is that they believe it will deteri-
> orate character, and the reason why socialist economists seek socialism is
> their belief that under individualism character is deteriorating.
>
> (Stefan Collini, 'The Idea of "Character" in Victorian Political Thought',
> quoting an unspecified socialist commentator from the 1890s)

Previous chapters have argued that, in the design of public policy, policy-makers have to consider how the people who implement those policies are motivated.[1] In doing so, consciously or unconsciously, they tend to work with either of two crude assumptions about human motivation. One incorporates the belief that individuals are fundamentally motivated by their self-interest: knaves, in our terminology. Alternatively, policy-makers assume that individuals, especially those associated with the public sector, are motivated by a self-denying altruistic ethic that puts the interests of the people they are supposed to be serving above their own: not knaves but knights.

It was also argued that in recent years we have seen a shift in policy-makers' beliefs about the motivation of those involved in the public sector in general and the welfare state in particular. There has been a gradual erosion of confidence in the reliability of the public service ethic as a motivational drive and a growing conviction that self-interest is the principal force motivating those involved in public services. Since the market is the quintessential mechanism for corralling self-interest to serve the public good, this in turn has led policy-makers to develop the use of quasi-market mechanisms in the delivery of public services. These are mechanisms that rely on taxation or other revenues to finance the service concerned but that use market incentives to ensure that the service is provided in the most efficient and responsive manner possible.

The extent to which these changes in belief were well-founded and, more generally, whether the market-oriented policy changes to which they gave rise have had the desired outcomes will be discussed in subsequent chapters, and I shall not dwell further on these questions here. Instead, I concentrate on

---

[1] An earlier version of some of the material in this chapter appeared in Le Grand (2000).

a slightly different issue. Both sets of beliefs about motivation actually incorporate another assumption, one common to them both. This is that the balance of motivation—the extent to which individuals are motivated to behave as knights or knaves—is independent of the policy structures themselves. As Philip Jones and colleagues have noted, economists and other social scientists, as well as policy analysts and policy-makers themselves, often take as given the proposition that individuals have a certain basic structure of motivation; and that the task of policy-makers is to accept that structure and to adapt their policies accordingly (Jones, Cullis, and Lewis 1998). But what if the assumption that motivation is exogenous or external to policy change is incorrect? What if motivation is actually endogenous or internal to policy? That is, what if policy reforms, whether in a market-oriented or a state-oriented direction, affect the balance of motivation itself? It is to this key question that this chapter is addressed.

I begin with an examination of some of the research relating to the introduction of market incentives into areas where they did not exist before. Interestingly, this work does not all point in the same direction. Some parts suggest that the introduction of the market 'devalues' knightly activity, leading to a reduction in that activity, while other parts suggest the opposite: that market payments 'revalue' or validate the activity concerned. I then discuss a parallel thesis, the irony of which is apparent in the quotation with which this chapter opens: that it is not market interventions but state ones that shift the balance of motivation. On this view, it is government, not the market, that corrupts; it is the state that turns the knight into the knave.

## THE MARKET: DEVALUE OR REVALUE?

Many writers have claimed that the market corrupts, or, more precisely, that the use of market mechanisms reinforces the expression of self-interest and reduces the opportunities for altruism. So, for instance, Alan Ware (1990: 191) argues that, in societies that place a greater reliance on markets, 'habits, conventions and principles which support aid for others are weakened'. Fred Hirsch (1977: 82) claims that 'a market economy probably encourages the strengthening of self-regarding individual objectives and makes socially-oriented objectives more difficult to apply'. More fundamentally, the sociologist Richard Sennett (1998: 148) has argued in his book on the corrosion of character by modern capitalism that 'a regime which provides human beings with no deep reason to care about one another cannot long preserve its legitimacy'.

But perhaps the most prominent among the advocates of the view that the introduction of the market 'devalues' knightly activity—that is, that it turns altruists into egoists—is Richard Titmuss. His key work in this area was the study, mentioned in previous chapters, that explored the supply of blood in Britain and the United States, *The Gift Relationship* (Titmuss 1970/1997). Two economists had argued in a publication for the Institute of Economic Affairs that the solution to the then acute problem of Britain's chronic shortage of blood for transfusion purposes was to follow the lead of certain parts of the United States and to begin paying blood donors (Cooper and Culyer 1968). *The Gift Relationship* was Titmuss's magisterial response. There he argued that the introduction of cash payments into a system for supplying blood that previously relied upon voluntary donation, so far from leading to an increase in blood supply as the economists predicted, would lead to a diminution of altruistic motivation and in consequence to a reduction in both the quantity and quality of the blood supplied.[2]

More specifically, Titmuss had four basic arguments. First, a market in blood products was what economists would call allocatively inefficient. It was highly wasteful; it created shortages and surpluses. It was also inefficient in production, being bureaucratic in operation and administratively costly. In consequence it provided blood at a much greater expense than a voluntary system would.

Second, the use of the market led to the production of contaminated blood; that is, it damaged the quality of the product, with potentially disastrous consequences. This was because in a market the suppliers of blood had an incentive to conceal any aspects of their previous health history that might have led to their blood being unsuitable for transfusion purposes (such as contamination by hepatitis B or, currently, HIV); for otherwise they would not be able to collect their payment. This was different from a situation where blood was freely given, since there the principal motive of the donors was to help recipients; hence the incentive would be to reveal any history of bad health in case the gift of blood turned out to harm, not to help.

Third, the market was redistributive, but in the wrong direction. It distributed blood and blood products from poor to rich, from the disadvantaged and exploited to the privileged and powerful. The rich would almost literally suck the blood from the poor.

Finally, and of most relevance for our purposes, a market in blood was ultimately degrading for society as a whole. It drove out altruistic motivations for blood donation, replacing them with the cruder calculus of self-interest. Titmuss (1970/1997: 310–11) extended this argument to a broader critique of market incentives, arguing that

the private market in blood, in profit-making hospitals, operating theatres, laboratories and in other sectors of social life limits the answers and narrows the choices for all men. It is the responsibility of the state . . . to reduce or eliminate or control the forces of market coercions which place men in situations in which they have less freedom or little freedom to make moral choices and to behave altruistically if they so will.

*The Gift Relationship* is now thirty years old and, as I have noted elsewhere (Le Grand 1997a), some of these arguments have not weathered the passage of time. For instance, the argument that markets in blood are always wasteful

---

[2] For a detailed analysis of Titmuss's relationship with economists and the Institute of Economic Affairs, see Fontaine (2002).

and necessarily create shortages and surpluses, and its corollary that the voluntary system always does better, has not been born out by experience either in Britain or in the United States. This part of the argument was always a little suspect in any case because of its lack of a theoretical base. Titmuss offered no theoretical explanation as to exactly why a voluntary system would closely match supply and demand, nor indeed why a market system would fail to do so: a striking omission given that economic theory would suggest precisely the reverse.

The excessive bureaucracy argument has also lost its power. Later analyses suggested that the British blood service was almost certainly heavily *under*-managed at the time of Titmuss's investigations, with damaging consequences that became apparent a few years later. Hence more resources devoted to management would probably have been desirable and would have contributed to greater efficiency rather than detracted from it (Berridge 1997).

The redistributive argument was incomplete. In particular, it ignored the fact that, although paid donation may result in blood and blood products flowing from poor to rich precisely because it would be a commercial operation, this flow would be matched by a flow of money the other way. While the idea of the poor selling blood to the rich may be morally offensive, it was difficult to claim that the poor were actually made worse-off by the transaction. Indeed, in their own estimation at least, they were likely to be better off; otherwise, they would not have undertaken the transaction.

However, the arguments concerning the impact of introducing market incentives on motivation seem to be more robust. Titmuss relied on international comparisons of the performance of existing systems of blood supply (especially between the paid donor systems of the US and the voluntary system in the UK) to provide indirect support for his proposition that the introduction of cash payments into a voluntary system would reduce both the quantity and the quality of blood supplied. More direct empirical support comes from a study in which a sample of the (American) public was interviewed to discover their attitudes towards blood donation (Upton 1973; see also Lepper and Green 1978: 72). Part of the sample was then offered a cash inducement to participate in a blood donation programme and part was not. Of those who indicated they were interested in donating blood, those in the group offered cash compensation were less likely actually to supply it than those in the group that was not. For those who were not interested, the offer of cash compensation made little difference.

Titmuss's position is also supported by some interesting findings by Bruno Frey (Frey and Oberholzer-Gee 1997; see also Frey 1997). He studied the use of monetary compensation to persuade residents of certain communities in Switzerland to accept a nuclear waste depository located in their community. A survey of more than 300 residents found that more than half (51 per cent) supported the siting of the facility in their community, despite a widespread knowledge of the risks involved. The question was then repeated with the additional information that the government had decided to compensate all residents of the host community. Varying amounts of compensation were offered to different groups of respondents, some quite substantial (equivalent to 12 per cent of Swiss median income in the relevant year). Despite its magnitude, the offer of monetary compensation actually *reduced* the level of public support for the facility by more than half (to 25 per cent). This was not due to any change in the perception of risks involved as a result of the offer of compensation: the researchers checked respondents' perception of risk before and after the compensation was offered and found little difference.[3]

So it would seem that there is some empirical basis for the view that the introduction of market incentives does affect the balance of motivation and, moreover, that it does so in some way that turns the knight into the knave. However, other research suggests that things may not be quite that straightforward. In particular, there is a strand of literature in the area of informal care and voluntary work that points in a rather different direction. This literature discusses, among other things, the merits or otherwise of paying carers or paying 'volunteers' to care for people in need of such care (see for instance Evers, Pilj, and Ungerson 1994). Now some research on the payment of volunteers supports the Titmuss/Frey argument, showing that such payments erode the spirit of altruism. For instance, Frey himself, together with Lorenz Goette, has examined data on volunteering from the Swiss Labour Force Survey, and found that, while increasing monetary rewards led to increasing work, the mere fact of receiving a reward reduced work effort. The magnitude of this effect was considerable: at the median reward level, the volunteers, although working more than if they had received a smaller reward, worked less than if they had received no reward at all (Frey and Goette 1999; see also Evers 1994: 30).

But there is also some evidence to suggest that, in these situations, market incentives can 'revalue' or validate knightly behaviour.[4] For instance, Diana Leat (1990) interviewed eighty-seven people (mostly women) engaged in caring activities of various kinds. These included child minders, foster parents, adult family placement carers (carers who took mostly elderly people in need of care into their—the carers'—own homes), and agency carers (carers who provided day care for elderly people in their—the elderly persons'—own homes). She found that the carers did not provide care for strangers solely for the money, but also that few would have done it without payment; they regarded it as something that should not be expected of them without payment. However, the fact of being paid was more important to them than the level of pay for the job. Moreover, carers did not necessarily expect the market rate for the job; and sometimes they preferred their payments to be labelled 'expenses'. Further, as caring continued,

---

[3] It is possible, though, that respondents might have felt that, in agreeing to the offer, they would be signing away rights to further compensation.

[4] I am indebted to Clare Ungerson for this point and for drawing my attention to the relevant literature.

carers did what they felt a client needed, not what they originally said they would or would not do—and they did not demand extra payment for it.

So payment here seems to encourage rather than discourage the supply of the service concerned. Further support for this comes from an earlier piece of work by Leat. She and a colleague investigated attitudes in ten local authorities towards paying volunteers for care, where the paid individual was an 'ordinary person': something between a completely unpaid volunteer and a salaried social worker or waged home help (Leat and Gay 1987). In all cases the payment was low and could not be thought of as in any sense a wage for the job; indeed, sometimes it was described as expenses. Some of the officials interviewed were aware of the possible discouragement effect on unpaid family care of introducing paid volunteers. So, for instance, one said that 'families may feel a bit resentful—we pay other people to care and not them. Payment may devalue altruism and duty.' However, there was no mention of any negative impact on the care supplied by the volunteers themselves. Indeed the majority of those interviewed were very enthusiastic about the scheme, clearly feeling that, even if there were problems with respect to unpaid family care, they were more than offset by the increase in care supplied by the 'volunteers'. In such cases, Leat and Gay argue, carers know that what they are doing is worthwhile, that they would not do it for the money alone, but that money was not irrelevant to them: indeed, rather the reverse.

So one set of research results suggests that market incentives devalue altruistic activities, another set that they revalue them. Is there any way in which these conflicting results can be reconciled? One possible explanation lies in the gendered nature of the caring activities researched. The vast majority of the individuals concerned in the carers' research were women; and, as Janet Finch (1989: 223) observes, 'Altruistic qualities, especially in family relationships, are more frequently associated with women than with men, and therefore altruism is a concept which legitimises the many self-sacrifices women make for other members of their family.'

The question whether women are in general more altruistic than men is an open one. As James Andreoni and Lise Vesterlund have noted, research suggests that males and females have different patterns of philanthropic giving, although women do appear to be more responsive to changes in the need for giving. Further, the results from controlled laboratory experiments yield a complicated picture, with either sex on occasion emerging as the more altruistic. The work of Andreoni and Vesterlund is an example. This was a modified version of the so-called 'dictator game' where subjects decide how to allocate fixed pay-offs between themselves and others, with different prices for the different pay-offs. The results of the experiment showed that men tended to be more altruistic when the altruistic gesture was cheaper (in terms of their own pay-off), while women were more altruistic when altruism was more expensive. Also, men were more likely than women to be perfectly selfish or perfectly altruistic, whereas women were more likely than men to share evenly.[5]

More specifically, some of women's caring activities could be viewed as examples of 'compulsory altruism' or 'coercive socialisation'.[6] In some cases of family caring, especially where violent men are concerned, women may be physically coerced into caring activities; in other cases they may be pressured by family, friends, or an overriding internal sense of responsibility, and there is no one else who will do it for them. In other words, the individuals concerned do not feel they really have a choice between altruistic and self-interested behaviour. In that case their behaviour will not change whatever happens. However, if a payment for their caring activities were offered, then it would be viewed favourably, either because it offered some kind of symbolic recognition of the work they are doing or because it provided some (doubtless inadequate) compensation for that work. The payment is not viewed as a kind of bribe, and therefore morally devaluing, as it might have been if it could have changed their behaviour.

However, although this undoubtedly is plausible as an account of the coercive situations described, it does not quite capture the situations investigated in the research with which we are concerned here. In most of these cases—child minding, caring for unrelated elderly people—the women voluntarily chose the caring activity. Hence they do not seem to be examples of compulsory altruism in the sense that they faced a total absence of choice. So we have to look elsewhere for reconciliation.

A second possible explanation concerns the differences in the magnitudes of the situations being investigated. Blood donation has some costs associated with it; it takes an hour or two, there is a certain amount of physical discomfort associated with the actual process, and some people experience a temporary feeling of lassitude after it. However, these costs pale into insignificance when compared with the costs associated with foster-parenting or looking after elderly people on a long-term basis. Hence it would not be surprising if, although people are willing to undergo the minor degree of self-sacrifice required in giving blood without compensation, they are not prepared to do so for the much larger sacrifices required by caring. In short, there might be a 'threshold effect' whereby people are prepared to make sacrifices for the sake of others up to a certain level of sacrifice, but beyond that point they require some compensation.

There is surely something to this argument. It was always a weakness of Titmuss's claims concerning the essential altruism inherent in human nature that they were based on examples such as blood donation that required relatively limited self-sacrifice; and one should be careful before generalising

---

[5] Andreoni and Vesterlund (2001). This also provides a useful summary of other research on the topic.

[6] Land and Rose (1985), Folbre and Weisskopf (1998). See also Leat and Gay's comment that women do not 'choose' to care (1987: 59).

from this to cases involving much greater sacrifices. However, again the argument does not wholly resolve the paradox. There remains the Frey case where, for the sake of the community, people did seem prepared to accept rather larger sacrifices (such as an increase in environmental hazards and the devaluation of property) than in the case of blood donation; although the costs in this situation are perhaps still not as great as those involved in caring situations, they are not offset by any benefits in terms of feelings of tenderness or gratitude that might accompany caring. Moreover, the level of support actually dropped when compensation was offered, which is precisely the opposite of the effect that the threshold argument would predict. Also, there are features of the caring situation that remain unexplained by the cost argument: for instance, the fact that some people did not expect to receive a market wage for their activities and indeed preferred payments to be labelled as compensation or expenses rather than as wages.

And I think it is here that we have the explanation that resolves the apparent paradox. In cases of knightly activity that involve large sacrifices, people do value some form of payment both as a form of recognition and as partial compensation for the costs involved. However, that payment should not be so great as to compensate fully for the sacrifice, for if it did there would be no satisfaction from making the sacrifice in the first place. In fact, if people were paid an amount that fully compensated them—or more than fully compensated them—the effect might be perverse, reducing rather than increasing the supply of the activity concerned. I develop this further in Chapter Four as part of a more general theory of public service motivation.

## GOVERNMENT: MORAL ATROPHY OR ENCOURAGEMENT?

In an ironic counterpart to the 'market corrupts' thesis, it has also been argued that it is government rather than market activity that corrupts. More specifically, it has been claimed that government institutions such as the welfare state can lead to a reduction in knightly activity by individuals: what has been termed moral atrophy.[7]

This reduction could arise for a number of reasons. First, government intervention reduces the opportunity for altruistic acts. So, by providing for the poor, the welfare state makes it less necessary for people to behave altruistically by helping them. This has been termed the 'substitution effect' in the literature. Second, through the taxation it imposes in order to finance its welfare activities, it reduces people's incomes and therefore the resources they have available for performing knightly acts such as charitable donations. This has been described as the 'income effect' (Abrams and Schmitz 1978). Third, it reduces the availability of the mechanisms for performing knightly acts. So,

---

[7] The arguments in this section owe a good deal to Goodin (1993).

for instance, it has been claimed that the introduction of state institutions providing welfare eroded the voluntary organisations and charities through which people used to express their charitable impulses (Coleman 1990: 321; Green 1993; 1996). Fourth, governments may actually change the motivation of people to perform knightly acts, making them more selfish. This could be done by conscious exhortation or example: a right-wing government could emphasise self-help, for instance, while denigrating so-called do-gooders in both its rhetoric and its policies. Or government could shift the balance of motivation by an unintended consequence of other policies. Thus, compulsory redistribution through welfare taxation and spending may make people resentful and thereby more concerned to protect their own interests.

Much of the discussion in the literature has concentrated on the first of these reasons: the substitution effect. If altruistic individuals' only concern is with the welfare of others—that is, in the terminology introduced in the previous chapter, if they are act-irrelevant knights—then any help those others get from government should lead to a reduction *pari passu* in the help provided by the knights. That is, government intervention would 'crowd out' individual altruistic actions. But, as we have seen in the previous chapter, in the cases studied in the literature this did not always occur.

One explanation for the failure of the substitution effect to appear in empirical studies is that actually there is an effect working in the opposite direction: governments have a positive, or demonstration, effect on knightly behaviour (Jones, Cullis, and Lewis 1998). Psychological evidence suggests that observing altruistic behaviour can encourage observers to engage in more such behaviour themselves (Bryan and Test 1967). In that case, public policies aimed at, for instance, helping the disadvantaged could serve as a model for potential knights. Again, this would be a shift in motivation, although in an opposite direction to that discussed above.

The state could influence the balance of motivation through its legislative activities. So the government could indicate through the legal system social disapproval of knavish practices, and thereby help internalise that disapproval within individuals. Thus the institution of a minimum wage could signal social disapproval of employers knavishly exploiting their employees by paying them low wages, and perhaps thereby affecting employers' attitudes towards their employees.[8]

---

[8] Indeed, no less a thinker than Aristotle has argued that the legislators themselves could have a favourable moral impact on their citizens, thus: 'Legislators make their citizens good by habituation: this is the intention of every legislator, and those who do not carry it out fail of their object. This is what makes the difference between a good constitution and a bad one' (see Thompson 1976: 92). In fact, Aristotle was making three points: that legislators by their actions can influence the moral character of the people for whom they are legislating; that they do it by 'habituation'; and that this influence should be to improve the moral character of their citizens. I am grateful to Karen Wright for drawing my attention to this passage.

## GOVERNMENT MODELS OF SERVICE DELIVERY

But there is another way, of more direct relevance to the concerns of this book, in which governments may 'corrupt' those who work within public services. Many governments historically have tended to reject market mechanisms entirely in their dealings with public services, and to use non-market models of service delivery. The two most common forms of these can be termed 'command and control' or 'hierarchical' models, and 'network' or 'trust' models.[9] And both of these have the potential for affecting the motivation of those who work within them, as we shall see.

The most widely known non-market model that governments have adopted is command and control. This relies upon the state both funding and providing the service concerned. A state-operated administrative bureaucracy organises and delivers services. The state owns all the relevant assets and employs, directly or indirectly, all staff. Those at the top of the hierarchy set the aims of the service. Resources are allocated to meet those aims according to managerial fiat. Service delivery occurs through administrative processes, via instructions given by superiors to those lower down in the managerial hierarchy. Classic examples are the forms of economic organisation that characterised the Soviet Union and eastern European countries before the fall of the Berlin Wall. But elements of command and control appear in many countries' systems of public service provision, including health care in several western European countries and education in many parts of the United States.

The network or trust model is perhaps less widely known, at least under those labels, but is becoming increasingly fashionable among some analysts and commentators. It is similar to command and control in some respects, but differs crucially in one key factor. Here again the state owns all the relevant facilities and assets and provides the funding, and to that extent the model is similar to command and control. But there is no direct command or instruction mechanism to allocate resources. Instead, service delivery on the ground is undertaken by qualified professionals who are trusted to make the right decisions in allocating the service among users. Resource allocation is undertaken through collaboration between the relevant individuals and agencies, through networks of more or less complexity, with the emphasis being on social relationships and trust rather than on hierarchical management, as in the command and control model, or on impersonal economic exchange, as in market-oriented models.[10]

An illustration of this kind of model in action was the British National Health Service between 1948 and 1991. This has been described by many authors

---

[9] This classification has many parents. But key references include Williamson (1983), Ouchi (1980), and Thompson, Levacic, and Mitchell (1991).

[10] The term 'network' is used to describe many different forms of organisation, from the Sicilian Mafia to clinical networks among medical professionals. I shall use it only in the sense specified here. For further reading and discussion of the term, see OD Partnerships Network (2002).

(including the present one) as an example of the first model: command and control (Le Grand 1999*b*). However, this is misleading. For there were rather few commands and precious little control. It is better described as an example of the network model, one that relied upon politicians and civil servants to allocate resources at a macro level and gave medical professionals almost complete clinical freedom to make ground-level decisions as to which patients should receive what treatment. The British school education system pre-1989 is another case, with local authorities allocating the funds to schools but with teachers being given extensive freedoms to determine curricula and teaching methods.[11]

What of the impact of these models on motivation? In the command and control model, for subordinates within the hierarchy motivation is irrelevant. It is assumed that subordinates will simply carry out the orders and instructions that emanate from the top. Non-compliance is met with punishment. Agents are neither knaves nor knights but something closer to pawns.[12]

It dose not need much insight to see that this kind of system can be directly demotivating—especially if the agents are knights. Systems that treat knightly providers as pawns risks demotivating them completely or turning them into knaves in an attempt to dodge the system, with potentially dire consequences for the public interest. Many of the classic illustrations of this can be found in the innumerable anecdotes that emanated from the old command and control economic systems in the former Soviet Union and eastern Europe. A more systematic study is that of H. G. Barkema (1995), discussed by Bruno Frey and Reto Jegen (2000). This study investigated the behaviour of 116 managers in Dutch firms in a variety of circumstances, and found that the closer the degree of personal supervision the greater was the (negative) impact on work effort.

In the network model, those who work in the service are essentially assumed to be knights. Their chief concern is supposed to be with the needs and wants of the clients they serve, and all their resource and service allocation decisions are made with those needs and wants in mind. There are no conflicts between different self-interested groups or individuals, or even between self-interest and the public interest, because none of the individuals involved is supposed to be self-interested. All have as their principal concern the same public interest; therefore the public interest will be served. Hence there is no need for an exchange or managerial relationship of any kind between them: trust will suffice. Policy-makers simply give agents resources and trust them to allocate them as they wish.

---

[11] In practice, most public service delivery systems incorporate elements of some or all of the models. Even in cases where one model is dominant, it may not take exactly the form spelt out here: there are not only quasi-markets but quasi-hierarchies and quasi-networks. See Exworthy, Powell, and Mohan (1999).

[12] An alternative interpretation is that the agents are knaves and the relationship is a contractual one. However, unlike in the quasi-market case, the contract is between employers and employees, where time, not a specific service, is exchanged for income. And the principal motivational tools are fear of punishment, such as job insecurity, not service-specific financial reward as in the quasi-market model: sticks rather than carrots.

But reliance upon trust in this way can create problems. A network system that trusts the providers of public services to put users' concerns ahead of their own will break down if the providers are really knaves; for there will be no mechanism for preventing them simply serving their own interests by their activities. But that is not all. Even if agents are knights, for the system to work as the policy-maker intends they have to be of a particular kind: that is, the kind that completely identifies his or her knightly interests with those of the policy-maker. They would have to share the same view of what constituted the public interest. But there would be little guarantee of this. A doctor whose principal concern was only for the welfare of his or her patients, for instance, would not necessarily work to the same agenda as a policy-maker whose concern was all the patients in a specific geographical area. For giving priority to the doctor's patients (as this particular knight would do) might result in patients with more serious needs elsewhere in the area being neglected—which could run against the aim of the policy-maker. Similarly, a teacher whose aim was the (non-selfish) furtherance of some fundamentalist religion might undertake activities that worked against a policy-maker's aim of wider social cohesion.

Faced with problems such as these, network models often end up having to develop systems of monitoring and regulation. Inspection and regulation units are set up aimed at ensuring that all providers (whether knights or knaves) actually do behave in ways that the policy-maker wants them to. This again has consequences for motivation. As Michael Power (1999: ch. 5) has argued, in circumstances where they are regularly audited professionals feel (rightly) that they are no longer trusted; they feel resentful at the auditing requirements imposed on them by the inspection agencies; they become less committed to the service and more inclined to pursue their self-interest.

So government can corrupt, not only through its own activities but also through the model of public service delivery that it chooses to adopt. Command and control, network, and quasi-market: all have the potential for shifting the balance of motivation among the individuals who work in the public sector. The direction of the shift will depend on the context; but some shift there is always likely to be.

## CONCLUSION

As the epigraph of this chapter illustrates, concern about the impact of the policy environment on motivation (or 'character') has a long history. And, whatever the detail of the research results, it is clear that policy structures, whether governmental or market, can indeed influence the balance of knightly and knavish behaviour in the individuals affected. This is a truth that policy-makers must learn to recognise; for, if they do not, their policies are likely to fail, with unfortunate consequences both for those who implement the policies and for those who are intended to benefit from them. In Chapter Four I consider some of the theoretical and policy implications of this fundamental insight.

# 4

# A Theory of Public Service Motivation

> Oh good old man, how well in thee appears
> The constant service of the antique world,
> When service sweat for duty not for meed!
> Thou art not for the fashion of these times
> Where none will sweat but for promotion.
>
> (Shakespeare, *As You Like It*)

Chapter Three illustrated how policy structures and context can change the balance of motivation in individuals working in the public sector. In this chapter I draw together some of the arguments into a theoretical account of public service motivation, and try to draw out some of its implications for policy.

## A THEORY OF PUBLIC SERVICE MOTIVATION

As we saw in Chapter Two, most people, including and perhaps especially those involved with the public sector, are motivated to perform altruistic acts because they wish to help others and because they derive some personal benefit from performing the acts that help others. That is, they are act-relevant knights.

Now the benefit that an act-relevant knight derives from performing an altruistic act itself is likely to be related to a number of factors. These would include the extent of the help they can offer, the extent to which that help benefits the persons concerned, and, probably of no little consequence, the degree of approval that the activity concerned attracts from the outside world. However, and this is the possibly unexpected insight from the work we have been reviewing, the motivation to undertake an altruistic act also seems to depend positively upon *the degree of personal sacrifice associated with the act*. We might term this the act's opportunity cost: that is, the cost to the individual concerned of other opportunities for personal benefit that have had to be forgone because he or she has chosen to undertake that act.

The relationship between the benefit derived from an altruistic act and its opportunity cost will be complex. If the cost is too little, the benefit from making the sacrifice will also be relatively little and the individual's motivation to perform the act will be correspondingly reduced. For the activity to feel really worthwhile, people need to feel that they have made some effort to perform it—to have incurred some significant cost. Too great a cost, on the other hand, will also demotivate them; they will feel that there is a limit to the amount of sacrifice of their interests that they are prepared to make for the sake of others, and they will therefore feel less inclined to undertake the activity. In other words, there are cost thresholds such that, if the cost falls below the lower threshold or rises above the higher one, people are less likely to perform the activity than if the cost falls in between.

This 'threshold' account contains some simplistic psychological assumptions and is obviously quite stylised as a description of human behaviour. But it can offer some insights into the apparent contradictions in the research results concerning market incentives that we have discussed in the previous chapter. It will be recalled that these provided evidence from blood donation and public reaction to the siting of nuclear waste disposal facilities which indicated that the introduction of market incentives devalued that activity. This contrasted with evidence concerning voluntary carers' activities which suggested that they favoured some form of compensation and regarded it as revaluing, not devaluing, their activities.

Now the carers who welcome compensation and who do not reduce their activity when offered it (or even do more) may be in the situation where there is still some significant cost of the activity to them: that is, the payment does not fully compensate them for the opportunity costs they incur. Hence some sacrifice is still involved and in consequence they continue to 'value' the activity. Indeed, the compensation, through indicating a measure of social approval for the activity, may have actually increased the benefit they derive from it, and they may supply more of it. The paid blood donors and those offered compensation for the nuclear waste disposal facility, on the other hand, may be in the situation where the compensation is adequate or more than adequate to compensate them for their perceived sacrifice. Hence there is no net sacrifice, no altruistic satisfaction from the activity concerned, and supply is thereby reduced.

Of course, in the blood donation and nuclear waste compensation cases, if compensation were increased yet further, individuals' knavish instincts may begin to kick in and supply would increase again. In short, if financial payments for an activity are introduced at a low level where previously there were none, the supply of the activity may remain constant or even increase; as the financial payments are increased, the supply will be reduced; as they increase further, the supply will gradually increase again.

This theoretical account can be viewed as a special case of a more general theory put forward by Bruno Frey, whose pioneering work on community reactions to the siting of a nuclear waste disposal facility has been noted above.[1] This in turn is based on the psychological literature concerning the distinction between 'intrinsic' and 'extrinsic' motivation.[2] There it is argued that there are two kinds of motivation for action: one intrinsic or internal to the individual concerned and one extrinsic or external. This is usually applied to the workplace, where intrinsic factors are taken to include interest in or enjoyment of the work for its own sake, while extrinsic ones include wages and salaries, promotion, the threat of losing one's job, and direct commands or orders.

It is argued that there may be a trade-off between the two kinds of motivation, such that too heavy an emphasis on extrinsic motivation can drive out intrinsic motivation. So motivations activated by external factors, such as monetary incentives or direct orders (as in the hierarchical model of service delivery discussed in the previous chapter), can 'crowd out' motivations that are internal to the individual, such as more altruistic concerns. In particular, they will do so if they are viewed as controlling by the individuals concerned—as reducing their sphere of self-determination and self-esteem. However, extrinsic motivational factors can also reinforce intrinsic motivation if they are seen as supporting self-determination or self-esteem. In that case external motivation is seen as 'crowding in' intrinsic motivation.

This theory has a number of problems, including the difficulty of satisfactorily distinguishing between 'intrinsic' and 'extrinsic'. As Robert Lane (1991: 368) notes, 'the "reward" for intrinsic motivation is the inner feeling, but the information that produces that feeling is often extrinsic—and indeed may be manipulated by another'. Moreover, although it is tempting to read directly across from 'extrinsic' and 'intrinsic' motivations to 'knavish' and 'knightly' ones respectively, this would not be correct. Extrinsic motivational factors do include what we might consider to be the knavish ones of cash payments or fears about job security, but could also include forms of recognition by the outside world of the merits of altruistic actions. On the other hand, many aspects of intrinsic motivation could include essentially self-interested factors such as enjoyment of the task itself, satisfying one's curiosity, and so forth, as well as the gratification received from performing knightly acts.

However, the concepts are nonetheless useful for our purposes. To return to Frey, he argues that changes in the supply of any activity (not just altruistic ones) in response to changes in the financial rewards associated with that activity will be the product of the interaction of two effects: what he terms the Crowding-Out Effect and the Relative Price Effect. The Crowding-Out Effect occurs when an extrinsic reward is introduced for an activity (such as the introduction of financial payments) and thereby undermines the intrinsic motivation to perform the activity (which may include altruistic motivations,

---

[1] The best account of Frey's most recent thinking can be found in Frey (2000).
[2] See, for instance, Lepper and Greene (1978), Deci and Ryan (1985), Lane (1991: 371–4).

but may not). The Relative Price Effect increases the 'price' of not undertaking the activity relative to that of undertaking it (that is, it increases the money forgone through not doing it) and hence encourages a greater supply of the activity. Which effect is dominant at any one time will determine the level of supply of the activity concerned.[3]

In Frey's terminology, what we are suggesting here is the following. (For those comfortable with supply and demand diagrams, a diagrammatic explanation is provided in the Annex to this chapter.) The introduction of financial payments for altruistic activities can lead to a crowding-out effect because it reduces individuals' perception of the sacrifices they are making to engage in that activity. However, that impact is not continuous, but begins to dominate only as the value of the payment gets close to fully compensating the individuals concerned for their sacrifices. Below that level it is more likely to be 'crowding-in' that dominates, with the financial payment indicating social approval of the activity and hence encouraging them to supply more of it. If, on the other hand, the value of the compensation is larger than the monetary value of the opportunities forgone by undertaking the activity (the cost), the relative price effect begins to dominate and again more of the activity will be supplied.

The central idea in this account—that the amount of sacrifice involved in undertaking a knightly act is an important motivating factor for the act—is contrary to much economic intuition. Thus Geoffrey Brennan and Alan Hamlin say 'it is a matter of *basic economic logic* that an [altruistic] act will be undertaken more extensively . . . if it is less costly to the actor in terms of other desired things forgone'. And Nancy Folbre and Thomas Weisskopf argue 'a higher price cannot, *by definition*, elicit a greater supply of labour motivated by altruism'.[4] But, as we can see, in fact there is no logical or definitional objection to the idea that individuals may be motivated to undertake altruistic activity by the fact that a measure of sacrifice is associated with it—or indeed to the idea that the greater the sacrifice, the more of the activity that may be undertaken (at least up to a point).[5]

The sacrifice account may not be consistent with 'economic logic' but it is consistent with some work done in a related context: the public perception of what constitutes a volunteer. Studies by Cnaan and colleagues show that the perception of who is or is not a volunteer is related to the extent to which the public sees the individual concerned as incurring a 'net cost' (total costs minus

---

[3]  Frey has extensively reviewed the empirical evidence for crowding-out and crowding-in. See Frey (2000) and Frey and Jegen (2000).

[4]  Brennan and Hamlin (1995); Folbre and Weisskopf (1998: 181). Emphasis added in both cases. See also Brennan and Hamlin (2000: 19): '[T]he desire to act morally will be more decisive the lower the opportunity cost.'

[5]  The key factor for economists is that the amount of sacrifice involved is not simply a function of the constraints that individuals face, as is normally assumed; instead, the degree of sacrifice actually enters into their utility function and thereby affects their underlying preference structure for knightly and knavish activities.

total benefits) from the activity concerned (Cnaan and Amrofell 1994; Cnaan, Handy, and Wadsworth 1996). The greater the net cost—what we have termed the sacrifice—the more 'pure' is the volunteer. Although this does not say anything about what actually motivates volunteers, it does demonstrate that in the public perception there is a link between the amount of sacrifice and the exercise of altruism, at least as altruism is expressed through volunteering.

The theory is also consistent with the social psychologists' argument that crowding-in reflects a reinforcement of intrinsic motivations, and crowding-out a controlling of those motivations. It will be recalled that external factors can reinforce intrinsic motivation if they are seen as supporting self-determination or self-esteem. In that case external motivation is seen as crowding-in intrinsic motivation. In the cases where individuals value payment, it is plausible to suppose that this is because they feel reinforced in their actions because, through the provision of payment, the outside world is recognising—and appreciating—the sacrifices that they are voluntarily making. In the cases where individuals appear to regard payment as devaluing their altruistic motivation, they may be viewing the payments as controlling—as reducing their sphere of self-determination and self-esteem—and hence they will be demotivating. The individual is no longer making a sacrifice, and has thereby lost a measure of autonomy in what he or she is doing.

## IMPLICATIONS FOR SERVICE DELIVERY

If this analysis is broadly correct, what are its implications for the discussions in the previous chapter, especially those concerning the corrupting effects of markets and financial payments? The analysis suggests that market payments can be employed to good effect but that they need to be employed with care. If they are small, then they need have no crowding-out effect on altruistic motivation; indeed, they might even complement it. If, on the other hand, they are too great, they may well erode people's sense of sacrifice and thereby reduce their intrinsic motivation to perform the activities concerned. Supply will fall. Of course, as market payments increase further, they will increase extrinsic motivation: that is to say, they will appeal to individuals' self-interest, and hence induce further supply of that activity that way.

The amount actually paid in any given situation will depend on the level of demand and on the positions of the thresholds for the individuals concerned. If these are known, then the payment issue is relatively simple. If the demand for the activity is relatively low, then the level of altruistic supply, coupled perhaps with a little extra supply crowded-in by some small extrinsic reward, may be sufficient to meet the demand. That might have been the situation in the 1960s for blood donation. If, on the other hand, demand is relatively high, then the amount paid will have to be sufficient to induce a level of supply through knavish motivations that is more than sufficient to compensate for any fall due to the crowding-out of altruistic supply (these arguments are illustrated diagrammatically in the Annex).

There are moral issues involved here. In the situation of high demand, is the social gain of having sufficient of the activity to meet the demand worth the social cost of a partial or complete crowding-out of altruism? In the situation of low demand, are the altruistic suppliers being exploited by receiving lower levels of reward than they would have done if they had been more knavish? These are important issues, but proper treatment of them at this point would deflect us from the main analytic argument. Hence I postpone that discussion to the end of the chapter.

So it is possible to use this kind of analysis to structure the payment system so as to induce the right amount of the activity—if the positions of the thresholds for the individuals concerned are known. But this condition is strong. In practice it may be far from easy to gain the information necessary to fulfil it. What if, as seems much more likely in real policy situations, the thresholds' locations are not known, or, at least, are not known with sufficient precision to enable the tailoring of payment structures in the manner proposed? How then should the incentive structure for the delivery of public services be constructed?

## Knightly Strategies

One answer to the problem of ignorance concerning motivation and one that, as we have seen in the previous chapter, has often been adopted in the provision of public services through the use of the 'network' model, is simply to assume that everyone is a knight. Those working in the public sector receive flat salaries and are trusted to provide the service with little or no monitoring of performance.

The principal difficulty here, as discussed in the previous chapter, is that, if in fact all the individuals concerned are really knaves, then the provision of low-quality, high-cost services is inevitable. For the knaves will exploit their position of trust to further their own ends, reducing uncomfortable effort and thereby reducing outcome, lowering both the quality and the quantity of the service provided. Moreover, problems remain with this strategy, even if there are many knights and the knaves are only a few. For, as the knights observe knaves' exploitation of the situation, they may feel their goodwill is being exploited. They will feel exploited themselves and perhaps start behaving more knavishly. Knights will turn into knaves. And this process may be cumulative; for as more convert to knavishness the incentives for the remaining knights to do likewise become even more intense.

Peer pressure may alleviate this to some extent, especially in the early stages of the process. The knights may engage in verbal or other forms of social disapproval to keep the knaves under control. But the effectiveness of this will be hampered by the fact that much of the activity (or inactivity) of public services is not readily observable by peers, taking place as it may in the individual classroom or practice surgery, for instance.

Again as mentioned in the previous chapter, similar problems also arise if the individuals are indeed knights but different kinds of knights from the policy-maker (the doctor concerned only with his or her patients, the teacher of fundamentalist religion). Again the public interest will not be served, at least in the policy-maker's terms. Here peer pressure is likely to operate in a way that exacerbates the problem, for an individual's immediate peers are likely to share his or her values and to resist the imposition of other values by outside authorities.

Now institutions have developed that attempt to address these problems (Arrow 1963). One is that of the profession, in which professional organisa-tions establish codes of ethics designed to prevent exploitative behaviour and try to enforce those codes on their members. The problem here is that the pro-fessional organisations have a tendency themselves to become knavish in their approach. Although designed to protect the users' interests, they too often end up protecting those of their members. And, once they are perceived as doing that, the trust that they are supposed to be reinforcing has gone.

Another institution for trying to prevent exploitation is the government-appointed regulator or monitor. But, again as we saw in the previous chapter, monitoring, even with a light touch, can also have the effect of turning the knight into the knave. If people feel they are not trusted to provide a quality service and, moreover, are forced to undertake elaborate activities to prove that they are in fact doing a good job (such as filling out forms, writing reports, and so forth), they often become either demoralised and demotivated or else motivated to behave in a more self-protective manner. Regulation and trust are difficult to reconcile.

### Knavish Strategies

An alternative that could be considered is that, in a situation of ignorance con-cerning the motivational structure of individuals, it would be safest to adopt public policies based on the assumption that everyone is a knave. For a knav-ish strategy will do little harm if people are actually knights; and it could pay off dramatically if they are knaves.[6]

The point can be illustrated by an example. Take a particular group of people involved in some public service institution, say, doctors in a hospital. Now suppose that most of these doctors are in fact knights, doing the best they can for their patients, often at considerable personal sacrifice. Moreover, the reward structure of the hospital is actually based on that assumption, with automatic payment of salaries and with no monitoring of doctor behaviour or performance review. But suppose, too, that there are a few specialists that are knaves, spending their time on the golf course or managing their investment portfolios, to the obvious detriment of their patients. And suppose further that this behaviour, despite the fact that it is characteristic of only a small number of doctors, is damaging the performance and reputation of the hospital as a whole, and thereby threatening its survival.

---

[6] For a critique of these arguments, see Hausman (1998). See also Goodin (1996: 41–2) and Pettit (1996: 72–5).

Now suppose in this situation that a system is introduced of performance-related pay. Since they are not motivated by economic self-interest, it could be argued that this will leave the knights' motivational structure untouched: they will still derive the same reward as before from doing good to patients. They will therefore carry on undertaking to the best of their ability all the activities that are part of what they perceive as their duty to patients. The knaves, on the other hand, will see that it is now in their self-interest to perform their duties properly and will react accordingly. What the new structure will have done, therefore, is bring the knaves into line, ensuring that they perform as least as well as the knights. Everybody, knights and knaves, is now performing to the best of his or her ability; and the hospital is saved.

However, in practice things may not always be that simple. The principal problem with the example is that it assumes the introduction of the knavish strategy will have no impact on knightly behaviour. But if the effect is to reduce the sacrifice involved in their work for the knights, then, if their activity levels are such that they are between the two cost thresholds referred to above, then, as we have seen, this may crowd out their intrinsic motivation and lead to a reduction in activity.

Now it could be argued that in one sense, even if something like this does occur in these situations, it does not matter. Any fall in activity can be overcome by increasing the rate of performance pay (on the assumption that this is economically feasible) until the erstwhile knights have crossed the threshold where the relative price effect begins to dominate. Then, so long as the incentives for knaves are the right ones, performance will continue to improve.

But there is a problem. This argument assumes that the knaves' strategy is watertight; that there is no way of getting round the system in a way that furthers self-interest except, on this occasion, at the expense of the public good. So, for instance, a system of performance-related pay would require reliable and accurate procedures for measuring and monitoring performance: procedures that cannot be fiddled to indicate better performance than is actually happening or that more effort is being made than is actually the case. But such systems are often difficult, if not impossible, to construct or maintain, especially for services such as health or education, where quality can be difficult to measure. As we saw in the previous chapter, this was one of the central points of Titmuss's critique of the use of market incentives to increase the supply of blood. Because it was so difficult properly to monitor quality in blood donation, market incentives would inevitably lead to the provision of low-quality blood. So, by extension, for public services: if quality cannot be properly assessed by the purchaser of the service, the knave will have every incentive to lower quality.

### Incentive Contracts

In recent years economists have developed mechanisms for contracting between the purchaser and the provider of a service that try to address some of these problems, especially those concerned with the asymmetry of information concerning cost, quality, and effort between purchaser and provider. These mechanisms can result in the provider's revealing some of the necessary information and thus minimising some of the difficulties illustrated above. They are often termed 'incentive contracts' on the grounds that they are contracts that incorporate incentives for providers to reveal information. The analyses use the language of 'principal–agent' theory, where the principals are the purchasers or commissioners of services, such as health care, education, and social care; while the agents are those who deliver the service on the ground, such as medical professionals, teachers, or social workers.

Avinash Dixit has shown how incentive contracting can help resolve three kinds of information problem that principals face.[7] First is the so-called moral hazard problem. The agents are contributing to the production of an outcome that the principal values. The principal wishes to encourage the agents to produce more of the outcome and is prepared to pay them to do so. But the principal does not know how much effort the agents have to put in to achieve the outcome and how much is due to the factors outside the agents' control. Hence the principal does not know how much to reward the agents for improvements in the outcome. The principal also wants to make sure that the agents remain in the business of provision; they do not want to set up payment structures that result in people leaving to go to other work that, say, pays better or gives more security.

An example might be a situation where a government agency wishes to improve a school's exam results. A good set of exam results could be due to the teaching efforts of the school and its staff; but it could also arise from factors connected with the school's intake of pupils such as differences in the socio-economic area in which the school is located or in their innate ability. In this situation any reward structure that is tied too closely to, say, exam performance would not necessarily encourage more effort by staff in schools whose intake is such that already exam results are good; and it might actively demotivate staff in schools with a poorer intake who see little hope of achieving the results necessary for the rewards. Rewarding accorded to value-added might be one solution in those circumstances; but the information requirements for that are high.

One possible solution is to give the agent a fixed amount and then a bonus per unit of the outcome achieved. The fixed amount is to ensure that whatever happens to outcomes the agent still receives an income; in effect it partly shifts the risk of a poor outcome due to factors beyond the agent's control to the principal. The size of the bonus would depend upon the probability of outcomes being influenced by the agent's own efforts; the lower that probability, the smaller the bonus. And the size of both the fixed amount and the bonus would depend on the agent's likely income in alternative employment and on all the relevant parties' attitudes to risk.

---

[7] Dixit (2002). Much of this section is based on this very useful paper.

A second problem, known as adverse selection, arises where the agent has private information that would benefit the principal, but the principal cannot access that information. For instance, some hospitals or schools may have low operating costs but are able to conceal this from the purchasers, who could therefore end up paying substantially more for hospital or educational services than they need have done.

In this situation, one solution is to offer the agent a menu of contracts. If the contracts are properly designed, the choice of contract made by the agent indirectly reveals the information concealed. For instance, suppose a purchaser knows that a hospital's activity can be supplied at either of two cost levels: high or low. The purchaser wishes to make a contract with the hospital but does not know whether the hospital faces high or low costs. In the absence of any contractual sanction, the hospital, if managed by knaves, will obviously claim that it faces high costs and therefore should be paid a price for the activity that will cover those high costs, regardless of whether it is in fact low-cost or high-cost. For, if it really is high-cost, it will need the contract price to be at the higher level because otherwise it will lose money; and, if it really is low-cost, it will make a greater profit the higher the price.

Now suppose the hospital is offered a choice of two contracts. One is an agreement to buy a small amount at a price equal to, or slightly above, the high-cost level. The other agrees to buy a larger amount at a lower price. The lower price is set at a point where, if the hospital has low costs and accepts this contract, it will make a slightly larger overall profit than if it had accepted the other contract. If the hospital has high costs, it will accept the first contract; if it has low costs, it will accept the second. If the hospital actually faced low costs, the purchaser will not have done quite as well as it would have done in a world of perfect information, for it will have been forced to pay above that cost; but it will have done better than if it had paid the original (high-cost) asking price. And, either way, it will have forced the hospital to reveal the truth about its cost structure, information that will be useful for subsequent contracting negotiations.

Third, there is what Dixit calls the costly verification problem. This is the case where the principal can verify whether or not an outcome has been achieved only through some expensive auditing or inspection procedure. Examples might be the more qualitative aspects of hospital care, such as consideration to patients, or cases where there are opportunities for fraud, such as schools leaking exam questions to pupils before an exam. In such cases, one solution is to have a scheme that does not audit agents if they report their worst possible outcome, but in which the probability of an audit rises with the quality of the reported outcome. If the audit reveals that the agents told the truth they are rewarded; if it reveals that they lied they are fined. The probability of an audit for a given reported outcome and the rewards and fines are all calculated in a way so as to ensure truthful revelation by the agents at the least cost to the principal.

All of this assumes that the agent is a knave, or at least is concerned only with his or her own financial state. Martin Chalkley and James Malcolmson (1998) have analysed the situation where agents are wholly knaves, wholly knights, or partially knights and knaves. The knights are act-irrelevant; they have direct concerns for the users of the services they are providing, but they get no special satisfaction from performing the acts themselves. An additional complication of Chalkley and Malcolmson's analysis is that they postulate agents whose efforts can be directed in any of three directions: quantity increasing, quality increasing, or cost reducing.

If agents are knaves, all effort in their analysis has a purely negative effect on their overall utility. The problem then is similar to that described by Dixit but has the additional complication that the ideal contract would encourage not only the correct degree of effort but also the correct direction of effort (into cost reducing, quality increasing, or quantity increasing). Chalkley and Malcolmson's conclusion is that in fact it is not possible to construct a contract that will do both of these things and instead one must accept that either quality increasing or cost reduction will be minimal and construct a contract to maximise the other variable given that fact.

If agents are knights (that is, if their aims are identical to that of the principal), then the simplest thing for the principals to do is to give agents a fixed budget and allow them to spend that budget as they will. This is basically the network model discussed in Chapter Three. For if the hospital is given a fixed budget it will spend it in the same way that the purchaser would like it to without any additional incentives or scrutiny. Thus a simple block contract is the optimal solution in this situation.

A partially knightly hospital will be different from a totally knightly hospital in that it will get less satisfaction from efforts towards improving the quantity and quality of treatment and/or the balance it seeks between these two will be different. In this situation, Chalkley and Malcolmson conclude, it makes sense to have some cost reimbursement in the contract, so long as monitoring the actual cost incurred is not too inaccurate or itself too costly.

As the reader will readily recognise, these are highly stylised situations and there are many complications to be surmounted before these kinds of ideas can be usefully applied in the real world. These would include the fact that, in that world, negotiations are repeated over time, giving the opportunity for 'repeated games' and the opportunities for strategic behaviour and learning that these give; that there are usually multiple outcomes, multiple principals, and multiple agents; and that many public services have outcomes that are even vaguer and less measurable than in the examples used above. There are developments in principal–agent analysis that have tried to take some of these complications on board, and there is hope for more.[8] But the aim was not to argue that this kind of analysis yet has the answer to all the problems that we are addressing, but simply that it indicates a promising direction of travel.

---

[8]  Again these are usefully summarised in Dixit (2002).

### Non-profit Organisations

Another way of resolving some of the motivation problems that confront the delivery of public services that has been widely advocated is to place a greater reliance upon non-profit or voluntary organisations as providers of services.[9] To take two recent British examples, Ed Mayo and Henrietta Moore under the auspices of the New Economics Foundation have advocated converting hospitals and schools into what they term 'mutuals' or social enterprises, while the Public Management Foundation has advocated the setting up of 'public interest' companies.[10] In fact the non-profit label is a broad one, embracing not only mutuals, social enterprises, and public interest companies but charities, faith-based organisations, consumer and employee cooperatives, and—in the United States—public benefit companies.

These organisations are very diverse in their governance structures. Some are run by employees: workers cooperatives. Some are controlled by users: consumer cooperatives. Some are managed by representatives of the local community, some by large charitable or faith-based organisations, such as churches. Others are managed by some or all of these, with representatives of the various stakeholders on the board. But they all share one characteristic. This is not (as the non-profit label might seem to imply) that they do not make profits. Rather it is that any profits or surpluses which they do make are not distributed to shareholders. Instead, non-profits' surpluses are retained and reinvested in the business. This characteristic is often termed 'the non-distribution constraint'.

The reason why organisations with non-distribution constraints are regarded as a possible solution to some of the problems that confront public service delivery concerns information and motivation. Those who run the organisation are by definition not motivated by the need to distribute profits to shareholders. Hence, it is argued, if contracted to provide a public service, they will not exploit their informational advantage to the detriment of the public interest. If users or purchasers (if the user is not the purchaser) cannot effectively monitor the quality of the service they are purchasing, they may prefer services provided by non-profits because they trust them not to reduce quality in search of shareholder profits. A related argument is that, because the people who work in non-profit organisations are usually prepared to take lower wages than those who work in for-profit ones, non-profits are likely to have lower costs of service delivery. For both reasons, principals contracting with non-profits could expect to get a higher quality of service for the same cost, or the same quality for lower cost, than if they contracted with for-profit firms.

---

[9]  Rose-Ackerman (1996: 716). This article is the most comprehensive recent review of the literature on non-profits.

[10]  Mayo and Moore (2001), Corrigan, Steele, and Parston (2001), and Brecher (2002). In fact this is all part of what Jeremy Kendall (2000) has called a 'mainstreaming' of the third sector into public policy in England in the late 1990s.

However, there is a problem relating to the motivational assumptions that underlie this argument. It seems to be assumed that the major reason why for-profit firms will behave in exploitative ways in a quasi-market situation is that they have to generate profits to distribute to shareholders. Hence organisations that do not have that possibility—that have a non-distribution constraint—will behave in a more altruistic fashion: that is, they will operate in the public interest. But this is a non sequitur. Whether in fact these organisations do conform to this assumption will depend crucially upon who actually manages them and what the motivational structure is for the managers. Employee cooperatives, for instance, will have a different set of motivations from consumer cooperatives, faith-based organisations different motivations from secular community ones, and so on. In each case there is no guarantee that they will be motivated to serve the public interest—or, if they are, it will be their own conception of the public interest, one which may be very different from that of the purchaser or principal.

Take employee cooperatives, for example. The aim of such an organisation must be the collective welfare of its members. The cooperative may have broader social objectives, but this would only be because those objectives are held by individual members, not because they are inherent to the organisation. And actions designed to maximise the collective welfare of the organisation may not be consistent with broader conceptions of the public interest. For instance, economic theory predicts that employee cooperatives will tend to restrict employment, to be less innovative, and to invest less than their for-profit counterparts. All these outcomes may be quite undesirable from a social perspective (Estrin 1989). Further, there is no reason to suppose that an employee cooperative pursuing the collective welfare of its members will be more reluctant to exploit an informational advantage it may have over the users or purchasers of its services than one driven by the interest of shareholders.

Or consider faith-based organisations. Their aim in, say, running a school may be altruistic in the sense that those in charge of the organisation are not motivated by the desire for personal gain. However, the form their altruism takes may not be consistent with the interest of the wider society. Thus, they may offer high-quality schooling, but in a fashion that is coupled explicitly or implicitly with a separatist moral or religious agenda that may be destructive of the wider community. It is possible that the morality associated with their faith may be such that they would not seek to exploit any informational advantage they may have over users; but there is no guarantee of this.

A possible way of overcoming some of these problems is to have no one specific group running the enterprise, but to have an organisational structure in which all stakeholders are represented. Attractive as this may sound at first sight, again motivational issues would have to be sorted out before it became a practical proposition. Different groups would have different motivations, some knightly, some knavish. Some mechanism would have to be introduced for reconciling these differences in a manner that was acceptable to all parties; and that may not be easy to find.

Another possible avenue is through the use of incentive contracts. Dixit (2001), for instance, has shown how to design a contract with a faith-based organisation, aspects of whose faith the principal dislikes. More specifically, he takes a case where an agent is producing both a product which the principal values but also a by-product from which the principal gets no or a negative value. The result is one in which the pay-off to the principal from the contract can be significantly reduced if the principal dislikes the by-product sufficiently, suggesting that the principal may be better-off contracting with an organisation with a different motivational structure (such as a for-profit firm) even if the latter has higher costs.

It is worth noting that non-profits may face other problems as service deliverers. They can raise capital only through issuing debts which may increase their vulnerability to economic downturns. Some forms of non-profits, especially those where no one 'owns' the surplus, may have little incentive to be efficient in their use of resources. And since there is no market in ownership shares, they lack the market discipline that the fear of takeover can provide. But at the end of the day it is the actual structure of motivation that will be the principal factor determining outcomes; and it is this that needs understanding before non-profits are judged to be the answer for public service delivery.

### Robust Incentives

So strategies that appeal either only to knaves or only to knights are unattractive; and incentive contracting and the use of non-profit organisations have some way to go before they can be useful policy tools. Another approach, and one that seems preferable if we are ignorant about what actually motivates people, is to try to design what might be termed 'robust' incentive structures: strategies or institutions that align knightly and knavish incentives. Such structures would not be dependent on a particular assumption concerning motivation and hence are robust to whatever assumption is made.[11]

Put another way, any incentive structure for public sector institutions must nurture individuals' non-material concerns. It should avoid setting up opposition between altruistic rewards and the material self-interest of those working in the public sector. It must not be constructed on the assumption that altruism does not exist, both because the assumption is false and because such cynicism may be self-fulfilling. But incentive structures must also not assume naively that such altruism is unlimited, and not in need of encouragement and reinforcement.

Although finding a robust incentive structure in this sense of the term is far from easy, it is also far from impossible. I hope to demonstrate this in the first

---

[11] To avoid possible confusion I should make it clear that this is a different terminology from that used by Robert Goodin when he deals with the broad issue of institutional design. For him, a 'robust' strategy is one that is robust to change, involving policies that are 'capable of adapting to new situations' (1996: 40–1). What I call a robust strategy is closer to what Goodin would term a strategy as 'sensitivity to motivational complexity' (1996: 40–1).

two chapters in Part III. However, some issues have surfaced in the discussions that have a moral dimension and it seems appropriate to conclude this chapter by looking at these in a little more detail.

## MORALITY AND MOTIVATION

There are two moral issues that need addressing. First, we noted earlier that, in a situation of high demand for an activity, the 'price' of having sufficient activity supplied to meet that demand might be the partial or complete crowding-out of altruistic supply of the activity. If altruistic acts are regarded as socially desirable, then paying this price will have social costs. Are those costs sufficient to outweigh the gain from having a supply that is sufficient to meet demand?

The principal advocate of relying upon altruistic motivations to deliver public services, Richard Titmuss, was able to avoid this problem by using as his principal example the situation with respect to blood donation in Britain in the 1960s, where altruistic supply did appear to be sufficient to meet demand. However, as we have seen, there is no reason to suppose this will always be the case; and indeed it was not so ten years later when Britain had to import blood supplies from the United States.

The other moral issue concerns the danger of exploitation. Blood donation involves people giving for free a commodity that, had they been less altruistic, they could have charged for (assuming that they were in a system that permitted the sale of blood). This parallels the situation of public sector professionals where, because of their commitment to public service, they are paid less than they would have to be paid if they were more self-interested. Generally, is it morally correct to pay people less to provide a service than they would have been paid if they had been less altruistic?

More precisely, suppose there are two possible payment levels, each of which would generate enough supply of the service to meet the demand for it, but one of which relies on altruistic motivations and hence is lower than the other, which relies upon self-interest. Put another way, suppose that public sector workers motivated in part by knightly considerations are paid less than they would need to be to generate the same work effort if they were completely knavish. Are they being exploited?

Some are in no doubt. Thus Nancy Folbre and Thomas Weisskopf (1998: 186) argue that 'many workers in care service jobs are exploited in the sense that they are being paid less than they would be in a world entirely lacking in altruism, responsibility or intrinsic enjoyment of helping others'. And indeed there is evidence that this kind of phenomenon is widespread. Robert Frank (1996) has analysed the wage differentials of a cohort of graduates from Cornell University, concluding that a person employed by a private-for-profit firm earns a salary more than 13 per cent higher than she would if she was employed by government. Paula England and colleagues have shown that the more caring a job requires, other things being equal, the lower the wages paid, and that care work in general is done by workers, mostly women, who earn less than they would in other jobs requiring the same education and experience.[12]

It is apparent that, in dealing with both these issues, there is a potential clash of several moral principles. Relying upon financial incentives to deliver public services may reduce the number of altruistic acts and increase the number of self-interested ones, which would be morally undesirable. However, it may also lead to the provision of more public services, which, other things being equal, would be morally desirable. And it could be seen as being less exploitative, which again would be desirable on moral grounds.

Now unless one is prepared to assert unequivocally that one of these principles lexicographically dominates the others—that is, one principle has to be served in all circumstances even if in doing so all other principles are violated—there is no general resolution of this issue. So, if some people believe that the only moral value that has to be served is that concerning the intrinsic moral superiority of altruistic acts, then they will judge the use of self-interest to be morally inferior to the use of altruistic providers—even if the result is fewer (or worse) public services being provided. Motivation is morally valued; outcome is not. If, on the other hand, they believe that society's only concern should be about the level of public service provided and if they also believe that the use of self-interested providers will increase that, then they will support the use of these providers regardless of the impact this has on the stock of altruism in the society. Outcome is the only matter of moral concern. Or, if their only concern is to prevent exploitation, then they will support all arrangements that reduce exploitation, even if the result is both fewer public services and less altruism.

However, in practice few of us are that lexicographic in our moral judgements. Most people would recognise that different circumstances yield different answers. For instance, if the result of relying purely on voluntary blood donation or on low-paid nurses was that a large number of patients died from a lack of blood available for transfusion or from a lack of appropriate nursing care, then we might be prepared to sanction a change in those arrangements that resulted in a substantial improvement in outcomes, even if the result was less opportunity for the exercise of altruism. If, on the other hand, a switch to less altruistic modes of provision led to relatively little improvement, then we would be less likely to approve such a change. In the real world, each case has to be examined on its merits and a decision taken as to whether, in that case, the movement towards realising one principle more than outweighs any movement away from another.

The idea that moral principles or values may have to be 'traded-off' against one another is a major insight of modern philosophical discourse.[13] Yet it is alien to many people, especially, it would seem, some of those engaged in debates concerning the delivery of public services. Ideological stands abound,

---

[12] England (1992), England and Folbre (1999), England, Budig, and Folbre (2001).
[13] For further discussion see Barry (1965: ch. 1) and Le Grand (1991: ch. 3).

brooking no compromise and allowing no possibility for trade-off. Yet in fact these kinds of trade-off are inevitable in all policy debate and implementation. In this case, it is impossible to say that, in all circumstances, the morality of altruism should always be in the ascendant over that of positive service outcomes, or that either should dominate the avoidance of exploitation. The exact balance will have to be a matter of judgement.

## CONCLUSION

Individual motivation is complex, especially where those working in the public sector are concerned. The evidence concerning the relationship between financial rewards and the supply of public services suggests that there may be reward thresholds above and below which behaviour is rather different. Below the lower threshold, financial rewards may be viewed as reinforcing or crowding-in supply, since they signify social approval of the sacrifice the individual is making in pursuing his or her activities. Extra payments above that threshold, however, erode the magnitude of the sacrifice that he or she is making, and thereby partly erode the motivation for the act. Supply is crowded out. However, as payments increase further, another threshold is reached where the relative price effect begins to dominate the crowding-out effect and supply increases again.

If policy-makers know where the thresholds are for an individual or a group of individuals, it is relatively easy to design a payment system that elicits the supply of the activity that we want (although the impact of any payment system on quality as well as quantity has to be borne in mind). If we do not know the underlying motivational structure, then the best strategy is likely to be the adoption of robust incentive structures: ones designed to align knightly and knavish motivations and to appeal to both the knight and the knave. Although these may be difficult to design, it is not impossible to do so, as we shall illustrate in Chapters Seven and Eight.

### ANNEX: A THEORY OF PUBLIC SERVICE MOTIVATION: DIAGRAMMATIC REPRESENTATION

Consider an altruistic activity that, if an individual undertakes it, he or she benefits others. An example could be blood donation; but it could also be the supply of any public service that has this property. Assume that he or she derives no direct personal benefit himself or herself for the activity and indeed incurs personal costs from undertaking it.

Suppose first that all individuals undertaking the activity are knaves: that is, they derive no benefit from the fact that the activity is of use to others. In that case, they will require some payment to undertake the activity, with the amount increasing as the amount of the activity increased. An aggregate supply curve for an activity might look as in Fig. 4.1: a conventional supply curve, with increasing activity as payment for the activity increases.

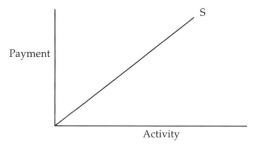

**Figure 4.1.** *Knavish supply*

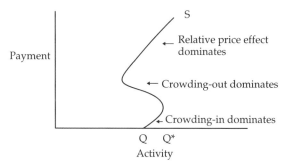

**Figure 4.2.** *Knightly supply*

Now suppose the individuals are all knights: that is, they derive some reward from the fact that others benefit from the activity. Suppose, too, that the reward they derive is related to the sacrifices that they themselves make to undertake the activity. In that case, the supply curve might look something like that in Fig. 4.2. That figure suggests that individuals are prepared to undertake some sacrifice and to supply a certain amount of the activity, Q, without payment. If they are then offered a small payment then they might regard this as a recognition or acknowledgement of their sacrifice and become even more favourably disposed towards the activity; hence supply is 'crowded-in', and increases to, say, Q*. However, as payment increases further, the sacrifice they are making in undertaking the activity lessens, and they begin to derive less intrinsic reward from undertaking it. Hence supply is reduced, with a 'crowding-out effect' dominating. This may, as in the diagram, reduce supply to a point where it is less than the original amount, Q, that people were prepared to supply without compensation. As payment continues to increase, however, the relative price effect begins to dominate, and supply increases again. The two turning points of the curve are the cost thresholds mentioned in the main text.

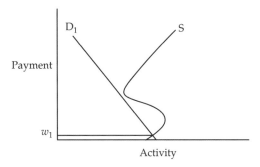

**Figure 4.3.** *Knightly supply and low demand*

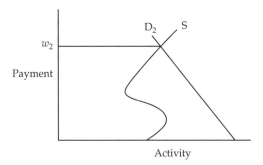

**Figure 4.4.** *Knightly supply and high demand*

If supply curves do look as in Fig. 4.2, then what are the implications for public policy? More precisely, how should altruistic activities be rewarded— or paid for? Unsurprisingly this will depend on the level for demand for the activity. This is illustrated in Figs 4.3, 4.4, and 4.5. At a relatively low level of demand where demand curve intersects the crowded-in section of the supply curve, the payment can be low: $w_1$ in Fig. 4.3. If demand is relatively high, so that it intersects on the relative-price-dominant section, the payment will be high: $w_2$ in Fig. 4.4.

If demand is such that, as in Fig. 4.5, the demand curve cuts the supply curve in several places, there is a dilemma. Should the payment be set at $w_3$ or $w_4$?[14] At $w_3$, there is more provided and consumers pay a lower price; but, because of the altruistic nature of the suppliers, the pay is low. At $w_4$, the suppliers receive a larger payment—which might be perceived as more 'just' and less exploitative—but consumers pay more and less is provided. In deciding

[14] The third intersection point is not an equilibrium and hence is uninteresting.

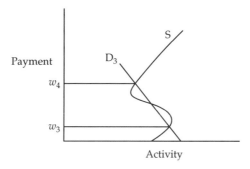

**Figure 4.5.** *Knightly supply and moderate demand*

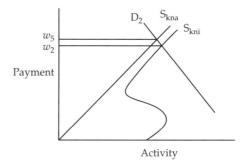

**Figure 4.6.** *Knightly and knavish supply and demand*

between $w_3$ and $w_4$, the policy-maker will thus have to trade-off his or her principles concerning the undesirability of exploitation, and the desirability of encouraging both altruism and the supply of the activity.

Finally, it is of interest to compare knightly and knavish supply situations. This is done in Fig. 4.6. The diagram assumes that the 'crowding out' is not complete: that is, the section of the knightly supply curve dominated by the relative price effect is to the right of the knavish supply curve, allowing for a measure of knightly motivation to remain even at those levels of payment. In these circumstances, with demand relatively high the appropriate knightly payment is $w_2$. This is lower than the payment, $w_5$, that would have been necessary if suppliers were knavish (or if the crowding-out had been complete). Again, as discussed in the main text, the question of exploitation arises: is $w_2$ exploitative as compared with $w_5$?

# PART II

# THEORY:
# OF PAWNS AND QUEENS

# 5

# Agency and Public Services

Your patient has no more right to all the truth you know than he has to all the medicine in your saddle bags. He should only get as much as is good for him.

(Oliver Wendell Holmes, talking to American medical students; quoted in Angela Coulter, *The Autonomous Patient*)

It is for the patient, not the doctor, to determine what is in the patient's own best interests. You may wish to recommend a treatment or a course of action, but you must not put pressure on patients to accept your advice.

(General Medical Council in 2002)

So far in this book we have been concerned primarily with motivation, and specifically with the motivation of professionals and other providers in the public sector. It is time now to turn to questions related to agency: individuals' capacity for action and choice. These questions are largely normative in nature: that is, they are not concerned so much with what is but with what should be. In the context of the public sector and indeed of wider social welfare, how much power should individual citizens have? Should users of publicly funded services have control over how much and in what way they make use of those services? Or should their use be largely determined by professionals or others involved in service provision, as often happens in areas such as health care and education? This chapter considers some of the more theoretical and philosophical issues concerned in trying to answer these questions.

The arguments differ from area to area, and any answers they generate will depend heavily on the contexts in which they are deployed. Hence I shall concentrate on the issues involved in the aspects of public policy that are the principal concerns of this book: publicly funded health care and education and (in the next chapter) personal savings and state provision for pensions and long-term care. In Part III, I discuss some of the practical issues involved in specific policies designed to empower individuals in the areas concerned: health and education quasi-markets, demogrants, partnership savings schemes, and hypothecated taxes.

## PATIENTS, PARENTS, OR PROFESSIONALS?

It is currently fashionable to advocate user empowerment in the context of publicly funded services such as health care and education. Many analysts feel that in these areas the professionals and managers who deliver the service concerned—the doctor, the nurse, the teacher, the bureaucrat—have too much power over decisions relating to the people whom the service is supposed to benefit—the patient, the parent, or the pupil.[1] Patient empowerment relative to the professional is the watchword for health services; parent, or more radically, pupil empowerment for education.

But power over what? The objects of power can be divided into the nature or type of the service to be offered, the quantity of the service used, and the provider of the service. The question then is who should have the power to make decisions over what (the nature of the service), how much (the service quantity), and by whom (the provider). Should the nature of a patient's treatment, the quantity of that treatment, and the hospital that provides the treatment be decided by the patient himself or herself or by the doctor—or indeed by someone else such as a manager or a civil servant? Should parents, teachers, or local education authorities decide on the type of the education a child should get, the amount of that education, and to which school the child should go? More generally, should the decision over all or any of these choices lie with the user or elsewhere? Should the user be pawn or queen?

There are three possible approaches to these questions: what we might term the welfarist approach, the liberal approach, and the communitarian approach. The welfarist approach tries to resolve the issue by referring to the impact on individual welfare or well-being: that is, whether individual users should be pawns or queens in different situations depends on which increases their welfare the more. The liberal approach is concerned simply with the impact on the individual's freedom: that is, whether users should be pawns or queens will depend on what ultimately gives them more freedom of action. The communitarian approach concerns the impact on the wider society of extending individuals' power of decision: will such extension ultimately benefit or harm the interests of the community as a whole?

To begin with the welfarist approach. In most contexts, welfarists would follow John Stuart Mill (1859/1982) in his classic discourse *On Liberty* and argue that individuals are the best judges of what would contribute most to their own welfare. Hence they should make as many decisions concerning

---

[1] Professionals themselves often feel this way. A *British Medical Journal* survey of visitors to its website (mostly medical professionals) found that 60% considered that the principal consulting style currently was one of 'doctor decides'. Just 7% thought that this style ought to prevail, while 87% considered that the preferable style was one where 'doctor and patient decide together'. www.bmj.com, 24 October 1999. Quoted in Coulter (2002: xi). Coulter's monograph is a useful source of information and argument on patient power and this chapter has made extensive use of it.

the factors that contribute to that welfare as possible, and should not have those decisions restricted by others. Nor should others make the decisions for them, for no one knows what would contribute to their welfare as effectively as the individuals themselves. In general, people should be queens, not pawns.

However, welfarists often also claim that this type of argument would *not* apply to some of the public services that we are considering in this book, particularly health care and education. There are a number of possible welfarist reasons why patients should not be permitted to make decisions for themselves with respect to medical care or indeed other aspects of their health; and there are similar ones with respect to parents making decisions with respect to their children's education.

The first, relatively trivial, welfarist argument for treating users as pawns is where they choose to be so. Some patients might prefer to place themselves in the hands of the doctor because they feel incapable of making the relevant decisions even if they are offered the opportunity to do so. Parents may feel that they know less about the appropriate education for their children than the teachers of those children; hence they may be prepared to delegate authority to those teachers. Although far from trivial empirically, particularly in health care (there is evidence that not all patients want to be involved in decisions about their own treatment; see Coulter 2002: 31–4), it is trivial analytically, because these are not really individuals ceasing to be queens. Rather, they are exercising their royal powers by delegating authority to someone else. The voluntary pawn is not really a pawn.

The more difficult arguments for a welfarist are those that form the case for not allowing an individual to make decisions even when he or she might wish to do so. The most well-known of these arguments is when the individual has poor or imperfect information concerning the likely outcomes of those decisions. Poor user information is an obvious characteristic of health care and education (Arrow 1963). Both doctors and teachers are trained professionals, much of whose training involves the acquiring of specialised and often highly technical information. Users of medical or educational services could not hope to acquire all this knowledge without undergoing the same training themselves.

However, the presence of poor information is not sufficient on its own to justify treating patients and parents as pawns on welfarist grounds. For this would be the case only if there were no relatively low-cost way by which that information could be provided to users. If the information relevant to the particular situation of the user can be given relatively cheaply to patients or parents, then, other things being equal, they are likely to be better-off making their own, informed decisions than if someone else makes those choices for them. I return to this point below.

Other welfarist arguments in favour of treating patients or parents as pawns concern what has been termed 'individual failure' (to distinguish it from market or other forms of system failure, such as poor information[2]). Bill New (1999) has identified four of these. The first is a technical inability to complete the necessary mental tasks. This inability could arise because the quantity of information is simply too great relative to mental capacity, or because the technological or causal connections are too difficult to make, again relative to capacity. This appears to be a special problem with respect to health care. For decisions concerning the appropriateness or otherwise of medical treatment often involve assessing the probabilities of benefit or harm from alternative forms of treatment (or from no treatment at all). And experimental evidence suggests that individuals often find it difficult to make rational decisions where weighing up probabilities is concerned (Tversky and Kahneman 1982).

A second source of individual failure identified by New is weakness of the will. This is where individuals know what they prefer in the long term but still make decisions that are not in their long-term interest. Again, there are obvious examples relating to health and health care. Individuals who are in the process of damaging their health through overeating or smoking often assert that they would really prefer not to engage in those activities, but find it impossible to stop doing so. Long-term compliance with drug regimes or other forms of treatment is another area where weakness of the will is often apparent.

A third source of individual failure is emotional decision-making. Becoming attached to certain choices allows emotions to distort decisions. This might arise because of a strong attachment to a particular outcome even though one knows that it is very unlikely to occur; or the decision may be made in a period of stress, such as that following bereavement. Again, health care raises this particular issue in an acute form; often treatment decisions have to be made at a time of considerable anxiety or distress, or in other situations that are not conducive to rational deliberation.

The fourth problem raised by New concerns the relationship between preferences and experience. Preferences over a set of decisions might vary depending on whether or not the individual has had actual experience (as distinct from abstract knowledge or information) of the outcomes of the decision concerned. Thus the decision whether to smoke or not might be different if it were possible for the individual concerned actually to have the experience of dying from lung cancer before the decision was taken. At first sight this resembles the imperfect information concern, and as such might be thought a system failure rather than an individual one. But it is not quite the same; for in these cases no system can supply the relevant information—even at high cost—prior to the decision being taken. No one can experience what it is like to die before actually dying.

As the illustrations given suggest, most of these kinds of system and individual failure apply with rather more force to health care than education.

---

[2] The distinction between system and individual failure has been challenged: see Calcott (2000). However, it is not crucial to my argument.

This would seem especially true with respect to those concerned with the technicalities of information: both the amount of information needed and the ability required to deal with it seem rather larger in the case of health care. However, there is a significant problem that does not apply when individuals are making decisions about their own health care, but does apply in education, especially where early school education is concerned. That is what might be termed 'parentalism'. In the case of education, at least in the earlier years, it is not the users themselves who are making the relevant decisions, but their parents. And parents may make decisions with respect to a child's education that further their own (or the rest of the family's) interests more than the child's. Thus the head of an impoverished family may decide that it would be better for the family income for a child to leave at the school leaving age and go out to work than for that child to stay on at school, regardless of his or her potential. Or the family may keep a child out of school so as to look after another family member in need of care. Such cases may serve the welfare of the family, but the welfare of the actual user—the child—may suffer.

So welfarists have a number of possible justifications concerning both system and individual failure for treating patients or parents as pawns. What of the liberal approach? At first sight, it might seem difficult to find any such justification from a liberal point of view; for, from that perspective, the desirability of individuals making their own decisions about factors that affect their own welfare arises from deontological, not consequentialist, concerns. That is, the promotion of freedom of decision is a desirable end in and of itself; whether or not the exercise of such decision-making power has the consequence of improving welfare (or indeed any other consequence) is irrelevant.

However, even here there may be cracks in the argument. What if a particular form of medical treatment or of education improves the decision-making power of an individual or the choices over which decisions can be taken—as, it has to be said, most successful forms of health care or education are likely to do? Suppose it improves his or her capabilities or functionings, in the terminology of Amartya Sen (1985)? Then would not the short-term restriction of patient or parental decision-making power be a price worth paying for the consequence of a long-term increase in the ability to take decisions or in the availability of choices?

Actually, the answer from a liberal point of view is, I suspect, probably not. From that perspective, an individual's freedom to take decisions should also include the right to decide not to enlarge his or her ability to do so. It would be wrong to override that decision, even in the name of subsequently generating greater freedom for decision-making. Of course, as with the welfarist case, information is important; the liberal would want the individual in making the relevant decisions to be fully informed about their consequences. And parentalism is a problem: what rights do children have, and at what age do they acquire the right to make decisions on their own behalf? But in general, from a liberal perspective, informed or not, the patient, parent, or—if old enough—pupil, should always be queen.

Finally, the communitarian case. Here the argument is still a welfarist one in the sense that it is concerned with people's welfare, but in this case the welfare of those other than the patient or parent. The argument here is that the decisions made by a service user may have (beneficial or damaging) consequences both for other users and for non-users: what economists term external benefits or costs or externalities.[3] Thus individual decisions to be vaccinated against an infectious disease reduces the likelihood of the spread of the disease, thus benefiting not only the individuals themselves but also all those with whom they come into contact. Parents' decision to send their child to an exclusive school may reduce social cohesion and thus damage wider social welfare.

In passing it is important to note that these externalities are a problem not only for publicly funded services. In a private market for goods and services, individuals consider only the private costs and benefits to themselves of their activities, and do not take account of any costs and benefits that may impact on others. Hence, from a social point of view, they are likely to undertake too few of those activities that confer external benefits and too many of those that create external costs.

But with publicly funded services there is an additional complication, one that arises even if there were no externalities. In a normal market situation, users purchasing a service pay a price for it. Under competitive market conditions, that price will reflect the opportunity or resource cost of the service. Hence they have an incentive to limit their use of the service to only those parts of it that benefit them more than the resource cost of providing them with the service.[4] However, if the service is funded from public funds and provided free, they have no incentive to restrain their demand for the service in this way. Rather they will overuse the service: that is, they will demand more of the service than would be justifiable from society's point of view. Every doctor is familiar with pushy patients demanding attention for their relatively trivial complaints at the expense of patients with more serious illnesses; every teacher with the parent demanding personal attention for his or her child at the expense of others who could benefit more. Meeting this 'excess' demand involves employing resources that, if put to another use, could have created higher social benefits elsewhere. There will be over-provision of the service concerned.

Further, with a free service users have less incentive to seek out the most efficient or most suitable provider for their needs. They do not have to pay for the service, and hence have no reason to look for the most economical supplier. Moreover, the fact that they are getting the service apparently for free can render users less critical or demanding of the service provider. Hence inefficient and unsuitable providers can continue in existence, wasting resources that could have been spent in other, better ways.

---

[3] So-called because they are external to the individual actually making the decisions.

[4] Strictly they will purchase the service up to the point at which the marginal cost to them of further purchases (including the price charged) exceeds the marginal benefit to them.

So the case for partly or wholly overriding individual decisions with respect to their use of public services is fundamentally a welfarist one. Individuals, if left to make their own choices with respect to health care and education, might make the 'wrong' decisions, both from the point of view of their own welfare and from that of the welfare of the wider community. That is, they might choose a service that is not suitable for their needs, or for the needs of the community; they might choose to use too much or too little of it, either from their own point of view or from that of society; and they might choose inefficient or unsuitable providers, again possibly harming their own welfare and that of society.

However, none of this establishes on its own the case for treating users of public services as pawns. For, although individual users may make mistakes, there is no guarantee that others—and in particular those to whom the power is often delegated, the professionals who provide the service—will do it better. To this we now turn.

The welfarist case for doctors to make decisions about their patients' care and teachers over their pupils' education is in some ways the mirror image of that for not allowing patients or parents to make their own decisions. They can correct system failure; and they do not suffer from individual failure, at least not in the same way or to the same extent as users do.

First, system failure associated with poor information. Medical professionals and teachers do possess the information about the technology of their craft that the users of their services lack; indeed, therein lies their claim to be professionals. Hence they are obviously in a position to correct system failures due to poor user information.

However, it is worth noting that there is a difference in scale. In health care, the doctor has to have knowledge of thousands of potential ailments, whereas the patient has to know only about those potentially or actually affecting himself or herself. Medical handbooks can aid self-diagnosis; and, once their illness is diagnosed, especially in these days of the Internet, patients can—and indeed often do—'train' themselves in their own disease. Similarly with respect to teaching: teachers have to be able to assess the educational requirements of thousands of pupils, whereas parents have only to do so for their own offspring, about whom they have considerable knowledge.

Rather similar arguments apply to the first element of individual failure that we discussed: technical inability to make decisions. Doctors and teachers are trained to make the relevant decisions and, moreover, are well practised at them since they have to do them every day. Hence they are much less likely to suffer from this particular difficulty. However, again scale matters. Patients and parents have to make decisions only for themselves or their families, and can therefore devote more attention and decision-making capacity to them.

Another argument for doctors and teachers as decision-makers can be made with respect to the second source of individual failure: weakness of the will. Such weakness is not a problem for a doctor or teacher making decisions for others, for the temptation of ignoring long-term benefits to the user in favour of short-term ones does not apply to them. There may be other, more self-interested reasons why a provider might adopt a short-term solution to a user's problem (such as a desire to get a demanding patient out of the surgery, or the complaining parent out of the classroom, so that the professional can get home). But they do not derive from the user's own inability to defer immediate gratification.

New's third concern was the role of emotion in distorting decisions. In this case it seems that professionals are likely to be as liable to this as anyone else. Considerations of professional pride, hubris, or maybe even excessive humility could all affect professional decision-making and thereby distort decisions made on behalf of users. This form of individual failure may be universal. However, since the emotional basis will different, the kind of distortion induced will be different from that associated with users. Also, since again the professional will be making many decisions affecting many people, the emotional commitment to any one decision involving any one user may be diluted and therefore less damaging to rational decision-making than the emotions of the user himself or herself.

Fourth, the question of experience. Now both the doctor and the teacher will have a kind of experience of people making the 'wrong' decisions. So, for instance, oncologists will have seen heavy smokers dying of lung cancer; teachers will have seen some of their most promising pupils ruin their lives through ill-considered career or educational choices. However, they will still not have actually experienced the consequences themselves. Hence this aspect of individual failure is present in the professional himself or herself, albeit to a somewhat lesser extent than in the user.

So far the welfarist case for professionals making the relevant decisions has been based on demonstrating that they could do better than the users themselves. But it is also based on another assumption, rarely mentioned in this context, but crucial nonetheless. This is that they *will* do better, given the opportunity. And this brings us back to motivation. Specifically, for the case to stand, professionals have either to be something close to knights or perfect altruists or to have personal interests that coincide with those of the user. That is, if they are to take decisions on a user's behalf that are going to promote that individual's welfare, then they must have the individual's welfare at the forefront of their concerns, or they must face no conflict between their own interests and those of the user. If neither of those conditions is fulfilled, there is no guarantee that professionals will use their decision-making power in the interests of users.

This is related to the currently fashionable debate concerning the role of trust and the public sector. The argument recently employed by, for instance, Onora O'Neill (2002) in her BBC Reith Lectures that we should be trusting public servants more and auditing them less is based almost entirely upon the assumption that the public servants concerned are knights. For if they are not—if they are self-interested knaves—then trusting them will result in users' welfare being improved only if the actions necessary to improve that welfare also improved their own welfare. So to trust professionals is to assume either that their interests and those of their patients coincide (or can be made to coincide), or that any situation involving a clash of such interests will always be resolved by the professional in favour of the patient.

What of possible liberal and community arguments in favour of professional power? It is difficult for the liberal to support professionals having control over users, except perhaps in cases where it is actually impossible for the user to make choices (such as a patient admitted unconscious into a hospital's accident and emergency department). The community arguments in favour of professional power depend upon the professionals taking the society's wider interests into account in making their decisions. The extent to which they do this will depend very much on the professional and the context in which they operate. The doctor will have a concern for all his or her patients, and the teacher for all his or her pupils. Hence he or she is likely to try to protect them from the consequences of any one of them being excessively demanding. However, there is no guarantee that their concerns will go wider than this, and that they will take into account the interests of the broader community or indeed of the nation as a whole.

## FROM PAWN TO QUEEN IN PUBLIC SERVICES

It is clear that there are a variety of conflicting arguments as to whether power should lie with users or professionals in health care and education. It is also clear that the resolution of these conflicts depends in part on the context. As noted, a patient admitted unconscious into a hospital's accident and emergency department is not going to be able to make any decisions even if he or she might have wanted to. The teacher of a child with a single parent in prison may have to make decisions on behalf of the child and the absent parent.

However, it does seem as though there is a convincing case for the user to have a measure of power, possibly considerable, over public service provision. For welfarists the motivational issue is paramount. The person who is most motivated to improve his or her health is the user himself or herself. Professionals may not be entirely or even largely knaves; but they can never have the same degree of concern for users as users have for themselves.

That said, the user's decision-making power cannot be completely unrestricted. There are system failures, especially with respect to information; and there are also individual failures to contend with. As argued above, these seem to be more powerful in the case of health care than education; moreover, they would seem to apply more to some choices than to others. Thus decisions over the nature and quantity of medical treatment seem potentially more subject to information and technical capacity failure than the choice of the provider of that treatment. Hence, in the case of health care at least, there may be a better case for giving users greater power over the choice of provider than over choices relating to treatment. It would still, of course, be necessary that the user had the appropriate information to judge the quality of the service offered by different providers.

What of the communitarian arguments? Again, these point against completely unfettered user power over decisions. But, as with the individual welfarist arguments, the communitarian arguments may lead to different conclusions depending on which kind of decision is under consideration. User choice over the nature of and how much treatment or education is provided is obviously subject to the communitarian objection concerning potential over-provision and hence overuse. The choice of provider for treatments of similar nature and amounts is not. User choice of provider, however, may result in the growth of selection and segregation damaging social cohesion, whereas this would seem to be a less likely consequence of user choice of treatment or education within the same institution.

So how should we design systems for public service delivery that offer an appropriate balance of power between user and provider? There are essentially two kinds of mechanism for empowering users: what are commonly termed 'voice' and 'exit'. These we must discuss in a little more detail.

## VOICE AND EXIT

If we accept that there is some case for empowering users, what is the best way of doing so? In Albert Hirschman's (1970) well-known dichotomy, there are two fundamental ways in which users may be empowered: through 'voice' or 'exit'. Voice is where users address their concerns directly or indirectly to the service provider. They can be collective (through voting or through other mechanisms of collective decision-making) or individualistic (through mechanisms such as complaints procedures). Exit mechanisms involve the user being in a position to leave or exit from his or her provider and go to another.

Both types of mechanism have their merits and demerits. Collective voice mechanisms have the advantage that they are indeed collective: that they take account of the interests of the community. On the other hand, they are clumsy instruments for dealing with the kind of individual decisions with which we are concerned here. Parents who are dissatisfied with their local school, or patients with their local hospital, can vote for local politicians who are promising to provide better ones; but, for their votes to be effective, a number of conditions have to be fulfilled. There has to be an election in the offing; their views have to be shared by a majority of other voters; the issues concerning the quality of schools or hospitals have to be the principal factors affecting the election; politicians promising better schools or hospitals have to be among the candidates; and, if these politicians are elected, they have to have some effective method for ensuring school or hospital improvement. Only rarely will all of these conditions be met.

Further, despite their collective nature, these mechanisms still suffer from the communitarian problems of over-provision and social segregation. Voters are rarely faced with the costs of meeting their service requirements. When they are not faced with those costs, they can simply vote to increase or maintain services at other people's expense. Indeed, this often happens when school or hospital closure proposals are put to a vote; the voters concerned usually do not have to bear the costs of keeping the institutions concerned open and in consequence usually vote the closure proposals down. And a majority can also vote to segregate a minority, excluding them by formal or informal means from the service concerned.

Individual voice mechanism such as complaints procedures also have their problems. They require energy and commitment to activate; they take a good deal of time to operate; and they create defensiveness and distress among those complained against. They favour the educated and articulate. Users who complain are not necessarily those who have the most to complain about, thus contributing to the overuse problem; and adversarial relations between professionals and users, especially tied to a threat of lawsuits as they often are, can lead to expensive and inefficient defensive reactions on behalf or providers.

These problems with voice mechanisms are well known. However, exit ones also require certain conditions to be met if they are to work effectively. First, there has to be at least one alternative provider to whom the user can go. Second, if the aim is to provide an incentive for increasing the responsiveness of providers to users' needs and wants, there have to be consequences for the provider of the choices made by the user: that is, providers from whom the user exits have to be penalised in some way while those to whom the user goes for service have to be rewarded.

An obvious way of ensuring that the right incentives are present is for the money to follow the user. So providers losing users would also lose resources while those gaining them would gain resources. But this leads to a further danger: that of polarisation, whereby poor performers lose income leading to yet worse performance, while good performers are able to perform even better through their increases in income. This outcome may be reinforced if good providers can 'cream-skim': that is, they can select users whose needs can be met relatively easily or cheaply. All this may lead to a widening gap between good and bad providers, with poor schools and hospitals in a vicious circle of decline while good ones steadily improve. Equity in a provision would suffer.

Another problem concerns parentalism: what if some parents decided to exit the system altogether and take their children out of school? Yet other difficulties concern the communitarian objections to user power. What if users used their power of exit to segregate themselves: parents in a religious cult sending their children to a school that propagated the values of that cult and only the values of that cult, for instance? Or what if users demanded more services from their new provider than was justified by their level of need—the over-provision problem?

However, there are ways of dealing with these problems while preserving the possibility of exit. Ways of dealing with the cream-skimming problem are discussed in Chapter Eight. To overcome the parentalism problem, parents can be required to send their children to school (as they are at present); and, to reduce the impact of the voluntary segregation problem, every school can be required to offer the same basic curriculum.

The overuse issue could be addressed by charging for services, so that individuals do face some at least of the opportunity costs of their decisions. However, charging for public services raises well-known equity problems, not least the potential such charges have for deterring genuine use of the service concerned, especially by the poor. A more attractive alternative is for individuals or their agents to be given fixed budgets with which to 'purchase' health care or education from different providers, thus allowing them the choice of provider but restraining them from demanding too much of the services concerned. Measures of this kind are discussed in greater detail in subsequent chapters.

## CONCLUSION

The arguments of this and earlier chapters lay the foundations for understanding what a successful system for a delivering a public service would look like. It would be one that treats the users of the service as queens not pawns: that is, it would have user power at its base. But it would also incorporate mechanisms that avoid the overuse or over-provision of the service concerned, or the use of the service in such a way that damages either the user himself or herself or the wider society. It would provide appropriate incentives for providers to deliver such a service, relying upon the appropriate balance of self-interested and altruistic motivations. Finally, it would do all this in as efficient a manner as possible, and in a way that did not violate equity or other social objectives that society might have with respect to the service.

The commonly used systems for delivering services, categorised here in terms of exit and voice, all have problems meeting these requirements. However, some of the more theoretical arguments sketched out in the penultimate section suggest that those with the most potential for doing so are the ones involving exit. But theory can only take an argument so far. Many of the issues involved are empirical ones that can be resolved only by a detailed examination of actual policies. That is the task of the next part of the book.

# 6

# Agency and Public Finance

If I'd known I was going to live this long, I'd have taken better care of myself.

(Eubie Blake, on reaching the age of 100; *Observer*, 13 February 1983)

Old age is the most unexpected of all things that happen to a man.

(Leon Trotsky, Diary, 8 May 1935)

I now turn to a different set of questions, but ones that also bring up agency issues in the context of the public sector. They concern not the delivery of public services but what we might think of as the cash or financial side of the public sector: that is, that part which is concerned with financing the provision of services and of cash benefits designed to support or to supplement people's incomes or capital assets. Again the arguments vary with the context, and I shall concentrate on some particular cases. Specifically, I shall address the question of savings, old age pensions, and the finance of long-term care.

With the exception of those who are lucky to acquire substantial wealth through inheritance or some other windfall, everyone will need to engage in some form of savings or capital accumulation to cover their future needs. In particular, all of us will need to have some form of pension or other form of income to be able to support ourselves when we are too old to work; some of us may become mentally or physically disabled and need more intensive forms of personal care. Others may require capital at earlier stages in their lives, for instance in order to start a business or to acquire a home.

We saw above that there was a prima facie case for users of public services to be queens not pawns, but that nonetheless some restrictions on user power had to be accepted in case users demanded too much of, or the wrong kind of, the service concerned. The situation is similar with respect to savings decisions in that there is a presumption that individuals should be queens not pawns, but that again there is a case for some limited intervention from outside. One difference, though, lies in the basis for that case: the concern here is not that too much of the activity concerned will be undertaken but too little.

## SAVINGS AND THE STATE

At first sight it might seem as though the case for intervention in individuals' savings decisions is difficult to make, especially from the perspective of turning pawns into queens. In particular, why should the state intervene to encourage savings for old age? *Pace* Trotsky, old age is after all eminently predictable. Except in the relatively unlikely event of early death, we shall all need an income to help support us when we are unable to work or when we are compelled to retire for other reasons; and there is a known probability of needing some form of long-term care as mental and physical infirmity take their toll. Since most people must know about both these eventualities, why do we not let people make their own arrangements for dealing with them? People can save for their old age; they can take out insurance against the need for long-term care. Surely the ultimate empowerment of individuals—the best way to turn a pawn into a queen—is to allow them to make their own decisions without any intervention at all from the state?

The presumption behind arguments such as these is that the principal threat to individual empowerment with respect to savings decisions is the state. But individuals operating in a free market can be disempowered too. This is partly because some individuals and households have too few resources to be able effectively to save. The appropriate strategies to explore in this case involve proposals for increasing those resources. The demogrant proposal of Chapter Eight is designed to do just this; and more details of the rationale for that particular proposal for turning pawns into queens are discussed there.

But there is a case for state intervention in the savings decisions of those individuals who are not disempowered through lack of resources. First, all individuals, wealthy or non-wealthy, face constraints and impediments in the relevant markets that limit their effective power: what are collectively known as market or system failures. Second, and perhaps more significant, there is an important group of individuals who are not directly represented in the current market and are therefore completely disempowered: our future selves. These arguments need to be discussed in more detail.

## MARKET FAILURE

The first set of arguments concerning the case for state intervention—failures in the savings and insurance markets—have been explored extensively elsewhere and so will only be summarised here.[1] So far as the savings market is concerned, the principal concerns are imperfect knowledge or information and transactions costs (Banks, Dilnot, and Tanner 1997). Potential savers often have little knowledge of the rates of return from, and the risks associated with, different

---

[1] An excellent exposition of the principal arguments can be found in Barr (2001), especially chapters 5 and 6.

ways of saving; hence they may find it difficult to decide on their savings portfolio, both in terms of its size (the overall amount they should save) and in terms of its structure (how much to hold in different assets). Transactions costs are the administrative costs incurred by operating in the market, such as charges and fees: many of these have a fixed component (for example, share dealing), and this puts barriers in the way of savings, especially for small investors.

Although not strictly a form of market failure, it is worth adding that problems with saving also arise because of other aspects of the welfare state. In Britain, people with savings above a certain level are disqualified from receiving state income support and, as we shall see, from help with the costs of long-term care. Inevitably this acts as a disincentive to save.

It should be noted that, although these problems are not due to poverty per se, they are likely to apply with particular force to individuals living in households with low incomes. Poorer individuals are likely to have limited educational skills; hence they are likely to have relatively little information on savings vehicles and to find it more difficult to process such information as they can obtain (Kempson and Whyley 1999). Fixed transactions costs will impact more on those with low incomes; and they are more likely to make demands on the state social security system, especially those parts that are already asset-tested (such as income support).

The insurance market has similar problems, especially with respect to information.[2] There are information problems for both consumers and insurers, especially concerning the future. Consumers trying to decide whether to take out insurance face enormous uncertainty. How likely is it that they will need care? What sort of care will they need, and how expensive is it likely to be? Should they insure against the need for residential care, domiciliary care (care in their own home), or both? What about developments in medical technology? Will improvements in the future make it less likely that they will need care through finding cures or effective palliative treatments for disability-inducing disease—or make the need for care more likely through prolonging old age into infirmity?

Insurers have problems due to so-called adverse selection: that is, high-risk individuals may be able to conceal their risk from the insurers. They will also confront another common insurance problem: moral hazard. This is the fact that the presence of insurance makes it more likely that the person will demand care. There is an additional problem in the long-term care case; for the family of the person concerned is also more likely to be involved and to behave differently if there is insurance than if there is not. As Mark Pauly (1990) has pointed out, in these circumstances it could be rational not to insure so as to guard against being put into care against one's will.

---

[2] Barr (2001: ch. 6). See also UK, Royal Commission on Long-Term Care (1999). Not everyone accepts these arguments: see Lipsey (forthcoming).

Insurers also face similar problems to consumers relating to improvements in medical technologies. Ironically, the one area where there are predictable advances to be made, the human genome project, also creates problems for insurance markets. If information concerning bad genetic risks is withheld from insurance companies there will be adverse selection, with only bad risks taking out insurance; but if the information is available to them there will be risk selection, and bad risks may be denied insurance. Neither outcome is desirable.

## MYOPIA AND FUTURE SELVES

But a more fundamental reason for state intervention concerns so-called myopia. Individuals may make wrong decisions about the best balance of present versus future consumption because they are too short-sighted to take proper account of the future. This argument needs closer examination.

Myopia is a common phenomenon. Those of a certain age may remember an advertisement for an insurance company of the 1950s called 'the five age view-points on a pension'. It consists of five line drawings of the same (male) individual at different ages, with captions expressing his attitude towards the pension arrangements associated with his job. At the youngest age (25), obviously about to take up the job, he is saying, with a smile on his face and a general air of insouciance, that 'they tell me that the job's not pensionable'. At age 35, he is slightly less sanguine, saying 'unfortunately, my work does not bear a pension'. At age 45, he is more worried, saying, 'How I wish I could look forward to a pension', and at 55: 'I dread reaching retiring age without a pension'. Finally, at age 65, his face riven with anxiety, he is saying 'without a pension *I really don't know what I shall do*'.

This advertisement captures the widely-held view that individuals' time horizons are limited. They do not consider the long term; they plan only on the basis of current events or on their predictions of the very immediate future; in consequence they do not make sensible savings or insurance decisions. In a word, they are myopic. Myopic individuals, as their lives unfold and they encounter unexpected vicissitudes such as unemployment or sickness, or even more predictable ones such as old age, have no personal resources with which to cope with them and experience massive drops in income in consequence.

It is important to distinguish between myopia and information failure of the kind already discussed. Working individuals may not save enough or take out enough insurance simply because they are not aware of the need to do so. They may underestimate how much they need to save out of current income in order to ensure that they have sufficient resources to provide for their retirement; similarly they may underestimate the probabilities of their need for long-term care and hence under-insure. If this is the situation, then the appropriate state response is simply to ensure that they have the correct information before they make the relevant decisions. But this is different from myopia, at least as I am using the term here. That refers to individuals' structure of preferences: their desire for present over future consumption. In economists' terms, a myopic individual is one with a high personal rate of time preference; that is, someone who, in order to satisfy current wants, is prepared to sacrifice a great deal of future consumption.

Now it might seem that myopia in this sense is not a form of 'market failure' since it is not the market that apparently fails in this situation. If people actually are myopic in the way described—if, in economists' terms, they have a high marginal rate of time preference—then the market will respond to those preferences in the way it does to any other structure of preferences. If, because of myopia, there is no demand for sickness insurance schemes or for old-age pension plans, then the market will not provide them; but that will not be inefficient, because it is only a response to what people want (or, in this case, to what they do not want). If anything is 'failing' in this situation, it is the individuals themselves who are behaving in a way that outsiders might judge as irrational (although they themselves presumably would not).

If this is a case of 'individual failure' rather than market failure, then this provides no direct justification for government intervention. For if individuals are myopic, then government may also be myopic. Certainly, there can be no presumption that the distribution of lifetime income as determined by myopic individuals working in a market context will necessarily be worse or more irrational than that which results from intervention by a government elected and run by the same myopic individuals. Indeed, even if governments did behave in a non-myopic fashion, arguably they should not; for to ignore the preferences of their electors would be undemocratic and paternalist.

However, here some of the arguments of the philosopher Derek Parfit (1984) concerning the nature of personal identity have relevance. Parfit's thesis is both weighty and lengthy, and I shall not be able to do justice to it here. However, a helpful guide to some of his reasoning has been provided by John Broome (1985). Combining Broome's insights with my own interpretations, Parfit's argument runs something like this. We normally invoke the concept of personal identity to link a person in one time period with the 'same' person in another, later period. But what does the concept of personal identity actually mean? It presumably does *not* mean what a possible literal interpretation of the words in the term 'personal identity' would mean: that is, the person in the first time period is identical in every respect to the person in the second. The person will have aged physically; external factors (such as income or family status) may have changed; tastes may have changed; aspects of personality may have changed. The extent and magnitude of these changes may be small if the distance between the time periods is small, but they are likely to increase with that distance: compare the physique, income, personal relations, and personality of an eight year-old with that of the 'same' person eighty years later.

So if it does not mean actual identity, what does personal identity mean? As Broome describes it, Parfit's answer is a reductionist one: that is, the 'fact' of personal identity can be reduced to some other facts that can be described without using the concept of personal identity. These facts, according to Parfit, are links of a psychological kind, principally those of intention and memory. For instance, a 20-year-old will have memories of her 19-year-old self; and certain features of her current existence will depend on the intentions and actions of that 19-year-old. These links are, according to Parfit, what makes the 20-year-old and 19-year-old the 'same' person. Similar phenomena would link the 8-year-old and the 88-year-old mentioned above; but here the phenomena (and therefore the links) would be much attenuated. Hence any argument that was based on the continuity of the self would be much weaker for the eighty-year gap than for the one-year gap.

What are the implications of this for the myopia argument? Simply that a certain degree of myopia may not be irrational. If people are related to their future selves by links that become progressively attenuated the more distant the future, then it seems quite rational to give those future selves less weight than their present selves. There is no individual 'failure' in the sense of irrational decision-making.

But this in turn means that there *is* a possibility of market failure. For there is now a group of people who are not participating in the market but who are affected by the decisions made by those who are participating in it.[3] An individual's future self is a person who is directly affected by that individual's current decisions in the marketplace. A 65-year-old may be poor because of myopic decisions taken by her 25-year-old self. Hence the 25-year-old is imposing costs on the 65-year-old through her decisions; but the 65-year-old has no say in those decisions.

An individual's future self is, of course, someone with whom her current self is linked. But the link is not as strong as that to her present self. Hence, in taking those current market decisions she will not give appropriate weight to the interests of her future self, in exactly the same fashion as if her future self was actually a different person. More specifically, because she is not giving her future self the same weight as that future self would if the latter were present at the point of decision, she will undertake actions relating to the balance of interests between present and future selves that are not 'optimal', for instance, by saving too little or by taking out too little insurance to cover eventualities that might adversely affect that future self.[4]

Again, one cannot deduce from this directly that government intervention is necessarily required. For, just as in the case of the irrational myopic individuals,

---

[3] This is what economists term an externality.

[4] This is a modified version of the argument I originally put forward in an earlier work (Le Grand 1995). There I argued that an individual's future self actually was in some sense a different individual from her present one. A personal correspondence with John Broome has convinced me that (1) Parfit would not have claimed that current and future selves are actually different people and (2), in any case, it is not necessary to make that claim. All that is required for the argument put forward here is that, for reasons that cannot be described as irrational, current individuals treat their future selves *as though* they were different individuals.

a democratic government will be elected by 'present' individuals who may give too little weight to their future selves in their collective decision-making, just as they do in their market decision-making. So governments may perform as badly as the market. Moreover, again, a government that overrode current preferences could be viewed as being unacceptably paternalistic.

However, the paternalism point is not exactly the same as that for 'irrational' myopia. There a government which overrode individuals' myopic preferences would be doing so only on the paternalistic grounds that it knew its electorate's interests better than the electorate itself did—a procedure that is indeed disempowering. But, if the absence of future selves point is accepted, a government could justify overriding present individuals' preferences on the grounds that those individuals are treating their future selves as though their future selves were different individuals, and hence not giving their interests sufficient weight. But those future selves have just as much right for their interests to be respected as present individuals, even if, for obvious reasons, they are not around to be able to express those interests.

## CONCLUSION

So, overall, there is a case for government intervention in individuals' savings and insurance decisions. This case is based, not on some individual failure, but on various forms of market failure: information problems, transactions costs, and the fact that all relevant interests, notably future selves, are not being represented in the market. All of these problems suggest that, if left to themselves, people will save, or insure for, too little. Hence the state needs to adopt methods of increasing people's savings. The exact forms this might take are discussed in Chapters Nine and Ten.

# PART III

# POLICY

# 7

# Health Care

What is the use of discussing a man's abstract right to food or medicine?
The question is upon the method or procuring and administering them.

(Edmund Burke, *Reflections on the Revolution in France*)

In Chapter Four I developed the proposition that, if policy-makers were largely ignorant about the exact form of the motivational structures of those who worked in the public sector, they should try to design policies that incorporate robust incentive structures: structures that align knightly and knavish motivations in a fashion that direct the individuals concerned towards producing the desired outcomes. Chapter Five argued that policies should also be designed so as to empower users of public services, on the assumption that users were queens not pawns. But it was also pointed out that there were problems concerning users' poor information base, their possible reasoning incapacity, and their potentially excessive use of the service concerned: problems that meant that unfettered user choice would not always be appropriate.

In this chapter and the next, I put some empirical flesh on the philosophical and economic bones of those arguments by discussing some specific policies in health care and education from their perspective. As noted in Chapter One, it is important to analyse specifics in this way: for only by so doing so can academic analysts escape the charge of avoiding the difficult decisions. So, for instance, it is relatively easy to say that we need robust incentive structures, or to say that user choice needs to be partly restrained; but it is much more difficult to specify what form the incentive structures or choice restrictions might take.

This chapter deals with health care and with two areas where these issues are important: the interface between primary and secondary care, and the payment of hospital specialists. Although the discussion is centred on British institutional structures, the problems addressed, as well as the proposed solutions to them, are of more general application.

## PRIMARY AND SECONDARY HEALTH CARE

Many of the recent debates on the organisational structure of the British National Health Service (NHS) have concerned the issue of incentives, motivation, and empowerment.[1] How can incentives be structured so that the agents who work within the NHS are motivated to use its resources to achieve the best possible health and health service outcomes? How many choices should patients have over their own treatment? And will increasing their choices lead to the best possible health and health service outcome? In particular, how should incentives operate at the interface between primary and secondary health care? Since, except in emergency, in Britain patients see their general practitioners first, these GPs inevitably have a large role in making the relevant decisions at that interface; and it is at this interface that there have been some interesting experiments with incentive structures.

General practitioners in the NHS are private contractors who provide primary health care for patients in exchange for a capitation fee paid by the government.[2] As independent businesses, GP practices are enmeshed in market relations. They sell their services—although the government rather than the patient pays and they are paid per patient rather than per service—and they purchase supplies and premises while hiring their own staff. The organisation is a delicate one, with many conflicting norms and motives. GPs have some monetary incentive to sign up as many patients as possible.[3] They also have a knavish material interest in limiting the services they provide to their patients.[4] This interest in neglecting patients is constrained partly by a (knavish) fear of losing them and the capitation fees they bring, but, probably more importantly, by strong norms governing the proper conduct of a GP and, in many cases, by personal ties to patients and a genuine knightly concern for them.

### Incentive Structures Pre-1991

In the NHS GPs serve not only as health care providers but also as gatekeepers who, except in cases of emergency, control patient access to secondary care. They also act as gatekeepers for patients' access to prescription drugs. Prior to the 1991 quasi-market reforms of the NHS, this gave them an inefficient set of incentives. The workload and cost of treatment that GPs provided fell on the GPs themselves, while the cost of treatments provided by others did not (and the costs of waiting for those treatments fell on the patient). So GPs had a material incentive to refer patients to others for treatment rather than providing treatment

---

[1]  Much of this section is based on Hausman and Le Grand (1999). I am grateful to Dan Hausman for allowing me to use this material here.

[2]  They also receive payments for certain specific services. They are in fact rather a peculiar form of private contractor; for instance, they are members of the NHS pension scheme. Many of these arrangements may change in a new GP contract that is being negotiated at the time of writing.

[3]  Bosanquet and Leese (1989: 13) hypothesise that these incentives are weak. However, the results of their survey suggest that in fact 'list size had an important effect on practice net income' (1989: 83).

[4]  GPs also have an interest in finding healthy patients who need little care. Government policy recognises this incentive to select undemanding patients and attempts to counter it by adjusting capitation fees for some demographic and socio-economic factors such as age and deprivation.

themselves.[5] In many cases this was reinforced by the knightly or caring concerns a GP might have, especially if he or she lacked confidence in his or her ability to provide adequate treatment for the patient concerned. Knightly and knavish motivations were aligned—but not necessarily in a direction that led to the most efficient use of health service resources or the best health outcomes.

In practice GPs were constrained from over-referring (and over-prescribing) by a number of factors. There was the worry that they might be seen as over-referring by the local consultant; more generally they had a need to 'keep in with' the consultant.[6] There was their sense of self-worth as doctors; thus the referral decision has been modelled as the outcome of a conflict between a GP's concern that he or she could not diagnose or treat a patient and the impact on his or her self-esteem of admitting this.[7] There was a concern that patients might have to wait too long for treatment. And knightly motivations did not always indicate hospital referral in cases where the best interests of the patient lay in his or her receiving treatment in a primary care setting.

Even when referrals were unquestionably appropriate, there was still a problem because GPs had little interest in economising on their patients' use of outside medical resources. A GP would be no richer or no better-off in other ways if a patient in need of hernia surgery waited only a few weeks rather than a few months or saw a more skilled rather than a less skilled surgeon; and, although a complaining patient was a personal hassle, so was bargaining with hospitals and specialists. If GPs were only self-interested, this system would have neglected the interests of patients. Even if a fear of losing patients would keep self-interested GPs from neglecting their primary care, knavish GPs would have relatively little incentive to promote their patients' interests with hospitals and specialists. Moreover, even if GPs were knightly, the situation was not much better. GPs who identified with their patients might, in fact, have created a stronger bias toward unnecessary increases in medical costs than GPs who are materially self-interested. Given a choice between one treatment and another that is slightly more effective and much more expensive, GPs who cared about their patients and who did not have to bear the costs would choose the more expensive treatment. Patients, if offered the choice, would have agreed.

To summarise, prior to the service reforms of 1991 the NHS had a serious institutional flaw. Although GPs had an incentive to economise on the services

---

[5] Since investment in new equipment and costly innovations in GP practice brought no higher capitation fees and often were unlikely to pay for themselves in time saved or in case-load increases, the system also created a bias toward under-investment within GP practices. Policies were instituted to combat this tendency toward under-investment, for instance by giving relatively generous grants or loan subsidies to encourage the improvement of premises or the purchase of new ones and for the installation of information technology, but these arguably distorted the structure of investment towards the subsidised areas (especially premises).

[6] Good relationships with consultants were very important, and indeed still are (Clemence 1998).

[7] Dowie (1983). In this context it is of interest to remember that not all referrals are for hospital admission. For instance, Coulter, Noone, and Goldacre (1989) found in a study of referrals in the Oxford Regional Health Authority that 28% were simply to establish diagnosis.

they provided, they had little incentive to economise on secondary care. Given a choice between reaching into their own pockets and into other pockets to pay for services, GPs had an incentive to reach into those other pockets. And since what GPs individually did had little effect on what was left in the other pockets for them to spend, GPs had little incentive to spend that money carefully and sparingly. Identification with the NHS itself, and recognition that an unwise use of resources for one patient diminished the resources available for others, might have mitigated the problem to some extent, but it would be unrealistic to suppose that this general identification would have solved the problem. Not only are such motivations typically weaker than more specific concerns for patients and self, but they also do not provide the information and institutional structure that facilitates the necessary economising.

### General Practitioner Fund-Holding

Among the quasi-market reforms of 1991 introduced by the Conservative government of the time, the institution of GP fund-holding was in part an attempt to address these problems (Glennerster, Matsaganis, and Owens 1994). Under the scheme, GPs could volunteer to become fund-holders. GP fund-holders were given a budget with which to purchase drugs and certain hospital and specialist treatments for their patients. The treatments concerned were chiefly elective surgery and comprised about 30 per cent of total referrals to secondary care. The size of their budget was determined by the GPs' patterns of referral in the year preceding their taking up of the fund-holding option.

   Fund-holding created a new institution for rationing health care. The hard rationing choices that every health-delivery system has to make—is cataract surgery for Mrs Jones more important than a hernia operation for Mr Brown?—were decentralised and assigned to individual GPs who knew Mrs Jones and Mr Brown and who were supposed (in many cases correctly) to have the interests of them both at heart. Although rationing by GPs must of course be constrained by centrally determined priorities and by norms requiring consistency, impartiality, and fairness, there are tremendous advantages in decentralising decision-making in this way. In so far as patients trust their GPs, such a system should make patients more willing to accept waits or denials of service than if these decisions are made by an impersonal bureaucracy. Knowing individual patients, GPs can be sensitive to details that a bureaucracy could not know or respond to. The decentralisation itself provides a measure of flexibility and encourages patient choice, since patients can move to practices with different priorities.

   But more important from the point of view of this chapter was the change in the incentive structure. Knightly fund-holders who were concerned about their patients' health consequences now had a strong incentive to use the funds as efficiently as they could. Since the fund was fixed, more needs could be met if the fund were used efficiently. But even self-interested GPs had some incentive to use the funds efficiently, party because they would wish to limit complaints and bother for themselves, and partly because, since patients could move, their case load and ultimately their incomes depended on the level of regard for their practice, including the success of their hospital referrals.

An important element of the incentive structure was that GPs could spend on their practices whatever portion of their funds they did not spend on outside services. This surplus was supposed to be used for the benefit of the patients but, since investments in the practice would otherwise come out of the GPs' pockets, the fund surpluses could easily redound to the income and comfort of GPs. Optimists could take comfort from the fact that the arrangement diminished the incentive to refer patients to others for services rather than providing them one-self, while pessimists were alarmed at the possible incentive to restrict access to secondary care. But, however one saw the arrangement, it bridged the gulf sep-arating the costs of services provided within a practice and services provided outside it. If GPs could keep the surpluses, then referring a patient for treatment out of the practice, like treating the patient within the practice, had to be paid for and, whether self-interested or concerned for patients' well-being, GPs had an incentive to be economical in their referrals. The incentive structure was robust, in that it appealed to the knight and the knave, and also created incentives for economising on expensive treatments.

If we refer back to the opening of this chapter, it should be apparent that the scheme met the requirements for good policy design in the health care area that were specified there. The incentive structure was robust. With respect to patient choice, patients had the choice of primary-care provider, the GP; and through that choice, although they did not have the direct power of choice over secondary-care provider or over the nature and amount of treatment, they could choose the agent who would make those choices for them. Moreover, those agents—the GP fund-holders—had a fixed budget, which meant that they had an incentive to avoid overuse of the system by one or more of their patients.

### Fund-Holding in Practice

The health care quasi-market evolved over time, especially on the purchasing side. In particular, fund-holding moved from being largely a fringe activity to one that took centre stage. By the time the Conservative government lost office in 1997, over half of all GPs were working in fund-holding practices. Many of the remaining GPs were part of so-called commissioning groups: groups that did not hold a budget but that nonetheless advised their local health authority on purchasing decisions. The fund-holding scheme itself changed to allow different levels of fund-holding. At one end, small practices were allowed to purchase only community services; at the other extreme, some experimental 'total purchasing pilots' were introduced where a practice—or, more com-monly, groups of practices—were allowed to purchase all forms of secondary care, including accident and emergency treatment.

So what were the effects of the scheme? Although there was some anecdotal evidence of abuse, in practice the surpluses of fund-holders were small and seem to have resulted more from shortages of specialist services and the need to ration the funds so as not to run out at the end of the year than from any desire to run a surplus for personal benefit (Goodwin 1998). Indeed, in many cases the surpluses were used to reduce waiting lists in the following year.

More importantly, there were improvements in the quality of treatment (Glennerster, Matsaganis, and Owens 1994; Goodwin 1998). There was a greater provision of outreach services by fund-holders than non-fund-holders. They obtained quicker admission for their patients, significantly reducing waiting times (Dowling 1997; 2000; Propper, Croxson, and Shearer 2002). Fund-holders also kept down prescription costs relative to non-fund-holders (Harris and Scrivener 1996; Goodwin 1998: 45–8). In fact, generally fund-holders appeared more successful than other forms of purchasers in obtaining responsiveness from hospital providers. However, on the more negative side, there was no evidence of increased choice for their patients (Fotaki 1999).

Whether the improvements in quality generated by fund-holding outweighed in value terms any associated increases in costs (and thereby led to an increase in efficiency, properly defined) is not known. There is also controversy as to whether fund-holders' relative success derived from their being more generously funded than health authorities. However, the best evidence suggests that this was not so, and that in fact it was their ability as purchasers, not increased resources, that led to their success (Dowling 1997; 2000).

One of the expectations of the fund-holding scheme was that fund-holders would find it cheaper (and arguably more effective) to treat patients out of hospital than in it, and hence would reduce the number of patient referrals to hospital. The evidence as to whether this actually occurred is mixed. Early work suggested that it did not (Goodwin 1998: 48–50); but a recent sophisticated study by Mark Dusheiko and colleagues showed that fund-holders did reduce referrals and, moreover, did so by a significant amount (Dusheiko *et al.* 2003). Of course, it is controversial whether a difference in referral rates represents a positive or a negative difference in the quality of care; but in some ways the interest for our purposes lies not so much in this question as in whether the financial incentive structure underlying the GP fund-holding scheme actually changed doctors' behaviour.

Reinforcing the view that the incentive structure did lead to a change in GP behaviour is an interesting study by Bronwyn Croxson, Carol Propper, and Andy Perkins (2001). This found that potential fund-holders 'gamed' the system, increasing referral rates in the year before they became fund-holders in order to get a larger budget (their initial budget being determined by their pattern of referrals in that year) and reducing them after they became fund-holders.

Finally, it is worth noting that there was little evidence of cream-skimming: the deliberate selection of patients by fund-holding practices who were easier or less costly to treat in order to protect budgets (Scheffler 1989). Given that fund-holding offered incentives for engaging in this kind of selection, it is not immediately obvious why it failed to materialise. It may have been the result of knightly motivation. Alternatively, the absence of cream-skimming may have been because there was an 'insurance' scheme by which fund-holders were not liable for the extra costs associated with very expensive patients: a fact which significantly reduced any incentive they may have had to exclude such patients from their lists.

On balance, then, it would seem that the robust incentive structure for GP fund-holding did change GP behaviour and did so in a fashion that, mostly, led to tangible benefits. In this it was an improvement on the previous structure of GP incentives that did have elements of robustness about it in that some knightly and knavish motivations were aligned, but that, due to the division of budgets between primary and secondary care, had undesirable consequences. One lesson to be learned from this is that it is not sufficient for incentives to be robust for there to be desirable outcomes; they must also be coupled with appropriate budgetary design.

### Primary Care Trusts

Finally, it is worth comparing the incentive structure of GP fund-holding with that of its successor: the primary care trust. When the Labour government took power in 1997, it officially abolished the internal market. The purchaser/ provider split was retained, but the emphasis was now to be on cooperative relationships, not competitive ones. However, as a last resort, purchasers could still switch their purchasing away from their providers. New purchasers were introduced: Primary Care Groups, soon to evolve into Primary Care Trusts (PCTs).

PCTs are now in place. They are independent trusts, directly providing primary and community care services and purchasing other services, including hospital care, from specialist providers. They are funded by central government, and will control up to 75 per cent of the NHS budget. All GP practices are required to join PCTs. They are geographically specific, often serving large populations (350,000 or more).

The PCTs can keep any surpluses they make on their budgets. These can be shared between the PCT itself and the individual practices within the PCT. The PCT has considerable freedom in how it can spend its share; the only real requirement is that it spend 'strategically . . . to develop primary care' (UK Department of Health 1998*a*: 23). Practices, on the other hand, are more constrained: they may spend the share of their surplus only on a prescribed list of activities including the purchase of equipment used for patient treatment, investment in existing premises, and non-recurring staff costs. There seems to be no uniform procedure for sharing any surplus between the practices and the PCT itself.[8]

---

[8] One was suggested in a Department of Health circular at the beginning of the process (UK Department of Health 1998*b*: 24–6). Under this scheme, each practice would have its 'activity

Although supposedly replacing fund-holding, the PCTs can be viewed as in many ways a partial successor to the scheme. In fact they bear many similarities to the total purchasing pilots: groups of fund-holders who, as mentioned above, were given a budget to purchase all hospital and community health services for their registered populations (Mays *et al.* 1998). Hence many of the arguments above concerning fund-holders' incentives should carry over to PCTs. However, the incentive structures are different in some key ways, notably in the sharing of surpluses and in the external environment.

If one supposes that the most important concern of GPs in a PCT is the caring one of promoting the health of *all* the patients for whom the PCT provides services, then the PCT will have an incentive to use its resources efficiently, regardless of how the surplus is shared out. In particular, it will allocate its budget in such a way that it will equalise the marginal health gain from each use of its fund, whether the use involves purchasing secondary services or investing the surplus in primary care. In principle the outcome could be more efficient than fund-holding, since all the relevant resources (including all primary and secondary care as well as community services) will be under the same budget. Under fund-holding, in contrast, there were separate budgets for primary care, secondary care, and community services, and the secondary-care budget for most forms of fund-holding did not cover the most expensive categories of secondary care. In addition, PCTs should avoid the inequities in care that resulted from the fact that some GPs were fund-holders and that some were not.

However, even knightly GPs may not be motivated by an impersonal concern for the welfare of all patients. Both the norms governing medical practice and their personal attachments are likely to make them more concerned with the health of *their* patients than with the health of others. So, even without material self-interest, there would be conflicts of interest among the GPs in a PCT, and these could give rise to problems, with GPs tempted to free-ride on others' activities. This will, of course, be even stronger for purely self-interested GPs.

However, a structure of incentives that involves a sharing of the surplus is one that should appeal to both the practice-interested GP (whether knightly or knavish) and to the GP whose concern is with the general PCT interest. Of course, some problems will remain. Very successful practices may resent not receiving all of their surplus, especially if it is used to offset others' deficits. Less energetic practices may be tempted to free-ride if they know that deficits

share' of the secondary-care budget calculated on the basis of its existing use of secondary care in its area. If it managed to spend less than its share, then it would be entitled to the whole of the first £10,000 of any surplus, half of the next £70,000 with the other half going to the PCT, and nothing from any surplus over £80,000. The maximum it could earn from making a surplus would thus be £45,000. If the PCT overall was in deficit, then all its part of the practice's surplus would be set against that deficit; however, the practice could still keep its share. So far as I am aware no PCT has implemented this scheme.

will be covered. Resources devoted to adjudicating the resulting disagreements and to implementing the administrative machinery needed to minimise and regulate the conflicts are resources that are not being used to treat patients.

But on balance the principles underlying the internal incentive structure seem to have merit. However, the external situation seems less satisfactory. What is to prevent a PCT that consists of largely self-interested GPs from exploiting its capacity to generate surpluses at the expense of patient care? An external disincentive to such behaviour that *was* present for fund-holders will not be there for PCTs. Fund-holders, unlike PCTs, faced the risk of losing their patients to another commissioner. Since a particular PCT covers all the population of a particular area, patients who are unhappy with the treatment they receive (or the lack of it) can only complain. In Albert Hirschman's (1970) terminology discussed in Chapter Five, they can exercise their voice, but they will not be able to exit. Although in practice patients of fund-holders rarely used the exit option, GP fund-holders were aware of the possibility, and it undoubtedly helped to align the self-interest of GPs with the interests of their patients.

The absence of the exit option will be partly addressed by government monitoring through a regulatory agency.[9] However, here the impact of policy on motivation becomes important. Heavy monitoring and the threat of penalties associated with failure may shift the balance of motivation in the wrong direction: towards greater self-interest. If people are treated as though they need to be whipped to achieve results, then they may behave as though they do need to be. As we have seen earlier, the threat of sanctions can debase a previously voluntary activity, arousing resentment and lowering morale. It encourages the development of evasion and avoidance techniques, and it leads to concentration on whatever is monitored at the expense of what is not, regardless of the relative importance to patient care.

An alternative way of coping with the absence of an exit option is to rely on a more conventional interpretation of Hirschmann's voice: patients' complaints procedures. But, as we saw in Chapter Three, these are blunt instruments for motivating change. They require energy and commitment to activate; they take time to operate; and they create defensiveness and distress among those complained against. Patients who complain are not necessarily those who have the most to complain about, and an adversarial relation between doctors and patients, especially if it is accompanied by threat of lawsuits, leads to expensive and inefficient defensive medicine.

Overall, it is here that the biggest weakness of the PCT structure is to be found. The methods that will be used to try to hold largely self-interested PCTs accountable to their patients are likely either to be ineffective or to encourage more of the kind of self-interested motivation that led to the

---

[9] Currently the Commission for Health Improvement; soon to become the Commission for Healthcare Audit and Inspection.

problem in the first place. It would be better to reinstate the exit option: to allow patients to choose their own PCT, as they could choose their fund-holder.[10] This has the obvious danger that PCTs could cream-skim; however, this could be prevented by putting restrictions on PCTs' ability to turn people away.

## THE PAYMENT OF HOSPITAL CONSULTANTS

Hospital consultants in the British NHS are currently paid on a salary basis to work a number of sessions per week in the NHS. However, if they are prepared to work (and be paid) for one fewer session per week, they are allowed to work in addition as much as they like in the private sector—where they are paid on a fee-for-service basis. Other countries have similar arrangements.

Such systems can create perverse incentives, at least from the point of view of the public service. This applies particularly to situations where physicians are paid for fee-for-service in the private sector and on a salary basis in the public sector. Thus a British consultant confronted with a public sector patient who needs an operation has a (largely knavish) incentive to encourage the patient to 'go private'. For if the patient remains in the public sector the consultant will have to do the operation without any extra reward whereas, if the patient goes privately, the consultant will be paid.

And the best way to encourage the patient to go privately is to have a long wait for a publicly funded operation. So, if the aim of policy is to have public sector waiting lists as short as possible, the existence of the private sector running alongside the public one directly undermines the latter's ability to achieve that aim.[11]

Can this be rectified? Can a robust incentive scheme be devised that would overcome these problems? Suppose that, instead of being paid exclusively by salary, the physicians concerned were paid on a fee-for-service basis for treating public sector patients above a baseline case load. So, for instance, for each case treated above the baseline, they would get 80 per cent of the current private rate. The extra payments could be made in addition to the present pay structure or could substitute for some aspect of it.

Why 80 per cent of the private rate and not 100 per cent? This is to allow for an element of knightly motivation. By opting for public sector work under this scheme, physicians would be better-off than if they did not do the extra work, so there would be a direct gain to themselves from working harder. But they

---

[10] As has been suggested by one of the original architects of the internal market, the economist Alain Enthoven (1999).

[11] This is not a theoretical danger. These perverse incentives do appear to distort consultant priorities in practice. For instance, a study of the extent of private practice by the UK Audit Commission (1995) found that the 25 per cent of consultants who do the most private work carry out significantly less NHS work than their colleagues.

would also be making a sacrifice through not doing the same work in the private sector at a higher rate, thus meeting public service objectives but at some opportunity cost—a feature of the scheme that as was argued in Chapter Four should appeal to the knight. So both altruistic and self-interested motivations would be working in the same direction.

Would changing the payment system in this way empower patients? In one sense it would, for, under fee-for-service, consultants' incomes would depend on the amount of services they provided for patients, in a way that it does not under a salary system. So consultants would have a direct incentive to meet patients' needs and wants or, as under the primary-care budget-holding scheme, their primary-care physician's interpretation of those needs and wants.

But there is a danger. Any fee-for-service system in medical care may encourage what economists term 'supplier-induced demand'. That is, physicians have a (knavish) incentive to encourage patients to have more medical care than they need: pressure that patients, from their position of relative ignorance concerning their actual need, may find difficult to resist. However, the fact that the system allows for an element of knightly motivation would act as a brake on this tendency. In addition, if the system were coupled with primary-care budget-holding, this would be a source of further restraint. For the cost of meeting demand would fall on the relevant budget, thus providing primary-care physicians with a strong motivation to approve only treatments that were strictly necessary.

There are two other possible objections. First, there is a fundamental assumption underlying the scheme (and indeed the primary-care budget-holding schemes discussed in the previous section): that doctor behaviour responds to changes in financial payment schemes. This could be challenged. But, in fact, there is overwhelming evidence from an enormous variety of studies that financial incentives do impact on physician behaviour and, moreover, that they do so in the manner that would be expected (Chaix-Couturier *et al.* 2000; Rodwin 1993).

Second, the shortage of specialists in the private sector could result in an increase in private sector rates. In consequence, if the price paid were always 80 per cent of the private rate, the scheme would end up being more expensive for the public sector. However, fixing the price as a high proportion of the private rate would discourage private rate rises, since it would be apparent to the private sector that this would be largely self-defeating. Further, the private sector is limited in the extent to which it can raise rates because of the knock-on effects on private health insurance premiums and out-of-pocket payments.

## CONCLUSION

This chapter has demonstrated that it is possible to design policies for publicly funded health care that offer robust incentives to medical professionals, that go some way towards empowering patients, but that avoid the problems of unfettered patient choice. Devices such as allowing budget-holding professionals to keep surpluses on their budget, providing those surpluses are spent in a way that improves patient care, or paying professionals fee-for-service at a rate that incorporates some sacrifice compared with alternatives, help align knightly and knavish motivations. Primary-care budget-holding coupled with fee-for-service for hospital consultants allows decisions concerning patients' treatment to be made closer to the patients themselves. At the same time it makes use of professional knowledge and expertise, and confronts decision-makers with the opportunity costs of their decisions. Although, of course, there are many ways of designing public health care systems, one that incorporates these kinds of features—or, at least, features that take proper account of motivation and agency issues—is likely to be more successful in creating appropriately motivated professionals, satisfied patients, and ultimately better health care than one without.

# 8

# School Education

Headmasters have powers at their disposal with which Prime Ministers have never yet been invested.

(Winston Churchill, *My Early Life*)

The previous chapter discussed the design of policies aimed at motivating professionals to produce quality services that balanced user and professional power with respect to decision-making in the context of health care. This chapter undertakes a similar task with respect to school education. It will be seen that, although there are fundamental similarities between the two cases, some of the more detailed proposals are rather different. Again, the chapter concentrates on the British case; again, though, the ideas and policies discussed are capable of more general application.

## PRIMARY EDUCATION

As outlined in Chapter One, state school education in England and Wales, like health care, underwent an organisational transformation in the late 1980s. Prior to that, the school education system in England and Wales relied upon a combination of command and control and professional trust. The local government of the area where a school was located had control of all schools' budgets and admissions. Budgets were set essentially on a historical basis and admissions were determined according to the local government's own criteria (usually related to geographical proximity and capacity). Schools had little flexibility in the way they could spend their budget; they had little control over who attended their classes. On the other hand, they had considerable freedom over what and how they taught. Parental choice was heavily constrained, with little choice over where their children went to school and what their children were taught when they were there.

The motivational and agency structures were thus a combination of knight and pawn. Local government officials were assumed to be knights, making budgetary and admissions decisions in the public interest. School head teachers and their staff were supposed to be pawn-like in their acceptance of these decisions but knightly in the way that they devised and implemented their curricula and teaching methods. Any head teacher or a member of staff who was essentially a knave thus had considerable freedom to exploit the situation to serve his or her own interests. Even those who were knights could freely indulge their conception of knightly behaviour, untrammelled by worries about users' concerns. For those users—parents and children—were essentially pawns, their power limited to an occasional exercise of 'voice' through complaints to the head teacher or the governing body. Finally, since the school had no control over budgets, neither knight nor knave had any interest in promoting efficiency in the way that resources were used.

All this changed following the 1988 Education Reform Act passed by the Conservative government of Mrs Thatcher.[1] Under the so-called LMS (Local Management of Schools) initiative, control of schools' budgets and other important decision-making responsibilities were taken away from local governments and given to schools themselves. School governing bodies were to decide upon the numbers and composition of staff and became responsible for hiring and firing decisions (including those relating to head teachers). If they so chose, schools were allowed to opt out of local government control altogether. Schools could keep surpluses on their budgets provided they used them to hire staff or improve facilities.

Under the new system, schools' budgets were predominantly determined by the number of pupils they had on their rolls, with the school concerned receiving a fixed amount per pupil depending on the pupil's age. Parents could choose where to send their child to school—in theory at least. All schools, except for religious and selective ones, had to accept as many pupils as their physical capacity would allow. However, an oversubscribed school was allowed to use published admissions criteria. The most frequently used criteria were geographical (proximity of the child's home to the school), sibling-related (the child's siblings already attending the school), and medical; but schools were also allowed to select a proportion of their pupils according to academic criteria.

In effect, this set of arrangements amounted to the equivalent of an educational voucher system. Under such systems, parents are given a voucher with a monetary value that they present to a school of their choice for educating their child. The school then redeems the voucher for cash from the relevant government department of education. The resources that a school can attract therefore depend on the choices made by parents. So, too, in these quasi-market reforms. In theory at least, parents could choose their child's school and the money would follow their choice. Schools that were successful in attracting pupils would thrive; those that were not would decline.

In addition to these changes encouraging parental choice, information systems were set up to enable parents to make more informed choices. Performance testing of children at ages 7, 11, and 14 was introduced, with the results by

[1] For more detailed descriptions see Barrow (1998), West and Pennell (1997; 1998), and Woods, Bagley, and Glatter (1998: ch. 1).

school to be published. Each school's results in national examinations at ages 16 (GCSEs) and 18 (A-levels) were also published.

These changes led to a significant shift in the structure of motivation towards one that both involved robust incentives and empowered users. Parental choices were the driving force. The possibility of competition means that a school whose head teacher and other staff were driven primarily by knavish concerns would now have an incentive to meet the wishes of parents and children and thereby encourage pupils to attend the school. For that would bring in more resources and perhaps more status, and their self-interest would thereby be served. Moreover, they would want the school to be run efficiently so that a surplus could be generated: a surplus that could be used to improve facilities that could make their working lives more comfortable or to hire extra staff so as to make their work less onerous. But a school run by knights would also wish to generate a surplus in order to provide a better service for pupils and parents. This would be true especially of altruistic teachers whose concern for the welfare of users took the form of wanting to meet their expressed needs and wants. Even other kinds of knights would want to attract pupils; for they would want the school to stay in business so they could exercise their knightly concerns.

It is worth noting that the Labour government that took power in 1997 left these arrangements largely untouched. Indeed, as Howard Glennerster (2002: 126) has argued, 'the Thatcher education reform package was retained and, if anything, strengthened. More of the budgets were devolved to schools. There was no let up in performance testing or publication of results.' This is not to imply that the Labour government was inactive. Glennerster listed sixteen major government policy initiatives in school education between 1997 and 2001. However, none of them involved rolling back the quasi-market reforms (Glennerster 2002: Annex 1). Indeed some of them could be interpreted as designed to improve the operation of the quasi-market, such as the Fresh Start programme aimed at closing failing schools and opening new ones on the same site. Others were mostly adding non-competitive measures to the quasi-market such as Education Action Zones (clusters of schools working with local businesses and others to overcome barriers to learning in areas of high social and economic deprivation) or command and control ones such as the Numeracy and Literacy Hour in primary schools (compulsory time to be set aside in the school week specifically to teach numeracy and literacy).

## PERFORMANCE

So how did the quasi-market perform? In an early study, Anne West and Hazel Pennell (2000) found that the average point score of pupils at GCSE and GNVQ (national exams taken by most pupils around the age of 16) went up between 1992/3 and 1996/7 in England by 8 per cent. Interestingly from the point of view of equity, the score for the top tenth of pupils increased by 7 per cent, but that for the bottom tenth fell by 13 per cent. Overall, there has been a steady improvement in performance in GCSE and A-level results over the period, as measured by the percentage of the age group achieving good passes. However, these trends have been apparent since the early 1970s; and there is also an (unresolved) controversy as to whether standards have changed over that time (Glennerster 1998).

In work that is of more direct use for our purposes, Howard Glennerster (2002) used the performance of pupils in the relatively new national attainment tests (tests taken by all pupils at ages 7,11,14, and 16) to assess the effects of the quasi-market. His conclusions were striking. First, the percentage of pupils reaching a given level of achievement in England steadily increased from 1995 (the first full year of tests) to 2001, especially at the end of primary school. Some of the improvements were remarkable; for instance, the percentage of pupils gaining the expected level of competence in maths at the end of primary school moved from 45 per cent in 1995 to 70 per cent in 2001. This should be set against the fact that the best available evidence suggests that there was no improvement in the maths skills of children in the early years of secondary school for thirty years prior to 1995. Second, these improvements were not confined to good schools; in fact, the lowest-performing schools in 1995 were the ones to show the greatest improvement by 2001. The same is true of schools ranked according to the wealth of the area; over the period schools in poor areas were catching up with schools from rich ones.

Some caution in interpreting these results is needed here. There are anecdotal stories of 'teaching to the test' and indeed of outright fraud. Unpublished results from the University of Durham found little improvement in reading skills for year six pupils from 1999 to 2002 and in vocabulary between 1997 and 2002. However, they assess only reading, whereas the national tests include assessments of writing, spelling, and handwriting as well as reading. Moreover, the same team did find a 5 per cent improvement in science and a 9 per cent improvement in maths between 1997 and 2002.[2]

A less desirable potential outcome of the quasi-market concerns selection by schools: what we have earlier termed 'cream-skimming'. Cream-skimming occurs where an oversubscribed school selects pupils of high intrinsic ability so as to improve the school's performance in examinations at relatively low cost.[3] The problem with cream-skimming is that it can lead to polarisation or segregation in terms of ability, with able pupils being increasingly concentrated in high-performing schools and less able pupils in low-performing ones.

A summary of some of the evidence on the operation of the quasi-market in its early days cites several studies that show evidence of the growth of cream-skimming practices (Whitty, Power, and Halpin 1998).[4] Notable among these

---

[2]  http://cem.dur.ac.uk/pips/StandardsOverTime.asp
[3]  For a description of the various ways in which schools can select and an elaboration of the potential consequences of that selection, see West, Pennell, and Edge (1997).
[4]  See Perri 6 (2003) for a more recent review of the literature.

is the work of Sharon Gewirtz, Stephen Ball, and Richard Bowe (1995), who studied the development of quasi-markets in London. They found evidence that schools sought students who were able, motivated, and committed, with girls from middle class and South Asian backgrounds particularly favoured. However, they did not find any indication that less able pupils were being disadvantaged. Nor did they find overt cream-skimming in admissions policies. But there was what they described as 'social targeting': the promotion of the school to middle class and more able pupils. There did also seem to be a greater openness of schools to families and the local community, and an increased sense of their accountability. But the researchers were agnostic as to the extent to which these changes could be attributed to the quasi-market.

Stephen Gorard and John Fitz (1998a, b) examined the proportion of pupils eligible for free school meals in South Wales from 1991 to 1996 and found that while there was an initial increase in social segregation (as measured by a widening in the differences between schools in the proportion of pupils eligible for free school meals) this was followed by a significant decrease. They argue that the overall decrease in social segregation may reflect a kind of catching-up effect. That is, middle class families responded more quickly to the quasi-market changes than poorer ones, thus generating an initial increase in segregation, but with the poorer families gradually learning how to take advantage of the new freedoms and thus improving their children's ability to get into high-performing schools.

Philip Noden (2000) investigated segregation in English secondary schools from 1994 to 1999 and has challenged Gorard and Fitz's results. He used two measures of segregation: that used by Gorard and Fitz, and an 'isolation' index that again measures the spread of eligibility for free school meals but gives a greater weight to the existence of heavy concentrations of such eligibility. For both indices, he found an increase in segregation over the period, although the increase was not uniform over time or between local authorities. Noden now believes that his index has unsatisfactory properties, but, following comments by Gibson and Asthana, has shifted his criticism of Gorard and Fitz to one of using eligibility for free school meals as an indicator of segregation. The latter varies with the economic cycle, and this in turn could bring about changes in the index even if the underlying distribution did not change.[5]

So the micro-evidence on cream-skimming is mixed. But it is worth returning to Glennerster's more aggregated evidence summarised above, and noting that the improvements to which he draws attention applied to poor schools (whether defined in terms of poor performance or of the poverty of the areas in which they are located) as much as if not more than to good ones. If cream-skimming in relation to educational attainment were a serious problem, this would not have been expected.

---

[5] Gibson and Asthana (2000), Gorard (2000), Noden (forthcoming).

Whatever the doubts about the detailed statistics, it seems hard to deny that there have been some kind of performance improvements in English school education in the last decade. This was the decade following the quasi-market reform and the introduction of robust incentives; so, at first sight, it might seem reasonable to ascribe the improvements to that change. But would this really be justified? Might the changes not be due to increases in public expenditure on education over the period or to other changes in policy, such as the introduction of the numeracy and literacy hour or increased prominence of the regulatory agency Office for Standards in Education (Ofsted)?

Glennerster (2002: 122–4) examines the issue of resources and points out that public expenditure per pupil in England increased only a little over the period at primary school level, and was virtually static at secondary school; public education spending as a whole actually fell as a percentage of GDP. So not only were there improvements in outcomes over the period but, since these were achieved with little if any increase in resources, it seems as though there was also an increase in the efficiency with which those resources were used.

The question whether these improvements in both outcomes and efficiency were attributable to the operations of the quasi-market or to other policy initiatives is more difficult to resolve. There has been no systematic study of the impact of Ofsted on performance. Such work as has been done has concentrated on how parents, governors, and teachers feel about Ofsted, concluding that they did not find it effective in helping to develop schools;[6] but this is far from conclusive. Nor has there been any systematic study of the numeracy and literacy hour; but it is hard to resist the impression that its impact on performance has been considerable. Also, the instrument by which the quasi-market is supposed to create its behavioural effects is through the exercise of parental choice; and there is little evidence that parents actually shifted their children from school to school in search of better educational outcomes.

However, parents do not need to exercise choice in the simple sense of actually moving children to have an impact on school behaviour. Simply the possibility of choice and the threat that it might be exercised—what is often termed 'contestability'—may be sufficient, especially in a world where that threat can be informed by Ofsted reports and the publication of test and exam results. Also, professionals dislike being low down a league table, even if they are not losing custom as a consequence; and this on its own can act as pressure to lever up performance.[7]

Certainly most parents are aware of the possibility of choice and approve of it. A detailed review of both national and international evidence on school choice by Perri 6 (2003) found that the scheme 'appears popular with many parents and has achieved good satisfaction ratings from majorities'.

---

[6]  The evidence is summarised in Propper, Burgess, and Shearer (2002).

[7]  I am grateful to Will Cavendish (personal communication) for this point.

Whatever the exact mechanism through which competition exercises its effects, micro-studies of the performance of schools suggest that some at least of the efficiency improvements can be directly attributed to the competitive pressures arising from the operations of the quasi-market. Stephen Bradley, Geraint Jones, and Jim Millington (2001) investigated the performance of all secondary schools in England over the period 1993–7. They measured the performance of each school on two dimensions of 'output': school exam performance and attendance rates. They then related these outputs to various input measures, including the proportion of pupils ineligible for free school meals and the proportion of qualified staff, to calculate the relative efficiency of the schools concerned. These relative efficiency scores were related to selected characteristics of the school and the local area, including local education authority expenditure per pupil, staff/student ratio, type of school (local, selective, grant maintained, and so forth), gender composition (co-educational, boys-only, girls-only), the local unemployment rate, and the proportion of adults in profession and managerial occupations. Finally they were related to the extent of competition in the area, as measured by the number of schools of different types (including selective) within a two-kilometre radius.

The conclusions of the study were quite unambiguous. The relative efficiency of the schools was directly related to the amount of competition they faced. The greater the degree of competition, the more efficient they were. Moreover, the strength of the effect increased over time, corresponding to the evolution of the quasi-market. Competition also encouraged changes in efficiency over time: the greater the competition, the faster the rate of change.

Stephen Bradley has taken the argument further. With Jim Taylor he has used data from the Schools' census, the School Performance Tables, and the Youth Cohort Study to study the impact of competitive pressures within the English quasi-market on schools' exam performance (as a measure of allocative efficiency) and on exam performance per member of staff (as a measure of productive efficiency) (Bradley and Taylor 2000). Again they found an unambiguous positive impact of competition on both indicators, even when all other factors that might affect school performance were controlled for. Other studies of what could be interpreted as outcome improvements are less direct but nonetheless suggest an effect arising from competition. Philip Woods, Carl Bagley, and Ron Glatter studied three areas with eleven schools during a period from 1993 to 1996. They interviewed head teachers, other teachers, business managers and governor and parents. They concluded that there was a 'sharpening of focus on the academic in most schools and . . . further than this, a privileging of the academic. Significantly this is considerably less marked in East Greenvale [one of their study schools] where there are fewer competitive pressures' (Woods, Bagley, and Glatter 1998: 162).

As well as investigating efficiency, Stephen Bradley and Jim Taylor (2000) in their paper mentioned above explored the selection consequences of the quasi-market. They found that schools with good exam results experienced a reduction in the proportion of pupils coming from poor backgrounds (as measured by the proportion eligible for free school meals) while those with poor exam results experienced the reverse. However, the effect was not large. Moreover, the direction of causation is not unambiguous, with the results possibly arising in part because the reduction in the proportion of pupils coming from poor backgrounds promoted good exam results rather than the other way round.

Finally, it is worth noting that there is international evidence concerning the importance of competition in affecting school outcomes, both positively (in the sense of improving educational outcomes) and negatively (in the sense of encouraging segregation). Caroline Hoxby (2002; 2003) has reviewed the evidence on the impact on the performance of public schools in Milwaukee, Michigan, and Arizona of competition from 'choice' schools. All three of those areas have experimented with allowing parents to choose schools other than their local public schools through the mechanisms of either vouchers (Milwaukee) or charter schools[8] (Michigan, Arizona). It had been widely predicted that, because of cream-skimming, public schools in the areas concerned would suffer an overall drop in performance as the better students were sucked into the choice schools. However, Hoxby found evidence of strongly improved performance by the public schools, from which she concluded that the efficiency-inducing effects of competition were more than enough to offset any potential effects of cream-skimming. She also examined the effects of competition with private schools on public schools and of competition between public schools through parents choosing place of residence. Again she found that competition had a positive impact on performance.

New Zealand also experimented with competition in education, offering full parental choice of schools. However, in one difference from the British case, neither the costs of teachers' salaries nor all central support services were devolved to individual school budgets. An experimental fully funded option was opened up to all schools for a trial period.

There does not seem to have been any direct study of the impact of competition on the outcome and efficiency results of the New Zealand experiment, with most researchers concentrating on the effects on parental choice and the consequences thereof.[9] A summary of the earlier evidence found that parents were given more information about school programmes and children's progress, and parents did indeed exercise their right of choice over schools.

---

[8] Charter schools are similar to Britain's foundation (previously grant-maintained) schools, being within the public system but funded separately. Individuals, non-profit, and for-profit organisations can apply to a local school board for a 'charter' to run a school. The charters are renewable but depend on targets set out in the charter being met. The funding is on a per-pupil basis. There are currently around 350,000 pupils in nearly 2,000 schools in 36 States.

[9] A partial exception is Lauder and Hughes (1999: ch. 7). However, they did not investigate the direct effects of competitive pressures on school performance. Rather, they examined the effects on school performance of the polarisation that they claimed was due to markets.

However, a consequence of this was increased polarisation with schools in low-income areas suffering from decreasing resource and enrolment problems (Whitty, Power, and Halpin 1998). This has been confirmed by later research. Thus Helen Ladd and Edward Fiske (1999) in a study of the country's three major urban areas for the US Brookings Institution found that the effect of choice was to generate a system in which the gaps between the successful and the unsuccessful schools became wider and in which minority and poorer pupils were concentrated in the unsuccessful schools, a result confirmed by Hugh Lauder and David Hughes (1999).

Belgium and the Netherlands have long had a quasi-market system of education, with school choice coupled with public funding organised on a per capita basis according to school rolls. Again there have been no studies of the relative efficiency of the Belgian or Dutch systems in terms of educational output per unit of input. However, Vincent Vandenberghe (1998) has studied the impact of parental choice on school segregation by ability in the French-speaking community of Belgium. He found that the variation between the output of schools (as measured by the number of pupils who did not have to repeat a grade year) was not related to the degree of socio-economic inequality in the area, as might have been expected, but was directly related to the degree of school competition in the area (as measured by a concentration index). In other words, the more the competition, the more schools were segregated by ability: a result he described as both inequitable and inefficient.

Finally it is worth noting that a recent paper in the *Economic Journal* has claimed that, in most OECD countries over the past twenty-five years, pupil performance has remained broadly constant, even though spending per pupil in real terms has risen (Gundlach, Woessman, and Gmelin 2001). The researchers conclude that this suggests a significant fall in the efficiency with which resources are used, a fall that they suggest is due to the lack of competitive pressures in the countries concerned. But, as Glennerster (2002) has noted, none of this is now true for the UK.

## THE POSITIVELY DISCRIMINATING VOUCHER

So it would seem as though the motivational and empowerment structures implicit in the quasi-market in primary education in Britain and in similar competitive systems in other countries can succeed in raising standards overall. However, even if some of the critics' worse fears about cream-skimming may not have always materialised, there is clearly a danger here. Head teachers do have an incentive to try to manipulate the entrance requirements to their schools so as to further the school's and its staff's interests. Under certain funding structures, this could lead to their trying to select pupils from wealthier socio-economic backgrounds, which, perhaps because of better support systems at home or more highly motivated parents, could improve their schools' exam results for minimum effort.

But not under all funding structures. Several years ago I proposed what I termed the 'positively discriminating voucher' (PDV) (Le Grand 1989: 202–4). This would be a form of education voucher that favoured poor families. Under the scheme those living in poorer areas would receive a larger voucher, thus creating a positive incentive for schools to take them in. Schools that contained a high proportion of children from poor families would then have more resources per pupil on average than those with a low proportion. They would also have better premises and equipment and could attract higher-quality staff. The outcome would be either selective schools, with those that specialised in the education of the children of the poor being better equipped and staffed than those that specialised in the education of the children of the rich, or, if head teachers or staff did not want to engage in such specialisations, schools that contained a reasonable proportion of children from all parts of the social spectrum.

A difficulty with the PDV is that it would be necessary to find some way of identifying families from poor backgrounds. This could be done by means tests; but these have well-known difficulties, including administrative complexity and stigmatising effects. An alternative would be simply to give larger vouchers to families who lived in poorer areas. The wealth of the area could be determined by a sample survey of the value of the houses in the area. This would have the advantage of stopping the better-off from moving into a poor area simply to benefit from the higher value of the voucher. For if they did so in any numbers, house prices would rise and the value of the voucher would fall.

Samuel Bowles and Herbert Gintis (1998: 43; see also Brighouse 1998) have proposed an interesting variant on this idea. This is to make the value of the voucher depend not only on the socio-economic status of the family but also on the socio-economic composition of the school. Thus a voucher presented by a low-income pupil to a school with predominantly high-income pupils would be worth more, giving the school an incentive to attract such pupils. Similarly a voucher presented by a high-income pupil to a school with predominantly low-income pupils would also be worth more, again giving an incentive to the school to attract such pupils.

## CONCLUSION

It is of interest to conclude this chapter by comparing the policies discussed therein with those relating to health care of the previous chapter, especially primary-care budget-holding. Overall, both the GP fund-holding scheme and the quasi-market in state school education appears to have done a better job than the systems that preceded them. They appear to have changed the behaviour of providers, and to have done so for the better. Outcomes seem to have improved, as does the efficiency in the way that resources have been used. In education, at least, choice and responsiveness appear to have increased, as, on a less positive note, has cream-skimming, although the evidence on the latter is mixed.

The reasons for the success lie in the 'robust' motivational structure of the key actors. In a school, the relevant decision-makers are head teachers. In the quasi-market, they are motivated in large part by a desire to preserve or improve the financial health of the institution. This could be in part a knavish motivation: a desire to preserve their own jobs, and an awareness that this depended in large part on their ability to control the finances. But it also could have knightly components; head teachers believing that by improving the financial health of their institutions they would thereby benefit their pupils and staff. What is indisputable is that head teachers also have direct managerial control over their staff, with considerable freedom to hire, fire, and promote. They also have considerable autonomy over admissions and exclusions (West, Pennell, and Edge 1997). Hence they have both the motivation and the ability to respond to market pressures.

And those market pressures are quite intense. Parents, armed with the latest published examination results, seem prepared to exercise the choices open to them, even if they did not always do so. They are much closer to queens than pawns. And any school that faced the threat of losing pupils would lose resources; while schools that succeeded in gaining pupils would gain resources. Schools that gained resources had considerable freedom of action how to spend any surplus they generated. Schools that lost resources went into financial difficulty; head teachers in charge of schools that were in financial difficulty were in risk of losing their jobs.

GP fund-holders were under less market pressure, although some was exerted by patients' freedom to change their GP. But their incentive structure was clear: to spend their budget in a fashion that made the best use of hospital resources. They had an obvious knavish motivation for this, in that any surplus they made on their budget could ultimately be used to serve their self-interest. However, this would not necessarily conflict with a knightly desire to do the best for their patients, since that too could be served by not wasting resources on unnecessary hospital treatment. And, as with head teachers, they had considerable autonomy and thus were well-placed to undertake the necessary activities to meet their ends.

There is a clear difference, though, in the extent of user empowerment in the two schemes. In both cases users have a budget associated with them: one that limits potential overuse. However, in the education case, the parents are the active agents in charge of that budget, making choices on behalf of their children. In the health case, the active agents were the GPs: quite close to patients in many ways but not clearly in the same relation to them as parents are to their children. This in part seems to be a sensible reflection of the differences between the two cases in the extent of system and individual failure. As was argued in Chapter Five, the information available to users and their capacity properly to process that information is arguably less in the case of health care than education. Hence appointing an informed agent to make choices on behalf of users seems more appropriate for health care.[10] However, it is important that users can choose their agent: hence the recommendation at the end of Chapter Five that patients should be able to choose their primary-care trust.

Finally, what conclusions can we draw from all the discussion so far about the way to design policies aimed at improving the delivery of public services? There seem to be three major ones. First, we are unlikely to be able to rely solely upon pure knightly motivations—upon the public service ethos—to deliver public services to the level of quality and quantity that we require. However, rewards for public service should not be such that all elements of sacrifice are removed—otherwise we are content to have all public services provided by knaves. Second, knavish and knightly incentive structures should not work against one another but should be aligned in a 'robust' fashion. Third, and per-haps most controversially, if the aim is to have a service that treats its users more like queens than like pawns and, moreover, is relatively efficient in its use of resources, then it would seem that a system of quasi-market competition with independent providers run by public sector professionals and with users or their agents having fixed budgets is the best—or perhaps the least bad. There is a danger in such a system that providers will exploit any informational advantages they may have to lower quality or to cream-skim. However, this is likely to be to be restrained in part by their knightly instincts and in part by the judicious design of policy, incorporating such measures as the positively discriminating voucher.

## ANNEX: GOLDEN HOUSING

This is not a case involving the motivation of public service providers; nor is it about education or health care. But it illustrates the point about robust incent-ive structures so neatly that I cannot resist including it: a pioneering scheme by a housing association to improve the service and behaviour of its tenants.

Irwell Valley is a housing association: a non-profit organisation providing more than 6,300 homes in Greater Manchester.[11] In 1998, it pioneered a new way of dealing with the relationship between landlord and tenant: one that appeals to both knightly and knavish motivations in the tenant and, not coincidentally, goes some way towards turning pawns into queens.

Prior to 1998 the Association had most of the problems associated with social housing in poor areas. Low demand, property abandonment, anti-social behav-iour by tenants, drug dealing, vandalism, and high turnover rates characterised a small proportion of the housing stock; but that proportion dominated the

[10] Another difference between the two situations is that the budget is individual in the case of education whereas in health care the budget for many patients is pooled. This arises because of the uncertainty associated with the need for health care, necessitating some form of risk pooling.

[11] What follows is drawn from Irwell Valley Housing Association (2001). I am very grateful to John Hills for bringing this to my attention.

business. Around 80 per cent of resources were being spent on 20 per cent of the tenants. The Association's general management performance was in the median quartile of comparable performance indicators published by the housing corporation. Void rates and rent arrears were above average.

In 1998, the Association introduced what it termed 'Gold Service'. Tenants could apply to be Gold Service members if they met certain criteria for acceptance. These included payment of rent in full for six consecutive weeks and no breaches of their tenancy agreement. In return, they received a range of benefits, including a faster repairs service, various discounts at local stores and entertainment facilities, and a cash bonus every year. With respect to the last of these, if the tenants wished they could choose to have it paid into a tenants' association or group, in which case the Housing Association would match it with a grant of its own. The money would then be used for the benefit of the community.

The aim was thus to reward good tenants and, in effect, bring them into the business of running a successful housing project. The incentives were largely knavish, but not entirely: knights could pay their bonus into a fund for group benefit and indeed would be rewarded by a matching grant for doing so. So both knights and knaves had an incentive to behave.

The results have been remarkable. Rent collection has increased substantially; rent arrears as a percentage of rent receivable has been halved, from nearly 10 per cent to less than 5 per cent. Nearly 70 per cent of the Associations' tenants have no arrears at all, compared with 40 per cent at the start of Gold Service. Average arrears of those in debt were reduced by 13 per cent during the eighteen months of Gold Service. The average time for re-letting property has fallen to just over three weeks, at a time when that for other social housing providers was increasing.

Although this is not an example of incentivising public service providers (rather it is motivating the tenants), it is an illustration of what a mixture of knavish and a (small) dose of knightly incentives can do to change behaviour if they are properly aligned.

# 9

## A Demogrant

Money is like muck, not good except that it be spread.

(Francis Bacon, 'Of Seditions and Troubles')

*Higgins.* I suppose we must give him a fiver.

*Pickering.* He'll make a bad use of it, I'm afraid.

*Doolittle.* Not me, Governor, so help me I won't. Don't you be afraid that I'll save it and spare it and live idle on it. There won't be a penny of it left by Monday: I'll have to go to work same as if I'd never had it. It won't pauperise me, you bet. Just one good spree for myself and the missus, giving pleasure to ourselves and employment to others and satisfaction to you to think it's not been throwed away. You couldn't spend it better.

*Higgins.* This is irresistible. Let's give him ten.

*Doolittle.* No, Governor. She wouldn't have the heart to spend ten; and perhaps I shouldn't neither. Ten pounds is a lot of money: it makes a man prudent-like and then goodbye to happiness. You give me what I ask you, Governor: not a penny more, and not a penny less.

(Bernard Shaw, *Pygmalion*)

Income only maintains consumption, but assets change the way people think and interact in the world. With assets, people begin to think in the long term and pursue long-term goals. In other words, while incomes feed people's stomachs, assets change their minds.

(Michael Sherraden, *Assets and the Poor*)

The previous two chapters concentrated upon the delivery of public services and the questions raised by considerations of motivation and agency. I now turn to another, equally important set of issues concerned with the public sector: those associated with the cash benefits it provides and with its finance. Again I shall select a number of specific policy areas for detailed analysis: the finance of pensions and long-term care, hypothecated taxation, and, in this chapter, capital grants to young people: what I term 'demogrants'.

The demogrant idea is directed at changing the distribution of power, opportunity, and wealth within society. That the ownership of financial assets or wealth confers power—political and social as well as economic—is an obvious truth. From it follows the equally obvious truth that inequalities in asset ownership create inequalities in power of all kinds, and that reducing those inequalities would contribute to the goal of increasing the power of the relatively powerless: of transforming pawns into queens, in the metaphor that informs this book. Yet many proponents of equality or of the empowerment of the poor have paid relatively little attention to policies designed to reduce differences in the ownership of assets or wealth. Instead they have concentrated more on the distribution of income and on policies such as income taxation or the provision of cash benefits designed to reduce inequalities in that distribution.

However, there is now a growing interest in what is called 'asset-based egalitarianism' and in the policies associated with it. These are measures aimed at increasing the wealth-holdings of those with few assets and/or at reducing the holdings of those with a large amount. Examples include an annual wealth tax, inheritance and estate taxes, tax reliefs or partnership grants to encourage savings, and universal demogrants (also known as 'baby bonds' or 'stakeholder grants'). This chapter focuses on the universal demogrant proposal, Chapter Ten on partnership grants.[1]

## DEMOGRANTS

The idea of the demogrant is a simple one. It is that each individual at birth or on attaining the age of majority should receive a grant of capital from the state that he or she can use as a springboard to accumulate further wealth.

Although it may seem radical, the proposal has a long history. As with a number of other imaginative innovations in social policy (such as education vouchers), it seems to have originated with Tom Paine. He proposed that everyone reaching the age of 21 should receive the sum of fifteen pounds sterling out of a 'national fund' financed from a tax on inheritances. 'The subtraction will be made at the time that best admits it, which is, at the moment that property is passing by the death of one person to the possession of another . . . The monopoly of natural inheritance to which there never was a right, begins to cease' (quoted in Ackerman and Alstott 1999: 182).

In more modern times in the UK, similar ideas were discussed by Cedric Sandford (1971: 250–4) and A. B. Atkinson (1972: 233–6). Both explored the idea of a demogrant, although not one necessarily provided at birth or at the age of majority: Atkinson, for instance, discussed the possibility of including a capital element in the state pension.

---

[1] Those interested in some of the other measures for affecting the distribution of wealth, such as wealth and inheritance taxation, should consult the classic treatment of the subject by Atkinson (1972), and, for a more recent review, Fabian Society (2000: ch. 12). Tax reliefs and partnership grants are discussed in Chapter Ten. Much of and the material is taken from Nissan Le Grand (2000). I am grateful to my co-author, David Nissan, for allowing me to use the work in this way.

Unaware of these predecessors, a few years ago I published a proposal for a grant to everyone on reaching the age of majority financed out of a reformed inheritance tax, terming the idea a 'poll grant' (Le Grand 1989: 210). At that time, there was relatively little interest in the idea. But, in recent years, the proposal has acquired momentum in British policy circles. In 1995, Eamonn Butler and Madson Pirie of the Adam Smith Institute proposed a 'fortune account': a tax-subsidised savings account for every individual started by the government paying in £1,000 at birth (Butler and Pirie 1995). In 1999, a demogrant at the age of majority was discussed in several contributions to the *New Statesman*.[2] A few months later, Gavin Kelly and Rachel Lissauer (2000) of the Institute of Public Policy Research (IPPR) reviewed schemes designed to promote asset ownership and proposed a 'baby bond': a grant of £1,000 made at birth.

At the same time the Fabian Society produced a pamphlet by myself and David Nissan advocating a demogrant of £10,000 to every 18-year-old, to be financed from a reformed inheritance tax (Nissan and Le Grand 2000). It would be paid into a special ACE (Accumulation of Capital and Education) account. ACE accounts would be handled by a set of trustees, whose purpose would be to approve the spending plans of individuals before releasing any capital; hence individuals would be able to draw money from the account to spend only on approved purposes, as defined by the trustees. These purposes would include higher and further education, down payment on a house or a flat, the start-up cost of a small business, or beginning a pension fund.

In what is perhaps the most important development of all, the British government has committed itself to the introduction of a 'child trust fund'. The illustrations used in the government's consultation documents on the proposal suggest that the government will set up a child trust fund for each newborn child into which it will pay £400 in tranches: £250 at birth, followed by three payments at ages 5, 11, and 16 (UK Treasury 2001a, b). Children born to parents below a threshold income will receive more, up to £800. Parents can pay into the fund, which will be invested in a wide range of vehicles including equities. Neither parents nor children will have access to the fund until the child reaches 18; there will then be no restrictions as to use. Financial education will be provided to both parents and children.

The idea has also attracted attention in the United States and elsewhere. Robert Haveman has advocated a universal demogrant to young individuals to be used for human capital investments of their choice. The grant could be used to purchase education or medical services and, provided that it was not exhausted by retirement, could then be used to supplement other income sources. Roberto Unger and Cornel West have advocated a 'social endowment account' on which every individual should be able to draw at major moments

---

[2]  These included an article by the ex-US Secretary of Labor Robert Reich (14 June), an editorial endorsing the idea (13 September), and articles by me and David Nissan (26 July, 4 October).

in their lives, such as going to college, making a down payment on a house, or starting a small business.[3] The government of Singapore has announced a 'baby bonus' scheme, where second and third children are entitled to a capital grant at birth with regular supplements in later years.

Bruce Ackerman and Anne Alstott (1999) have recently put forward a more ambitious proposal. They recommend what they call a 'stakeholder grant' of $US80,000 to everyone at the age of 21 with a high-school diploma and no criminal record. Dropouts would still receive an annual return on their stake of $4,000 or so (at current rates); but they would not be able to use the principal except for a limited set of purposes (such as extraordinary medical expenses). Those convicted of an offence might be able eventually to claim their stake but only after a long period of rehabilitation. For everyone else the grant would be unrestricted in use; but it would be paid in tranches of $20,000 over a four-year period from the age of 21. The scheme would be financed by a 2 per cent tax on wealth paid into a 'stakeholder fund'. The grant plus interest would be paid back on death out of an individual's estate, if it was large enough; these payments would also go into the stakeholder fund.

Finally, it is worth noting other ideas that have underlying similarities. Samuel Brittan (1998: 29) proposed that shares in privatised industries should be allocated equally among the citizenry. John Roemer (1988) has suggested a demogrant, but one where recipients have access only to the income from that grant. John Hills (2000; see also Hill *et al.* 2002) has proposed that tenants of social housing should build up a capital stake in their homes through an equity share that reflects the value of their current expectation of paying rents that are below market value.

The demogrant idea is also related to that of a basic income, as championed in recent years by Philippe Van Parijs and others, whereby each individual receives an unconditional cash income every year (Van Parijs 1992; 1995; see also Fitzpatrick 1999). In their most unrestricted forms, the two ideas of a basic demogrant and a basic income are very similar, for, if capital markets were perfect, one could be readily converted into the other. Thus a demogrant can be used to purchase an annuity, thus generating an income for life; and a basic income could be mortgaged or borrowed against, thus creating a capital sum available for immediate use.

So the idea of a universal demogrant has several parents (and indeed many siblings). But is it a good idea? Answering this question will preoccupy the rest of this chapter. A major part of the case for the universal grant rests on the more general case for asset-based egalitarianism, so that is where the discussion begins; it then moves on to specific issues raised by the proposal itself.

---

[3] Haveman (1988), Unger and West (1998). I am grateful to Stuart White for drawing my attention to these; see White (forthcoming).

## ASSET-BASED EGALITARIANISM

The ownership of assets is currently very unequal in Britain, as indeed it is in most Western countries. The top half of asset-owners in the country own over nine-tenths of marketable wealth; the top 10 per cent own over half. And this inequality is growing. The Inland Revenue estimates that the share of marketable wealth of the top 10 per cent rose from 49 per cent to 54 per cent between 1982 and 1999, while the share of the top 50 per cent rose from 91 per cent to 94 per cent.[4] Alongside this the proportion of households with no wealth at all is also increasing; a recent study by the Institute of Fiscal Studies estimates that twenty years ago only 5 per cent of households had no assets, whereas a decade later 10 per cent had none (Banks and Tanner 1999). An already heavily unequal distribution has become even more so.

Moreover, the trend is set to continue. An increasing proportion of already relatively wealthy owner-occupiers are now inheriting the houses of their parents. Equity-sharing schemes and share options, encouraged by government policy, are likely to boost personal wealth further. But inevitably many will miss out. These will include not just the low-paid and the unemployed but also workers in the public and voluntary sectors, where there are no profits to share or equity to hold.

The sheer scale of this inequality, and the trend towards its getting even greater, are facts that almost on their own provide a prima facie case for some degree of asset redistribution. However, the case is not (completely) clear-cut. Some of the observed inequality is age-related. Over a working lifetime assets are built up through saving and other forms of investment, and then, at least partially, consumed in retirement. And some of the observed inequalities result from different patterns of work and effort, and hence might be thought to be justified on those grounds. Asset redistribution needs a more sophisticated rationale than can be provided by a simple knee-jerk reaction to the stark figures of wealth inequality.

In fact, asset-based egalitarianism and the measures associated with it can be justified on grounds that emanate from all parts of the political spectrum.[5] From the right, it forms part of the conventional arguments for a property-owning democracy or popular capitalism. Asset-ownership gives people a stake in a society. Spreading asset-ownership, especially to those who have few or no assets, makes society more stable and less prone to revolutionary upset. On the left, asset-based egalitarianism can be seen as a move towards reducing inequality, in the sense both of equality of opportunity and of equality of outcome. In particular, the current process of transmitting assets from one generation to another through family gifts or inheritances is both unequal and unfair, with some individuals, through no efforts of their own, starting life

---

[4] www.inlandrevenue.gov.uk/stats/personal_wealth/dopw_t05_1.htm
[5] See Sherraden (1991), Ackerman and Alstott (1999), and White (2001).

with far greater advantages than others. Hence any move towards enabling children from asset-poor families to acquire assets themselves will contribute to greater equality of opportunity. Moreover, so the argument runs, most asset-based welfare policies are likely to result in a reduction in the overall inequality in wealth-holdings, and thereby contribute to greater equality of outcome as well as of opportunity.[6]

More neutrally from a political point of view, several studies, both in the US and the UK, have shown asset-ownership to be associated with favourable outcomes in terms of individual and family welfare. Thus individuals and families who own assets tend to have better health, lower mortality, higher marital stability, less domestic violence, more self-employment, better educational outcomes for children, and higher savings when those children become adults.[7] Hence spreading asset-ownership more widely is likely to result in improvements in all these areas.

But the most fundamental justification for asset-based egalitarianism from the point of view of this book is that the ownership of assets contributes to greater capacity for agency. Indeed, although hard evidence on this is difficult to come by, it seems quite plausible to suppose that it is the psychological impact of these feelings of agency and independence that leads to the favourable outcomes reported in the previous paragraph. More specifically, asset-ownership gives individuals a greater degree of economic independence; it enables them better to weather the vicissitudes of life, and puts them less at the mercy of others' decisions. The tenant of a property can be evicted at the whim of the landlord unless he or she is legally protected. But the home-owner cannot be evicted by anyone (so long as any mortgage is paid). Individuals with significant savings, if made unemployed, do not have to rely on the state or on charity to find the wherewithal to feed themselves and their families. Elderly people with assets do not have to depend for their well-being entirely on a Chancellor of the Exchequer's decisions concerning pension uplifts or on a local authority's willingness to pay for domiciliary or residential care.

Of course, asset ownership does not confer complete independence. The usefulness of any asset will depend in large part on its market value and, except in rare cases, that will not be under the control of the owner. Shareholdings in a firm that goes into liquidation, a private pension from a financially precarious institution, dropping house prices, savings accounts with

---

[6] Samuel Bowles and Herbert Gintis (1998) have argued that asset-based redistribution is not only socially just but also productivity-enhancing. However, this claim seems to be based, not on a general proposition that this must be true in all circumstances, but on the potential for productivity enhancement of certain specific policy proposals (workers' cooperatives, education vouchers, home-ownership, and the assignment of limited property rights to children over the income streams of their parents). For an exposition and critique of their arguments, see the contributors to Wright (1998).

[7] For a summary of the US literature, see Kelly and Lissauer (2000: 9). The UK evidence is discussed in the next section of this chapter.

falling interest rates: all of these will reduce the owner's economic resources, and the immediate cause of the reduction in value—say, a downturn in the economy or a crooked director of a corporation—may be something about which he or she can do little. However, even in such situations asset-owners have some autonomy. In particular, they can affect the incomes they receive and the risks they take by managing their portfolio of assets appropriately. There may be cases where people's savings are completely locked into an asset that they cannot sell, but such situations are rare and usually temporary; more-over, they often follow asset-price bubbles where the owners concerned had previously made substantial windfall gains. Autonomy goes with responsibil-ity; and, although asset-owning individuals cannot be held responsible for the price changes in any specific asset, they do have a measure of responsibility for the pattern of assets in which they invest.

This could be challenged on the grounds that proper asset management requires skills and knowledge that the average middle-class individual does not possess, let alone the poor or very poor. However, even if this is true, it is in part a result of the current situation where asset-ownership is relatively con-centrated. There is no incentive to acquire knowledge or skills if there is no cause for using them. Indeed, this argument can be turned on its head: a major justification for asset-based measures is that they will encourage the spread of the skills and understanding of asset-management.

A more substantial argument against asset-based egalitarian policies is that their implementation may reduce popular and political support for other wel-fare measures. So, for instance, it might be thought that, if individuals receive help in acquiring assets, they do not need other forms of help, such as cash benefits or assistance with education and training. Further, acceptance of asset-based measures might induce a certain harshness towards those who fail to take advantage of them or who 'blow' any advantage they get, so that their eligibility for further help is reduced.

It should be noted that the first part of this criticism is one that could be levied against almost any proposal for improving a specific item of welfare provision. Any improvements in one area may weaken other areas, partly because they will consume resources that may have gone to those areas and partly because they may weaken support for them in the manner suggested. But such arguments cannot be used on their own as trump cards against the proposal under consideration. For their force depends on two conditions being fulfilled: whether the phenomenon of reduced support elsewhere is really likely to occur to a significant degree, and whether, even if it does, any consequences for the programme or programmes concerned will result in wel-fare losses that outweigh the gains from the asset-based programme.

With respect to the first of these conditions, as we shall see when we come to discuss them below, several of the asset-based proposals concerned are so small that it seems unlikely that they would pose a threat, in either resource or support terms, to other major welfare programmes; while the larger ones are usually accompanied by proposals for financing mechanisms that do not directly threaten those other programmes. Fulfilment of the second condition will depend on which programme is under threat and cannot be decided a priori. But it should be noted that there is a respectable case for saying that the two broad programmes mentioned—cash benefits and education and training programmes—may be, at current levels of spending, both close to the limits of their effectiveness even with respect to their own aims; that neither of them addresses the issue of wealth inequality; and hence that diverting extra resources from them into asset-based programmes could well yield higher returns in terms of overall welfare gains.

With respect to the harshness point, again it is useful to distinguish between large- and small-scale programmes. Small-scale ones seem unlikely to induce the kind of backlash predicted. Large-scale ones could do so, although not necessarily. But even if they did, this might not be so undesirable. It is not clear that those who, out of their own free choice, waste one form of generous state aid should be automatically entitled to another form. Of course, if 'blowing their grant' is not a result of their free choice but of factors beyond their control, then that is another matter. In those cases they should be entitled to as much additional aid as anyone else. However, with genuine empowerment comes responsibility; and if individuals do waste an opportunity then they may have to accept the consequences.

## DEMOGRANTS: SOME SPECIFICS

I now turn to a number of specific issues relating to the demogrant proposal, both theoretical and practical, that need examination. They concern: whether there should be a particular focus in turning pawns into queens on empowering the young; whether conditions should be imposed on the way the grant is spent; whether it should be offered on a universal or means-tested basis; how it should be financed; its timing (at birth or at the age of majority); and whether giving the grant might have adverse consequences for incentives to work and to save.

### Pawns and Queens

As noted above, the principal argument in favour of asset-based egalitarianism from the point of view of this book is that the policies concerned help turn pawns into queens: that is, they help empower individuals. This is particularly important in the early years of adult life. For it is then that lack of capital is a major factor inhibiting an individual's ability to take control of his or her own life. Starting a business, paying for higher education, putting a down payment on a house: all are ways of enhancing individual autonomy. But all require capital, a requirement that many cannot fulfil. A demogrant would help individuals to get their feet on the rungs of the mobility ladder: to help them help themselves.

Few young adults have pension schemes or equity in owner-occupied housing. What counts for them is financial assets, which can readily be used for any number of worthwhile purposes. Huge numbers have no access to such capital. James Banks and Sarah Tanner estimate that in 1997–8 in Britain, of the 22–29 age group, 45 per cent did not have a deposit account, and the median wealth of those that did was just £750. Fifteen per cent had National Savings, holders of these having median wealth of £1,050. Holdings of other financial assets such as shares and unit trusts were practically negligible. Moreover, the few owners of these more sophisticated savings did not have very much; their average wealth was between £3,500 and £5,000.

The impact of asset poverty among the young on their subsequent life chances has been graphically demonstrated by John Bynner of the Centre for Longitudinal Studies in London, using the National Child Development Study. This has data for a cohort of individuals on their savings and investments at the age of 23 and various social and economic outcomes for those same individuals at the age of 33. Bynner and Despotidou (2001) demonstrated that there were strong positive links between holding assets and time spent in full time employment between ages 22 and 33 for both men and women, between asset holding at 23 and earnings at age 33 for men, and between asset holding at 23 and general good health ten years later for both men and women. These relationships remained even when other possible causal factors were controlled for, including income, class, and indicators of personality type.[8]

So increasing the asset holdings of the young is likely both to empower them, not only directly by increasing their command over resources but also indirectly, through its beneficial effects on other factors that are themselves empowering, such as earnings and health. But how much empowerment is desirable? Is it always desirable to convert young pawns into young queens? More specifically, should a demogrant be given to the young with restrictions on how it should be used or should it be unconditional?

### Conditionality

The intention of a demogrant scheme is to encourage investment and hence the accumulation of assets (financial, physical, or human). Hence it would be desirable for the grants to be spent on investment opportunities. But, unless their use is restricted in some way, they may be used for current consumption instead. Indeed, some almost certainly will be; it is unlikely that each and every 18-year-old will be able to resist the temptation to spend some or all of an unrestricted grant on something offering immediate gratification. But is anxiety about this sufficient to justify the imposition of conditions on use, and, if so, what form should they take?

---

[8] See also Bynner and Paxton (2001) and, for a critique, Emmerson and Wakefield (2001).

The size of the grant may in itself be of importance here. While it may be tempting to launch such a scheme with a small grant to introduce the idea, as the British government is doing, there is a danger then that it is seen to be insignificant by the recipient, who might then feel quite justified in blowing it for a bit of fun. The sum needs to be seen as significant, providing a one-off opportunity that justifies careful consideration. Instinct says that a grant of a thousand pounds or so may fall between stools, being insufficient for most worthwhile investments. Hence my and Nissan's suggestion of a £10,000 grant.

Now it would be possible to make a respectable case for this level of grant to be given unconditionally on the grounds that ultimately adults do have to take responsibility for their own lives, and that young adults have to learn to do so. As it is, there would be plenty of social pressure on 18-year-olds not to blow their grants; to add to that pressure by confining the grants to only certain kinds of spending might be seen as unacceptable state paternalism.

Indeed, this is the argument put forward by Ackerman and Alstott, who do not put any restrictions on how their grant is to be used. Their argument is essentially a libertarian one; imposing conditions on use 'smacks of welfare state mentality inconsistent with the liberal spirit of stakeholding' (Ackerman and Alstott, forthcoming). However, they do make their position somewhat easier for others to swallow by setting the age of receipt for their stakeholding grant at 21 and restricting the recipients to those with a high school diploma and without a criminal record.

Interestingly, the possibility of the latter kinds of restrictions has not been raised in the British case. Nor should they be; for they would have the consequence of excluding precisely those who would most benefit from the scheme. However, the idea of delaying the age of receipt from 18 to 21 (or even later) is perhaps worth considering. It would create difficulties in paying for activities that usually begin at 18, such as higher education; but this could be overcome by allowing people to borrow against future receipt of the grant. A more fundamental objection is that it is not obvious why the receipt of a grant should be delayed beyond 18, when the age at which young people are allowed to engage in other responsible acts such as voting is not.

Although I find the arguments on both sides quite persuasive, on balance I favour the imposition of restrictions on the use of the grant. This is largely for political reasons: there would be no surer way to lose popular and political support for a system of demogrants than a few well-publicised cases of young people blowing their grants on cocaine or wild holidays. It is also possible that restrictions might also be preferred by the young people themselves; like everyone else they may perceive themselves as occasionally subject to weakness of will, and hence prefer to have the temptation of immediate gratification removed.[9]

---

[9] For discussions of the behavioural phenomenon of weakness of will and some of its implications for policy, see above Chapter Five and Elster (1989).

Currently the British government is proposing no restrictions on the use of its child trust fund at age 18. In that case, it is largely for practical reasons: the impossibility of policing the restrictions, an argument also used by Ackerman and Alstott. So it is important for those who advocate restricting use to spell out how the restriction process might work. As noted above, Nissan and I have suggested that the grants could be paid into a special ACE account held in the individual recipient's name either in a local commercial bank or in a local branch of a network of publicly owned savings institutions set up by the government specifically for this purpose and managed by a set of trustees.

Having quality ACE trustees would clearly be important to this aspect of the scheme. For they would have not only to vet the spending plans but also to ensure that the money was spent in the way proposed. They could be specially employed by the local institution to vet the spending plans of all the grants being given out by that branch; alternatively they could be drawn from panels of local business people and other community leaders on a voluntary basis.

What sort of investment purposes should they approve? One obvious possibility is higher and further education: a way of accumulating human capital and hence increasing an individual's value to the labour market. The grant could be used to contribute to the fees and maintenance costs for a university education or to the costs of more vocational forms of training. To ensure compliance, it could be paid through the educational institution concerned, in much the same way as the present student grant and loan scheme.

Another use for the grant might be for the down payment on a house or flat purchase. Unpublished research by Gavin Smart suggests that for many poor people the down payment is the biggest obstacle to home-ownership; once the down payment is made, people have a commitment to their homes and usually manage to keep up the mortgage payments regardless of any income or employment problems they encounter. Again, to ensure compliance the payment could be made directly to the vendor.

The grant could also form part of the start-up costs of a small business. The development of a business plan and its approval by the trustees would be essential—which makes it the more desirable to include local business people among the trustees.

What should happen if no worthwhile uses are proposed for an individual's ACE account? One option would be for the grant to be put towards a personal or stakeholder pension. The pension schemes could be drawn from an approved list, and payment made directly from the ACE account to the scheme.

Such arrangements could not prevent all abuse, and it would be pointless to pretend otherwise. Assets bought through trustee-approved distributions must at some future date be saleable, and use of the proceeds could not easily be monitored. It is not unheard of for the offspring of the wealthy to fritter away their fortunes; and it will always be in the nature of some of the recipients of our demogrant to do so. What counts is for everyone to get his or her opportunity. Thereafter, as in many other aspects of life, it should be up to them.

One way of minimising the role of the ACE trustee would be to ensure that each individual on receipt of his or her demogrant received training in asset management, as advocated by Stuart White (forthcoming). White draws attention to the success of financial education classes attached to the Individual Development Account schemes developed in the United States (discussed in Chapter Ten), and suggests that attending something similar could be a condition attached to receipt of the grant.

Indeed, this idea could be taken further. The grant could be combined with the allocation of voting rights and viewed as part of a larger coming-of-age event. Attendance at other classes could also be made a condition for grant receipt, including classes in citizenship and political awareness. A demogrant and the right to vote then become tangible expressions of young adults acquiring a stake in society while at the same time getting the training to exercise that stake effectively.

### Universal or Means-tested?

The children of the wealthy can look forward to help with assets throughout their adult lives, in the form of payment of university fees, housing deposits, and start-up capital for business ventures. But others, especially those brought up in poverty, are significantly disadvantaged by their lack of access to capital. Not only do their parents not have the wherewithal to supply them with that capital, they also find it difficult to borrow from other sources. Banks and other financial institutions are reluctant to lend to poor families, and indeed even to the non-poor if they live in poor areas.

These reasons would be enough to justify a demogrant to the children of the poor. However, there is also a case for a broader, universal grant: one going to the children of the poor and non-poor alike. This is partly because of the general case for universal benefits over ones targeted on the poor. Universal benefits contribute to the sense of national community, whereas targeted ones can be socially divisive. Also, targeted benefits require a cumbersome apparatus for determining eligibility: one that is expensive to administer and can be demeaning to the recipient. In contrast, universal benefits require only the information necessary to determine that the individuals concerned fall into the relevant category: in our case, simply their age.

In fact, targeting a demogrant would pose greater problems than are encountered with the array of means-tested benefits currently available. As its purpose is to distribute capital, the wealth of potential recipients would be the appropriate criterion. But if the grant were to be distributed to young adults, it is likely that almost all would have no capital, unless they had benefited from parental or grandparental gifts, or an inheritance. A means test based on wealth would be far more likely to lead to the gifts being deferred until after any deadline for assessment than to the exclusion of a sizeable number of beneficiaries. Other assessments could be made on, say, parental wealth or even grandparental wealth. But then there would be difficult and expensive problems of assessment, and, in denying someone a grant, an implication that their parents should make capital available.

But there is an additional, more fundamental reason for a universal grant at birth or at the age of majority. Everyone born into a developed country benefits from a share in a common inheritance: a set of capital assets, including buildings and other physical infrastructure, transport links, capital equipment, and agricultural land. The vast majority of these are the results of the labours and efforts of previous generations, whose members have struggled together to produce what is in effect a gift of wealth to the next. It is largely because of this inheritance that the current inhabitants of any developed country are as wealthy as they are; without that enormous accumulation of capital over the centuries, no amount of efforts by the current generation could generate the levels of current production that maintain our standards of living.

This idea, that the wealth of one generation is a common asset to the next, is important, for it cuts across the argument that individuals who have created wealth should be free to give it all to their children. Ownership gives personal command of resources, but it is not easy to justify this persisting beyond the grave, especially when, as we have seen, the life chances for many are reduced by lack of access to start-up capital. How can one argue that people have as great a right to inherited wealth as to, for instance, the income or profits that result from their own efforts? It would seem fairer if the right to our national patrimony were more equally distributed—as would happen if the proposal for a universal demogrant were implemented.

A standard argument used against any universal benefit concerns the rich: should the benefit be paid to the better-off, who are unlikely really to need it, as well as to the really needy? The answer is, in general, 'yes': for this is a price that has to be paid if the other advantages of universality are to be obtained and the problems of means-tested targeting avoided. Moreover, if, as I go on to discuss, the grant is financed through inheritance tax, so parents pay the tax, a significant portion of their wealth will now be going to pay for the start-up costs for thousands of other children as well as their own.

It is also worth noting that the children of the better-off already receive a form of grant through subsidies to higher education. Although with the introduction of tuition fees and student loans these subsidies are being reduced, they remain considerable. Most students come from middle-class backgrounds. Hence our proposal can be viewed as simply a means of extending an already existing subsidy to the better-off to those less fortunate. It also has the implication that higher education subsidies can be further reduced without making anyone worse-off, since one potential use for the grant could be to pay for tuition and living expenses while acquiring further education.

## Timing

Should the grant be given at birth in the form of a 'baby bond', as the British government and the IPPR have proposed, or at the age of majority, as Paine, Ackerman and Alstott, and I have argued? There are arguments on both sides. In favour of a grant at birth, less can be given up front since the money is to be invested for eighteen years. This would make the grant allocation easier politically because it apparently saves the government money (in reality, of course, there is no saving, since the government is simply losing the income that it could have earned by investing the grant itself). Another advantage is that the fund can be seen to accumulate by both parent and child, thus serving a useful financial educational purpose. On the negative side, this very visibility may make the fund unpopular with parents, especially poor ones, who will see money accumulating that they might feel they could have put to good use but which they are unable to touch. Also, depending on how each of the funds is invested, children may end up with different amounts on reaching the age of majority—an outcome that could be regarded as unfair.

This last point raises questions as to the appropriate investment strategy for a 'baby bond' and the related issue of who would manage the investment. Should the funds be invested in savings accounts, equities, or government bonds? Should government or private sector financial institutions manage the fund? What should be the role of the parents in managing the investment—or indeed of the children themselves?

As yet these questions have not all been settled in the British case. The government would prefer the private sector to manage the funds; the private sector, on the other hand, although interested for long-term reasons, is worried about the small size of the amounts involved and the difficulty of covering their fixed costs. This may be resolved by confining fund management to a few finance institutions from whose offerings parents would choose.

## Finance

Where would the money to finance the demogrant come from? The British government does not specify this in its proposals. Ackerman and Alstott (1999) finance their much more generous scheme from an annual wealth tax. Kelly and Lissauer (2000) finance their baby bond through reducing tax reliefs for pensions.

I have argued that the best way to finance this potentially popular spending proposal is by linking it to reforms to a hitherto unpopular and inefficient tax—inheritance tax (Le Grand 1989; Nissan and Le Grand 2000). Hypothecating, or earmarking, inheritance tax revenues to demogrants could provide the means for rehabilitating a much despised tax. As I shall argue in Chapter Ten, hypothecation in and of itself is often desirable, especially when viewed from the perspective of turning pawns into queens. Hypothecating the inheritance tax for demogrants in particular has an obvious popular appeal. For it takes the wealth of one generation and, in the spirit of Francis Bacon's quotation that opens this chapter, spreads it around like manure to fertilise the growth of the next.

Inheritance tax is a misnomer in the United Kingdom. What that country has is a tax on estates that bears no relation to the amount any individual inherits, either from the estate in question or over a lifetime. And the tax is largely voluntary. The Inland Revenue estimates that in 1999 total marketable personal wealth stood at £2,594 billion.[10] This measure excludes wealth that cannot be realised, such as accrued pension rights. In contrast, the yield from inheritance tax is pitiful, just £2 billion in 1999–2000.[11] Wealth passes almost untaxed between generations through lifetime gifts, through exempt items such as agricultural land and forestry, and through devices such as discretionary trusts which can defer tax liabilities for decades.

It is against this scale of wealth transfer that suggestions such as demogrants should be measured. In any one year, there are currently approximately 650,000 18-year-olds in Britain, so it would cost £6.5 billion to give them each £10,000. The inheritance tax yield in 1999–2000 of £2 billion would only pay for about £3,000 per 18-year-old, but, although this might be better than nothing, I have argued above that a demogrant may need to be bigger if it is to be used wisely.

Yields, and hence the grant, could be increased in subsequent years by reforms that have long been on economists' agendas but that have lacked popular support. These include shifting the basis for the tax from the donor to the recipient, and extending it to include lifetime inheritances and gifts. This would encourage the wealthy to pass on their wealth to those who have not already been substantial beneficiaries, as by so doing they could reduce the taxman's take. The system would require that everybody had a lifetime gift and inheritance allowance, say of £50,000, which could be received free of tax. Thereafter tax could be levied at progressive rates to maintain incentives for wealth to be spread around. A review of exempt items and trust law should also be undertaken to broaden the base of the tax.

In theory, receipts could collapse with such a tax if bequests were directed only to those who had not used up their inheritance tax allowance. However, if that occurred a fairer distribution of inherited wealth would have been achieved, and there would be less need of an additional system of grants. More likely, however, is that wider bequests would happen mainly at the margins, as people would continue to want to help their own children first. As they did so they would be taxed to pay for grants for those less fortunate.

It would not be necessary to impose penal rates of inheritance tax to finance a substantial reallocation of capital. Indeed, an ideal system would have rates that most regarded as reasonable, to minimise incentives for avoidance or evasion. What might such rates be? The inadequacies of the existing inheritance tax

---

[10]  www.inlandrevenue.gov.uk/stats/personal_wealth/dopw_t04_1.htm
[11]  www.inlandrevenue.gov.uk/stats/tax_receipts/g_t02_1.htm

mean we have very limited information indeed about the extent of wealth bequeathed or given on a year-by-year basis. But, following the methodology used by Nissan and myself in the Fabian publication, we can produce a crude estimate. Suppose we assume that all wealth is held by people over the age of 25 and that wealth is evenly spaced between the cohorts from 25 to 75.[12] In that case one fiftieth of personal wealth would be passed on in one form or another every year: £52 billion in 1999. Then a reformed inheritance tax would need to be levied at an average rate of around 12.5 per cent to finance £10,000 per young adult. If higher education subsidies were reduced *pari passu* (as they should be if equity is to be maintained), the savings from this could also be used to finance the grant and the inheritance tax rate could be lowered yet further. Since the participation rate of the relevant age group in higher education is now running at around one-third, this means that the inheritance tax rate could be lowered to 8 per cent. Alternatively, the rate could be kept at 12.5 per cent and the savings in higher education spending could be used elsewhere within the education budget or for other public services. In short, there is every opportunity here to levy a modest tax on gifts and bequests, and still make sure every young person has the capital needed to get off to a good start.

The insignificant contribution of inheritance tax to financing public spending, and the sense of the state as inherently wasteful, have meant that avoiding such tax has never attracted much moral opprobrium. The ease of avoidance of inheritance tax reflects the lack of public support for it. But if the proceeds of the tax were visibly distributed through demogrants, perhaps that perception could change.

### Contributions

One possible objection to the scheme is that receipt of the demogrant does not depend on any actions on the part of the recipient. It might be thought better to have a scheme that requires some form of matching contribution to the ACE account from the individuals themselves or from their families. So, for instance, the government could offer to match personal or family contributions at a rate of, say, a £1 grant for a £1 contribution, or at a higher (or lower) rate.

I discuss matching grants as a means of encouraging savings in Chapter Ten and so will not dwell on them here. But it is worth noting that they have the advantage of encouraging people to help themselves. They also mobilise private resources and thus can reduce the cost to the state of any given level of grant.

However, matching grants favour those who can contribute more and who are likely to be (although not necessarily) among the better-off. To overcome this, the matching rate could be varied with the income of the family (as in

---

[12] This assumption is of course unrealistic. Most studies of wealth distribution suggest that wealth is accumulated through a lifetime, so on average the elderly hold a higher proportion of the nation's wealth. Hence the qualification of the estimate in the text as 'crude'.

some US schemes): higher for poor and lower for better-off families, and perhaps even dropping to zero for the very well-off. Varying the matching rate in this way might make the scheme more politically acceptable but would have the disadvantage of requiring a means test. It might be better to have the same matching rate for all, but to cap the total amount of grant received by any one individual and to count it for lifetime inheritance and gift purposes. The well-off would repay their grants as further bequests came their way and were taxed at progressive rates.

### Disincentives

We have seen that the scheme could offer a number of positive incentives, especially towards greater capital accumulation by the poor. But are there also major disincentives associated with the scheme that would discourage otherwise socially or economically desirable behaviour? For instance, might not the tightened-up inheritance tax discourage parents from saving for their children, or even from working quite so hard to benefit their families? Might not the existence of the grant itself lead parents to cut back on what they were planning to give to their children? And might not the recipients of the grant be discouraged from saving for themselves?

These seem unlikely dangers. For effective inheritance taxes to weaken the economy in this way, taking care of the next generation would have to be the main motive for individual achievement. The tendency of the ambitious to delay having children and forge their careers first would seem to suggest that other factors matter more. Also, the amounts involved are not that great, especially when compared with the massive inheritances received by a few lucky children under the current situation, which almost certainly do have a discouraging effect on their subsequent work and savings activities.

## CONCLUSION

As we have seen, there are many possible ways in which a demogrant scheme could be set up. The amount, the age at which it should be received, the restrictions imposed on its use, if any, the contribution regime, the method of finance: all of these can vary and indeed do among the alternative schemes proposed. But all of these schemes do share a common core that it is worth re-emphasising. All are aimed at increasing the ability of a young person entering adult life to control his or her own destiny. Children in many ways are the ultimate pawns in our society; and one of the tragedies of that society is that too many of them stay as pawns on becoming adults. Demogrants at the age of majority are one way of encouraging everyone to develop from a passive to an active citizen.

# 10

## Partnership Savings

To be a prodigal's favourite—then worse truth
A miser's pensioner—behold our lot!
O man, that from thy fair and shining youth
Age might but take the things that youth needed not!
(William Wordsworth, *The Small Celandine*)

In Chapter Nine I presented an asset-based welfare scheme aimed at helping people to acquire assets at the start of their adult lives. This chapter examines schemes that help individuals accumulate assets throughout their working lives: schemes that help them to save. I concentrate on proposals for helping them save for their old age: for their pension and for their long-term social care, should they need it.

Again the focus will be on measures aimed at turning pawns into queens: that is, on schemes that increase the power of individuals and the sense of control they have over their own lives.

### COMPULSION VERSUS PARTNERSHIP

Traditionally, most developed countries have endeavoured to increase people's savings, especially for pensions, through some form of compulsion. This usually takes the form of compelling individuals to contribute to a pension fund administered either by governmental or by private organisations. So, for instance, in Britain the government compels all employees (and their employers) to save towards a pension by putting aside a proportion of their earnings for this purpose, either through occupational or private pension schemes or through the state earnings-related pension scheme.

The British government also taxes individuals through the national insurance system and uses the revenue to provide a basic flat-rate pension. However, this is not a savings scheme since, contrary to many people's perceptions, there is no savings fund into which payments are made and out of which, once savings have accumulated, pensions are paid; instead, current contributions are used to pay for current pensions. In fact the state basic pension is really an income-support device for alleviating the poverty that would otherwise ensue because people had not saved enough for their pensions. But its existence reinforces the case for other government interventions to encourage savings: for the presence of a state safety net to help people who reach retirement age with little or no pension of their own can have disincentive effect on pension savings (the so-called 'moral hazard' effect).

Now compulsion as a means of raising savings has a number of problems. First, there are transition difficulties. Almost by definition, compulsion really works only for people entering the labour market now; it would not be until people entering the labour market today had retired that the transition to a compulsory system could be said to be complete. Second, compulsory contribution systems do not fit well with changes in needs over the life cycle. So, for instance, compulsion makes no allowance for the costs of child rearing, and, given the introduction of student loans and the culture of owner-occupation, would tend to exacerbate the 'front-loading' of life-cycle burdens. Some have gone further, arguing that, if people cannot borrow against their savings due to capital market failures, compulsion will tend to reduce individuals' ability to invest in education as financial resources will increasingly be directed towards retirement.

More fundamentally, the fact that contributions are compulsory means that they infringe individual liberty. As an instrument for reducing individual power, it moves away from the goal of turning pawns into queens. The only kind of independent action that it encourages is the exploitation of techniques for avoidance and, ultimately, evasion—with heavy social costs in terms of legitimacy, policing, and reduced revenue. It helps turn the welfare state from what should be a noble enterprise helping people to help themselves into a repressive apparatus compelling people to do things that they otherwise would choose not to do.

An alternative to state compulsion is what might be termed state partnership. Here the state provides a positive incentive for people to save based on financial assistance rather than a negative incentive based on penalties for failure to comply with state-set requirements. Partnership thus does not suffer from the incentives to avoid and evade associated with compulsion. More generally, the state takes on the role of partner rather than that of policeman.

As with demogrants, academics and policy-makers in both Britain and the United States are already exploring a number of ideas of this kind. Michael Sherraden (1991: ch. 10) of Washington University in St Louis has proposed setting up what he calls Individual Development Accounts. These would be optional, earnings-bearing, tax-benefited accounts in the name of each individual initiated as early as birth and restricted to specific purposes. The grant would come from the federal government, matching or otherwise subsidising deposits made by the account holders themselves or, in the case of young children, by their families. The subsidy would be confined to the poor. It would be paid for by closing various tax loopholes, especially those in the welfare area directed at the non-poor, such as the tax reliefs associated with medical insurance premiums, mortgage interest, and social security benefits. IDA programmes of various kinds are in fact now being implemented on an experimental basis in several US States and have been rather successful (see Boshara 2001 and Beeferman 2001).

Moreover, the British government has begun to take tentative steps in this direction. It has proposed what is termed a 'Savings Gateway'. This is a single interest-earning account to be targeted at low-income individuals. The government will match any deposits made by the account holder at a rate to be decided up to a maximum. The consultation document discussing the idea suggests a 1:1 matching rate up to a £50 maximum per month. The account would be time-limited; the consultation document suggests three years (UK Treasury 2001*a*).

Elsewhere, I have developed more ambitious matching grant schemes for pensions (with Philip Agulnik) and for long-term care (Agulnik and Le Grand 1998*a*, *b*; Le Grand 1999*a*). These I now examine in more detail.

## PARTNERSHIP PENSIONS

The British government does already provide a kind of partnership scheme through an elaborate structure of tax reliefs for pensions and indeed for other forms of savings. Tax reliefs can be applied at various stages in the savings process: to contributions to the relevant savings fund; to income accruing from those funds (including income from interest payments, from dividend payments, and from capital gains); or to withdrawals from the funds. The current system of tax relief for pensions basically exempts the first of these (contributions); that for Individual Savings Accounts (ISAs) exempts the last two stages (accruals and withdrawals).

However, tax relief is a highly unsatisfactory way of getting the benefits of partnership. It is opaque; it appears in the form of tax not being paid, and the people who receive it may well be unaware that there has been a reduction in their tax bill because of it. Moreover, even those who are aware of the tax reduction usually do not see it as a form of state assistance; rather, they often view it as simply the government taxing 'their' money less and hence as involving a reduction in governmental malevolence rather than as an example of state beneficence. Also, tax reliefs are inflexible, with the amount of aid not determined by policy towards pensions but by parameters of the tax system, such as the structure of tax rates. Thus, if the Chancellor of the Exchequer decides that, because of, say, a surplus in the government's budgetary position, he or she will reduce income tax rates overall, then the amount of tax relief for pensions will fall; and this may reduce pension savings although that was not part of the Chancellor's intention.

Also, tax reliefs are less accountable than public expenditure programmes since, unlike those programmes, they are not subject to the annual Treasury spending round or any systematic analysis of value for money. And they undermine democratic oversight of the government's tax and spending priorities by departmental select committees and the like, leading to an excessive policy concern with the costs of direct public spending to the relative neglect of tax spending (Kvist and Sinfield 1996).

But perhaps the biggest problem with tax reliefs as an instrument of state assistance concerns their impact on the income distribution. They are open only to those who pay taxes; partly because of this, partly because of the existence of increasing marginal tax rates with income, and partly because the wealthy save more, they are highly regressive. For instance, it has been estimated that half the benefit of pension tax reliefs go to the richest 10 per cent of households and a quarter to the top 2.5 per cent (Agulnik and Le Grand 1998*a*).

A partnership scheme that would avoid most of these problems involves abolishing the tax relief system and using the revenue raised to finance a system of matching grants. That is, instead of giving tax relief on pension contributions, the government would match individuals' contributions with a direct grant. The matching rate could be pound for pound; alternatively, it could be lower, say, 66 pence or 50 pence of state assistance per pound contributed by the individual. To allay possible Treasury fears of an open-ended commitment, there could be a cap on the amount of contribution that could attract this assistance.

Partnership schemes involving matching grants have many advantages, especially when compared with the existing structure of tax reliefs. They are transparent; those who received them would know both that they were in receipt of state aid and how much aid they were receiving. As a form of direct public expenditure, they would be subject to Treasury and Parliamentary scrutiny. And they would be flexible, with all their parameters (such as the matching rate) under the direct control of the funding agency; hence the amount of aid could be tailored more exactly to the requirements of pensions policy.

Moreover, such schemes would be much more progressive than the present system of tax reliefs. Agulnik and I have made estimates of the distributional impact for two variants of the partnership scheme as applied to pensions. One, a less redistributive scheme, provided matching grants at the rate of 50 pence per pound contributed, and the other, more redistributive, used a 66 pence per pound matching rate.[1] Either version of the scheme would be much more

[1] The calculations are based on the assumption that abolition of the current tax relief system will result in a long-run increase in revenue of around £9 billion, a little over 1% of GDP. In fact, the amount of revenue yielded through abolishing the current tax relief system is a matter of considerable controversy. In essence it depends on what one considers to be the counterfactual: that is, the type of tax regime that would be in place if pension tax reliefs were abolished. In keeping with the Inland Revenue's own estimates of the cost of various tax reliefs, we assumed that this regime would be a 'comprehensive income tax', where all income, including investment income, is subject to tax. So abolition of this particular tax relief would not result in savings being diverted into other tax-exempt vehicles. The effect of alternative assumptions is discussed in Agulnik and Le Grand (1998*b*).

progressive than the existing system of tax relief. Under the 66 pence per pound scheme, the top 10 per cent of taxpayers would receive 18.5 per cent of the benefit (a quarter under the 50 pence scheme), as compared with half the benefit under the current scheme. The top 2.5 per cent would receive just 3.5 per cent of the benefit (5 per cent under the 50 pence scheme) instead of a quarter as they do now (Agulnik and Le Grand 1998*a*).

There are other possible variants of matching grant schemes. The matching grant could be confined to poor households, as with the British government's Savings Gateway proposal. More generally, the matching rate could vary with the income of the household, gradually tapering off to zero as that income increased. Such variants would be cheaper than a universal scheme (or, if the total cost were kept the same, would allow for greater help to the poor; but they would necessitate a household means test).

Alternatively, as has been suggested by Ros Altmann (2003), the matching rate could vary with the amount actually saved. Thus, the first tranche of savings would have a high matching rate associated with it, the second tranche a lower rate, the third a yet lower one, and so on, until the matching rate dropped to zero and any extra savings received no help. By concentrating help at initial levels of savings, this would help overcome any kind of threshold effect whereby people are deterred from making the jump from being a non-saver to a saver. It would also again allow the overall budget to be spread further than under matching grant schemes involving a flat rate for all savings; and, again as compared with those schemes, it would reduce the help given to the better-off (who, other things being equal, would be saving more).

Overall, therefore, there is a variety of ways in which matching grant partnership schemes could be applied to pensions, each of which seems fundamentally superior to other means of encouraging pension savings such as compulsory savings or tax relief. But the idea can be applied outside the pensions field to other forms of savings, and indeed to other forms of social assistance such as paying for long-term care. To this I now turn.

## PARTNERSHIPS FOR LONG-TERM CARE

There is an approximately one-in-four chance that anyone currently under the age of 65 will need some form of long-term residential care after passing that age. Not surprisingly, since it covers board and lodging costs as well as the provision of social care, such care is very expensive. In Britain, state aid is available to meet those costs; however, it is means-tested, with both an income and a savings cut-off.

It is clear that, in order to provide an adequate level of long-term care, it will be necessary to continue relying on private resources, both in financial terms and in terms of time and effort provided by informal carers. The trick is in some way to mobilise those resources (or to continue to mobilise them) in a fashion that (1) generates enough combined resources (public and private) to provide at least a minimum level of care and preferably a higher level if appropriate, (2) allows for users and carers to make appropriate choices over the kind and level of care provided (that is, enables them to be queens), and (3) does not provide incentives for evasion and avoidance.

The problem with the present means-tested system of state assistance is that it meets none of these conditions. The level of provision of long-term care is universally regarded as inadequate, especially for the less well-off, and offers little by way of choice to those involved. At the same time the means test, which requires the running down of assets until their value falls below a certain level, seems to penalise those who have had the foresight to save for their old age or for their children's inheritance. It is viewed as punitive and exploitative and encourages evasion and avoidance.

A royal commission has recommended that Britain follow the lead of Germany and Japan and introduce a system of social insurance to finance long-term care (UK Royal Commission on Long-Term Care 1999). Employers and employees would both make contributions to a fund that would pay for care for those who need it. However, several analysts, including members of the royal commission itself in a note of dissent attached to the main report, have criticised the proposal on the grounds of cost. Moreover, as we shall see in Chapter Eleven, social insurance has problems of its own, notably the narrowness of its tax base and the problem of non-contributors.

An alternative scheme would involve a partnership funding arrangement of the kind discussed above with respect to pensions. This could take either of two forms. It could involve grants matching individual contributions to an insurance policy to cover long-term care. Alternatively, the scheme could involve matching contributions made out of an individual's own resources, including her savings, to costs at the time of needing care. Either would involve removing the disincentives to save implicit in the present means-tested system.

The idea of the state matching an individual's contributions to an insurance policy for covering long-term care is broadly similar to the idea of matching contributions to a pension fund discussed in the previous section. Hence I will not examine that further here but concentrate instead on the second idea: that of matching contributions made at the time of care. This would involve a minimum level of public funding coupled with a system of matching grants for expenditure over that minimum. Under this system each person assessed as being in need of care would be entitled to a minimum level of care met from public funds. This minimum, although adequate, would be basic. For the payment of care above the minimum, the state would undertake to match pound for pound (or at some lower rate) the resources that individuals or their relatives can mobilise for their own care.

To keep spending under control, there would be an overall limit on the total amount of grant that could be received by any individual. However, this would not be sufficient on its own to ensure the scheme remained within cash limits; it would also be necessary to have some mechanism for limiting the number of individuals who were eligible for the scheme. This could best be done through the assessment process by which individuals are judged in need of care, and needs are compared with available resources. Indeed, in the spirit of case management, the people who undertake the assessment process could hold the budget for the scheme. They would then have a strong incentive to ensure that eligibility decisions were compatible with available resources.

Take the following example as an illustration of how the scheme might work. An elderly person currently living at home is assessed by a social worker as in need of residential care. For everyone so assessed, the state will automatically pay a minimum of, say, £250 per week. There are a number of possible homes in which she could be accepted, each offering different standards at different charges, from one providing a basic level of care at the government rate of £250 per week to others offering higher quality but charging above that rate. If she (or her relatives) opt for the home with the lowest charge, the state minimum payment will meet the charge and she does not have to pay for anything out of her own resources. However, if she chooses a more expensive home, then the state will match any extra resources she puts in herself.

Now suppose she chooses a home somewhat superior in quality to the minimum but which charges £400 per week. Then the state will pay £250 (the minimum) per week plus half the difference between the minimum and the charge, that is, £75 per week; the total amount paid by the state would then be £325, with the elderly person contributing £75 out of her own resources.

In this case the state is matching contributions at a pound-for-pound rate. However, it could choose to do so at a lower rate: say, 50 pence or 25 pence per pound personally contributed. In the 50 pence per pound case the elderly person paying an overall charge of £400 would contribute £100 out of her own resources while the state would contribute £250 (the minimum) plus £50 as a matching contribution. In the 25 pence per pound case, she would contribute £120, while the state would contribute £250 plus £30 as a matching contribution.

A major advantage of schemes such as these is that participation in them is cooperative rather than, as with a means-tested scheme, adversarial. People have no incentive to hide their assets, to give them away, or to engage in other forms of evasion and avoidance. Rather, they have an incentive to produce their own resources, resources that can be used in partnership with the state to improve their long-term care situation. If, on the other hand, people preferred not to contribute everything to their own care but to set aside some of their resources for their children to inherit or whatever, then they are at perfect liberty to do so; the only penalty is not benefiting from the matching grant that they otherwise would have received.

A related advantage of such a scheme is that the means test would be completely abolished. The intrusive, demeaning, and costly administrative apparatus of means tests could be dispensed with entirely. More importantly, those who did have the foresight to save and were prepared to contribute, instead of simply losing their savings as under the means test, would be rewarded for doing so by getting better community care. The carrot would replace the stick: arguably both better social policy and better politics.

The scheme is also quite practical. It is hard to see many difficulties in either introducing the system or administering it. It does not require an elaborate apparatus for assessing people's means; for these are contributed voluntarily. It does not require any information concerning contribution records, as social insurance schemes do. Again unlike social insurance, it does not require a waiting period while funds are built up; it could be introduced tomorrow.

The scheme would provide more benefit to those who paid more, and thus will be less targeted on the poor than the present means-tested scheme. But *any* reform proposal that involves a move away from means testing (including the introduction of social insurance as advocated by the royal commission) will have this feature. Moreover, this scheme would be 'progressive' at least in the sense that, the more expensive the care chosen, the lower would be the proportion of the cost met from public funds. For instance, in the pound-for-pound example given above, four-fifths of the cost is met from public funds. If the elderly person had chosen a home that charged £500 instead of £400, then she would have paid £125 and the state would have paid £375: three-quarters of the cost.

There is an extra point here. Strictly, it is not correct to say that the partnership scheme automatically gives more to the better-off. Rather, *the scheme gives more (in absolute terms) to those who are prepared to contribute more of their own resources to their own care.* Indeed, this is one of its perceived advantages: it helps those who help themselves. Now often, of course, those helped in this way may be the better-off; but they will not always be so. For instance, relatively poor childless individuals may decide to spend more on their care than better-off individuals with a family who wish to keep their children's inheritances intact. Spending on care, as with spending on anything else, is determined by needs and wants as well as by income; and the distribution of support under the scheme will depend on that spending, not on income per se.

A possible disadvantage is that, under the scheme, the state might end up funding aspects of care of which the state would not approve. If this did look like being a problem, institutional accreditation or 'approved expenditure' procedures could help resolve it. However, it is also important to recognise that people do have different needs and wants for long-term care. In this situation most universal schemes are faced with an unpalatable choice. They can provide a very basic minimum to everyone, thus keeping costs down but satisfying nobody; the consequence is likely to be a residualist scheme with the poor unhappily left at the minimum and with those who can afford it trying to buy themselves out. Alternatively, a universalist scheme can provide a higher quality and quantity of care, meeting the requirements of those who want or need rather more than the basic minimum, but at an exorbitant cost to the public purse. In contrast, the partnership scheme offers a minimum *and* help to those who want or need a higher quality and quantity of care; and, since it encourages people to volunteer their own resources, it can do so at less expense than a high-quality system with full state funding.

A final concern is over provider incentives. Would not providers have an incentive to raise their prices in the knowledge that the state would be meeting some of the cost? This is a problem for any system of state aid. However, the partnership scheme is less subject to it than most other forms of aid. Many of the latter involve the state (eventually) meeting whatever charges are levied, and thus isolating the individuals themselves from any increase in cost. But, even under the most generous version of the partnership scheme (the pound-for-pound matching rate), an individual would have to bear half of the cost of any increase in charges; under the less generous versions, they would have to bear two-thirds (the 50 pence per pound scheme) or four-fifths (the 25 pence per pound scheme) of the increased cost. These costs would be sufficient to constrain providers from any system-busting increases in charges and also to prevent users and providers colluding to defraud the system.

The scheme could be refined in various ways. One possibility, designed to help those with few or no financial resources, would be to allow for *non-financial contributions* that could wholly or partly substitute for financial contributions. These could involve time or effort put into caring; either by the relatives of the individual concerned or by the individual himself or herself caring for others at an earlier period. So, for instance, an individual could put in a year or more of community service of one kind or another, which could supplement or replace entirely his or her financial contribution. Obviously an exchange rate specifying how non-financial contributions could be nominally translated into financial ones would need to be determined.

Another refinement concerns the progressivity of the scheme. This could be enhanced by dividing the difference between the charge and the minimum into different bands and reducing the matching ratio from band to band, perhaps eventually to zero. For instance, instead of being uniformly 1 : 1 as in the above example, the public/private matching ratio could be 3 : 1 for the first £100 of the difference, 1 : 1 for the second £100, 1 : 3 for the third £100, and zero for the fourth £100. In that case, the elderly person in the example would pay £50, and the government £350 : 87.5 per cent of the cost. If she had chosen the £500 home, then she would have paid £112.50 and the government would have paid £387.50 : 77.5 per cent of the cost. This is more progressive than in the example with a uniform 1 : 1 ratio, with the government paying a higher proportion of the total cost for the cheaper option and a lower proportion of the more expensive one.

A problem could arise under this scheme if the individual ran out of her own resources to provide the matching contributions. If nothing were done, she might then be required to leave her residential home and move into one paying the state minimum: a traumatic change, especially since at the point where she runs out of resources she might be at a very advanced age. This danger could be overcome by making it a condition of the matching grant that the individual or her family use their own resources to purchase an annuity of a value sufficient to cover the costs of her contributions. In that way there would never be a shortfall in contributions and she would never be forced to move.

## CONCLUSION

Asset-based partnership schemes of the kind proposed here would have many advantages as a means of providing government help towards accumulating sufficient funds for a pension and for the funding of long-term care. It would provide a strong incentive for individuals and their families to mobilise their own resources. Unlike compulsion, it treats individuals more like queens than pawns. Unlike the present system for long-term care, there would be no means test with all its disincentives and distortions. Unlike tax relief, the schemes would be transparent, flexible, and accountable; and, since they would benefit non-taxpayers as well as taxpayers and because their value would not depend on the marginal rate of tax, they would be much less regressive. They would be relatively easy to implement. The details need refinement; but, overall, the ideas involved seem worthy of serious consideration.

# 11

## Hypothecation

*Moderator*: What comes into your mind when someone says 'tax' to you?
*Man*: Nicking my money
*Woman*: Sadness at the end of each month

(Fabian Society focus group)

'You've stolen my **** budget!'

(Chancellor Gordon Brown to Prime Minister Tony Blair on hearing
that the latter had committed the British government to
spending the European average on health
services in a television interview;
Andrew Rawnsley, *Servants of the People*)

One of the most obvious ways in which a country's citizens are treated as pawns is with respect to taxation. In large part this arises because of the nature of taxation itself. In the language of the libertarian right, taxation is coercive; and coercion is by definition inconsistent with individual freedom of action. Put less pejoratively, paying taxes is a legal obligation, and fulfilling that obligation necessarily restricts the autonomy of individuals to act as they wish.

The general question of the morality of taxation—more specifically, the moral legitimacy of the legal obligation to pay taxes—is beyond the scope of this book.[1] Instead, I want to focus on another important way in which governments' taxation and expenditure systems treat their citizens as pawns: as lacking the capacity for agency. This concerns the use of tax revenues.

### TAX REVENUES AND AGENCY

Outside of election periods, individuals are given little choice in how the income raised in taxation is used. The revenue disappears into the black box of

---

[1] For the record, I must make it clear that I do think there is a legitimate moral case for taxation, and that the fact that it involves 'coercion' does not thereby invalidate that case. There are occasions when it is morally correct to restrict individuals' autonomy, such as by imposing taxation for certain purposes (such as redistribution or to ensure an optimal provision of collective goods). For a discussion of these issues, see Fabian Society (2000: ch. 4) and Nagel and Murphy (2002).

government. True, it reappears as government spending programmes; but the way in which it is allocated between those programmes is determined by a complex web of governmental and parliamentary procedures, with little or no direct reference to the preferences of the people who paid the taxes in the first place.

Of course, this situation can be defended as simply part of the process of representative democracy. Practicality considerations mean that citizens cannot be involved in every decision concerning the governance of the state. Hence a system has evolved whereby every few years citizens elect representatives who make decisions on their behalf, including those concerned with taxation and spending. If citizens do not like the decisions made by their representatives, then they have an opportunity to vote out those representatives at a general election. In that way individuals' preferences and concerns about taxation and spending are taken into account.

However, elections are a blunt instrument for registering individuals' wants and needs. The choices are few. The election is usually between two or three major political parties that offer packages of policies that often differ from one another in relatively minor ways. Further, the packages are not just about taxation and spending but incorporate policies relating to other, non-fiscal areas such as civil rights and foreign policy. Hence the choice between the parties is as likely to be determined by preferences concerning those matters as much as by tax or spending issues. Perhaps even more importantly, elections are relatively infrequent; and the system offers little opportunity for citizens to express their preferences between elections.

These problems with elections as a tool of accountability for taxation and spending decisions would matter little if there were a high degree of trust between citizens and their representatives. If individuals felt that, even in the absence of direct electoral sanction, their representatives would broadly make the 'right' decisions—that is, the decisions they might have made themselves in the circumstances if they had all the relevant information—then the system could work effectively and citizens would feel connected with the decision-making process. Even if representatives on occasion made the 'wrong' decisions, but did so in a transparent and open way so that the reasons for the decisions were clear, it is probable that the connections between representative and citizen would be maintained. However, if even those levels of trust and openness do not exist—if representatives are viewed as making opaque decisions and ones that are probably more in line with their own agendas than with citizens' wants or needs—then citizens are likely to feel disconnected from the process and resentful of the decisions that emerge from it. More generally, they are also likely to feel relatively powerless in the face of those decisions: more pawns than queens.

Although to some extent these feelings may pervade citizens' attitudes to all decisions by governments where elections are relatively infrequent, they are likely to be particularly acute with respect to taxation. For people in modern societies are continuously reminded that 'their' money is being taken from them through various forms of taxation: income tax via their pay slips, value added tax (VAT) or other sales taxes through their sales receipts, local taxes through their annual tax demands. The powerlessness associated with both the manner of extraction and the way the money is subsequently used that citizens face is in stark contrast with the power they retain over their post-tax resources. Only if they fundamentally trust the government to do the right thing will they feel more like queens than pawns.

Unfortunately, in many countries it does seem that the predominant feelings among the citizenry with respect to government and taxation are not trust and connection but rather distrust and alienation. In Britain, as part of the work of its Commission on Taxation and Citizenship (of which I was a member), the Fabian Society undertook some extensive research into public attitudes towards taxation. The research used a number of techniques including focus groups, a large-scale quantitative survey, and a question in a separate opinion poll. The researchers found that:

Taxes were not merely unpopular: they were perceived as an unpleasant subject to discuss altogether, invoking negative feelings even among those who accepted their legitimacy in principle. Almost everybody acknowledged that taxes were necessary to pay for public services; but a commonly used phrase was 'necessary evil' with the emphasis on the evil. Taxation, it was widely remarked, had an almost punitive feeling with the Inland Revenue in particular regarded as a coercive or even threatening body.

Few people experienced taxation as payment for services rendered. Whereas everyone could say what they would do with the money if they had to spend it themselves, few felt that they knew what the government does with it. On the contrary for many people taxes seem to disappear into a 'bottomless' pit (others used the phrase 'black hole') with almost no visible connection at all to the things it pays for. (Fabian Society 2000: 45)

The Commission concluded that people did feel disconnected both from the taxes they pay and from the public services they finance. This disconnection arose partly from a lack of knowledge of what taxes are paid and where the revenues from those taxes are being spent, and partly from a sense that the revenues are not being spent properly. Both of these are well illustrated in the following dialogue from one of the Commission's focus groups (Fabian Society 2000: 51):

*Woman*: Do you ever believe anything they say?
*Woman*: I think the older I get the less I—I get quite a jaundiced view.
*Moderator*: But in principle, if you really believed that it was going into the Health Service, you wouldn't mind paying an extra penny in tax?
*Man*: No, nobody would.
*Woman*: No, I wouldn't, I wouldn't mind at all.
*Woman*: No not at all, no.
*Woman*: If I knew where it was going, not at all.

That individuals feel disconnected and hence relatively powerless with respect to government taxation and spending cannot be good for the health of the wider society. It fosters a resentment of government itself. It can provoke people into endeavouring to compensate for their lack of electoral power by elaborate schemes for tax avoidance and evasion. It may also ultimately lead to socially disruptive action outside the electoral process: demonstrations, strikes, go-slows, blockades. These in turn may panic governments into trying to buy off the protest through ill-considered concessions that serve only the interests of the protestors and ignore those of the wider society. Alternatively, they may provoke governments into a stern inflexibility, a refusal to be intimidated, which in turn may lead them to ignore genuine concerns and grievances over taxation, thereby fuelling even deeper popular resentment and perhaps even greater civil disorder. Either way, the public good is not being served.

So what can be done better to increase individuals' sense of power in relation to their taxes and government spending—in the terminology of Chapter One, to move up the agency axis from pawn to queen? One promising course of action is to earmark tax revenues for particular spending purposes: what is known in the jargon as *hypothecation*. The remainder of this chapter explores the justification and implications of this idea.

## HYPOTHECATION

A hypothecated tax is one whose revenues are earmarked for one particular purpose. The idea has a long history. The word itself comes from the Greek *hupotithenai*, meaning to give as a pledge, via the Latin *hypotheca* (pledge or deposit), and has as its original meaning the act of pledging (property) as security.[2] In fact, in classical Athens and imperial Rome all taxes were hypothecated, largely because of administrative convenience (Webber and Wildavsky 1986: 121). In medieval Europe, again most taxation was hypothecated: monarchs raised money to fund their armies. More recently, in Britain the road fund licence was a hypothecated tax, with its revenues being earmarked for road building; but this earmarking was ended in 1937 (Bracewell-Milnes 1991). In local government, separate rates funded different services until the 1930s. More currently, the BBC licence fee is a classic form of hypothecated tax: a poll tax whose revenues go only to the BBC and which is the sole source of tax funding for the Corporation.[3]

A more prominent current example of hypothecation, used extensively both in Britain and elsewhere in Europe, is national or social insurance. Employers and employees make contributions towards a fund that is used to pay for certain social services and benefits such as old age pensions, unemployment

---

[2] Definitions from the *Shorter Oxford Dictionary* and the *American Heritage Dictionary*. Interestingly, neither dictionary gives the meaning of the term as it is used here and more generally in the tax debate. The Fabian Commission preferred the term 'earmarking', reserving 'hypothecation' for what I term 'strong hypothecation': see below.

[3] The BBC has other, non-tax sources of funding, notably the income from its commercial arm.

benefits, and (in some countries in continental Europe, though not in Britain) health services. Here hypothecation is usually combined with some form of contributory requirement: the benefits funded from the hypothecated tax revenues are available only to those who meet certain conditions concerning the amount of contributions they have made.

Recently, as the Fabian Tax Commission noted, hypothecation has undergone something of a revival in Britain (Fabian Society 2000: 156). When John Major's Conservative government introduced the National Lottery in 1994, the revenues raised for the public purse were allocated to supporting the arts. The first tax measure of the Labour government elected in 1997 was to introduce an earmarked tax: a windfall tax on privatised utilities to pay for the New Deal programme for helping the unemployed get back to work. Subsequent budgets have earmarked increases in tobacco duties for increased health spending, and various environmental taxes have had their revenues earmarked for improving the environment. Outside of government, over the last decade various versions of the idea have been advocated by the Liberal Democrats, the Institute of Economic Affairs (1991), the BMA (1994), and the leading journalist and commentator Samuel Brittan (2000).

So hypothecation is an idea with a pedigree, and one in which there seems to be increasing interest. But it is far from uncontroversial. Proposals for extending it to other areas of government funding, such as health care and education, invariably arouse vigorous opposition. The Treasury and other ministries of finance strongly resist the idea; and it has little support among public finance economists. So what are the relevant arguments?[4]

## WHY HYPOTHECATE?

There is one good argument and one bad argument for hypothecation. To begin with the bad. This is the common belief that hypothecating tax revenues for some popular services, such as health care and education, would lower the electorate's resistance to tax increases. Now the reason why this is a bad argument is not that it is incorrect. On the contrary: that certain kinds of hypothecation would lead to a reduction in taxpayer resistance is indeed quite likely, at least in the current British context. This is again borne out by research done by the Fabian Tax Commission.

In the survey undertaken by the Commission on attitudes to taxation, respondents were asked their reactions to specified increases in the rate of income tax. In each case the implications for the absolute amount of extra tax payments that they would have to pay were spelt out. The results were striking. If the extra tax revenue raised were to be spent on unspecified areas, then 40 per cent of respondents supported a one percentage point increase in the

---

[4] Useful reviews of the principal arguments for and against can be found in Teja and Bracewell-Milnes (1991), Jones and Duncan (1995), and, especially, Fabian Society (2000: ch. 8).

standard rate of tax and 34 per cent a two percentage point increase. But if the money were to be spent on the National Health Service, the proportion supporting the increases virtually doubled: to 80 per cent for a one point increase and to 71 per cent for a two point increase. If the money were to be spent on education, then the proportions were 68 per cent for a one point increase and 61 per cent for a two point one (Fabian Society 2000: Table 2.3). Nor is this simply a phenomenon specific to Britain; there is evidence from other countries to suggest that similar results would hold there too, at least so far as health spending is concerned (Hoffmayer and McCarthy 1994).

So, if it is not factually incorrect, why is the lowering of taxpayer resistance a poor argument for hypothecation? There are two reasons. First, the factual conclusion that hypothecation would lower such resistance is time- and context-specific. At other times, and with spending being allocated to different kinds of uses, it could well be that revealing the cost of spending in this way could increase taxpayer resistance rather than lower it. Further, even if taxpayer resistance were reduced for rises in a hypothecated tax for one popular service, it might be reduced for taxes perceived to be funding less popular ones. And such attitudes exist. So, for instance, analysis by John Hills and Orsolya Lelkes (1999) of the 1999 British Social Attitudes Survey found that more respondents thought that the government should spend *less* on unemployment benefits (35 per cent) than those who thought the government ought to spend more (22 per cent).[5] More generally, an analysis of the 1995 British Social Attitudes survey found that, when people were given the specific tax consequences for themselves of higher spending on particular programmes, a majority remained for increases in health and education spending; but this was not the case for other items such as police, the environment, and defence (Brook, Hall, and Preston 1996).

So the claim that hypothecating taxes will automatically lower tax resistance, while perhaps correct at the time of writing in Britain for certain specific programmes, is not necessarily true in general. But there is a second, more fundamental, objection to the argument. It is unprincipled. For it simply assumes that raising spending is a good thing and hence anything that furthers that end has also to be good. But there can be no presumption that, at all times and in all situations, raising public spending is desirable; there are going to be occasions when even the most ardent advocate of the public sector might feel that reductions in expenditure would be appropriate (defence spending after the conclusion of a war, for example). And, even on occasions when more spending is desirable, it cannot simply be assumed that the end justifies the means, especially when, as we shall see, this particular means has costs associated with it.

So what is the good argument for hypothecation? The fundamental reason why hypothecation is desirable is related to the central theme of this book: that it turns pawns into queens—or at the least that it goes some way towards

---

[5]  40% thought that the same amount should be spent.

doing so. It does this in two ways. First, if properly administered, it makes citizens aware of the costs of public services, both in general and to them personally. The opaqueness consequent on the pooling of revenue would be lifted. Information is an essential element to being an active and autonomous citizen, and hypothecation is a way of ensuring that a key part of that information is available. Second, it restricts the power of government relative to that of its citizens. Governments cannot simply do what they like with the tax revenues; instead, they have to allocate those resources in a pre-specified way. The balance of power between citizens and their government is shifted in the direction of citizens.

It could be argued that hypothecation, although increasing the relative power of citizens by reducing government flexibility, does little to increase citizens' absolute power. For they can still express only their preferences for changes in the hypothecated taxes and the associated levels of the public services that the taxes fund every few years at a general election, and then only via voting on a bundle of services and taxation. To rectify this, we could follow the suggestion of some analysts of combining hypothecation with a system of popular referendums on spending (see, for instance, Buchanan 1963). So individuals could be asked in a set of binding referendums how much tax they were prepared to pay to fund a particular service or services via taxation. Government decisions would then become even more representative of citizens' views. Continuous referendums have their disadvantages, however, not least in terms of their practicality; and, although attractive as a means of increasing citizen power, it is probable that, at least in the short term, the practical difficulties involved in implementing such a suggestion rules it out.

So the case for hypothecation rests fundamentally on the increase in the power of the citizen relative to that of the government. What of the case against? There are a number of more or less powerful objections.

First, there is an argument in favour of government flexibility. Spending needs change, the economy fluctuates, there are all kinds of outside events and shocks that affect both spending and the economy in the long and short term. Governments, it is argued, must be able to respond to these changes and hypothecation reduces their ability to do so. However, this argument can be turned on its head. It is precisely the intention of hypothecation to reduce government flexibility. It is governments' use—or, as some would argue misuse—of that flexibility that has sown the seeds of mistrust between government and people. Losing the benefits of flexibility may be the price we have to pay for restoring a measure of power to individuals and thereby reducing a source of disconnection between them and their government.

Of course, this raises the question as to how far the hypothecation would go. How many government programmes should be funded by hypothecated taxes? Clearly the greater the number of such programmes—more accurately, the higher the proportion of revenue that is earmarked in one way or another—the less flexibility the government has in disposing of revenue. It may be that hypothecation or earmarking comes to a point where the costs of extending the process further begin to outweigh the benefits. But where this point is reached is impossible to decide a priori. Rather each hypothecation proposal has to be assessed not only on its own merits but also in terms of its impact on the overall budget position of the government.

A second objection relates specifically to the fluctuations in the economy. An important role of taxation is to stabilise the economy over the economic cycle. In boom times, other things being equal, tax receipts increase, consumer demand is curbed, and the boom is moderated. In recession, tax receipts fall, consumer demand is stimulated, and the recession alleviated. But if a substantial portion of the tax system is hypothecated there is no guarantee that this stabilisation role can be properly fulfilled. On the contrary, during a boom tax rates may have to be lowered or expenditure will have to be increased to keep tax receipts in line with expenditure; either would add fuel to the boom. In a recession, tax rates might have to be raised or expenditure cut, thus exacerbating the recession.

This is part of the more general argument in favour of government flexibility. So in large part the counter-argument is simply that, as observed above, the loss of this flexibility is a price that has to be paid in order to get the benefits of hypothecation. Moreover, given that the use of fiscal tools as an instrument of macroeconomic stabilisation in this way is no longer thought to be as important as it once was, the price might not be all that great.

However, if it is felt to be a serious problem in a particular case, than it can be handled by a stabilisation fund. This would be a fund into which any excess of revenue over expenditure was paid in boom times, and which was used to top up expenditure during recessionary periods when tax receipts fall. The hypothecated tax budget would be balanced not over a particular year but over the economic cycle. In that case it would not be necessary to change tax rates in line with the cycle; stability could be maintained.

It has to be acknowledged that the idea of a stabilisation fund is not unproblematic. The principal danger of such funds is that, as they accumulated in good times, they would be raided by government to be used for other purposes. This happened to the British Road Fund in the 1930s and led to its eventual demise. Constitutional safeguards against this kind of raiding would have to be built into any stabilisation fund proposal.

This problem is actually part of a third source of objection to the idea of hypothecation: the genuineness or otherwise of the hypothecation. On this argument, hypothecation, whether or not accompanied by a stabilisation fund, is almost invariably a cosmetic exercise. What happens in practice, the argument runs, is that, if funds are earmarked for a particular use, then government notionally allocates the funds to that use. But it does not relate the revenue raised to the amount of spending it makes, deciding that amount independently. If the revenue raised by the hypothecated tax is more than the expenditure requirement, then it siphons off the extra revenue for use elsewhere; if the revenue raised is less, then it uses general revenues to make up the difference. Either way, effectively the government is simply using the hypothecated tax as part of general revenue, and the hypothecation is a sham.

In responding to this, it is useful to distinguish between two kinds of hypothecation: strong and weak. Hypothecation is strong when the revenues from the tax concerned are used only for funding one particular government programme or area of expenditure, and when there is no other source of tax funding for that programme. Hypothecation is weak when either or both of these conditions do not hold: that is, either when any surplus revenues from the tax are used to fund some programme other than the one for which it was earmarked, or when revenues from other taxes are used to top up spending on the designated programme. Of the examples given earlier, the BBC licence fee is an example of strong hypothecation. Most of the others are forms of weak hypothecation, either because they are supplementing revenues raised from other sources, as with the revenues from the National Lottery for the arts and the increases in tobacco duties for the National Health Service, or because the programmes funded receive on occasion top-up funds from other sources, as with the UK national insurance fund.

The distinction is important in this context, since the 'sham' objection refers only to weak hypothecation. This is obvious in the case when the revenues are used to fund services in addition to those specified in the hypothecation arrangement. Then the government is simply using the tax as one way of raising revenue for general purposes and all the transparency and other disadvantages of that way of doing things will come to the fore. But it is also the case when other revenues are used to fund the service in addition to the hypothecated tax. Then there will be no automatic link between changes in expenditure on that service and changes in the hypothecated tax and again the transparency and other benefits will be lost.

This suggests that, for a hypothecated tax to succeed, the hypothecation must be strong. The revenue must be genuinely circumscribed. That is, it must be the sole source of funds for the service concerned; and it must be used only for funding that service. A surplus in the hypothecated fund should not be used to fill gaps in the funding of other services. Rather, it should be carried over for use in the next year (perhaps through the mechanism of a stabilisation fund) either to increase the level and quality of the service concerned or to reduce the hypothecated tax rates. The corollary also holds: if there is a deficit in any one year, revenue from other sources should not be used to fill the funding gap. Instead the deficit should be carried over and rectified by appropriate changes in the hypothecated tax rate the following year. Again this is crucial for maintaining individuals' trust in the system. If there is no automatic link between the hypothecated tax payments and the level of service delivery, then the allegedly hypothecated tax becomes simply one among a battery of government fund-raising measures and the advantages of hypothecation are lost. For, with weak hypothecation, individuals can no longer be sure that the money they pay through the earmarked tax will be used in exactly the way they have been told it will; and, once that certainty is gone, the trust that the hypothecation is meant to cement between individuals and government will disappear.

A fourth potential difficulty concerns the impact of earmarking revenues for one particular programme on other programmes paid for out of general revenues. We have seen earlier that some programmes, such as health and education, are more popular than others, such as unemployment benefits. Hypothecating revenues for the popular programmes could reduce political support for general taxation, and hence reduce the potential for supporting the less popular programmes.

However, here there are two points. First, the argument is predicated on the presumption of deception. Political support for taxation is generated by fooling taxpayers into thinking that their taxes are largely going to service the programmes they favour—whereas in fact many of the revenues are siphoned off to fund programmes that they do not. This is not an argument that would commend itself to those who wish to turn taxpayer pawns into queens.

Second, the 'nesting' of popular programmes within a budget funded from general taxation could actually have a similar effect to that feared by opponents of hypothecation: the driving down of funds available for unpopular ones. There is a danger that 'nesting' acts as a cuckoo in the nest, with the political imperative of the popular programmes being so dominant that little room is left in the budget for the remainder. That this danger is a real one is graphically illustrated by the quotation from Gordon Brown, the Chancellor of the Exchequer, at the beginning of this chapter, namely, that the Prime Minister had stolen his budget through committing the British government to matching continental European levels of health spending in a television interview.

A final concern about hypothecation is ideological. Hypothecation is said to be anti-collectivist in nature: an advantage to some on the political right, but a demerit to those more sympathetic to government involvement in the economy. In their history of taxation and expenditure in the Western world, Caroline Webber and Aaron Wildavsky put the point as follows: the use of earmarking 'indicates strong tendencies towards competitive individualism. Separation of revenues by source and allocation of receipts by function in modern governments in effect converts collective goods into individual ones, for such specificity permits calculations of losses and gains by private people' (Webber and Wildavsky 1986: 121).

But, although this sounds plausible at a rhetorical level, it is not clear what it really means. In particular, it is not obvious how earmarking or hypothecation turns collective goods into individual ones. Roads were not any less collective goods when they were funded by the road fund licence than they are now; nor is the BBC any more or less a collective good through being funded by the licence fee. The collective insurance function of the National Health Service would remain if it were funded by a hypothecated tax. The nature or otherwise of a collective good does not depend on whether it is funded from general or hypothecated taxation.[6]

What perhaps this argument is expressing is the fear that, once the purpose of a tax is made clear through hypothecation, people may prefer not to pay it, especially if they perceive themselves as getting no direct benefit from the service concerned or if they think they could get a better deal outside the public sector. In effect, to use terminology from earlier in the book, hypothecation may turn collectivist knights into individualistic knaves.

But this is not a necessary consequence of hypothecation. Even if people do not get any immediate personal benefit from a service, they may be prepared to continue paying for it, either because they have altruistic concerns for the actual beneficiaries of the service or because they perceive themselves as possibly needing the service themselves in the future. And those who do get an immediate personal benefit may not necessarily think they will get a better deal outside. In Germany, where wealthy individuals are offered a choice of remaining in the statutory health insurance sector or opting out and taking private insurance, a large majority stay with the public sector—largely because they think it is better (Thomson, Busse, and Mossialos 2002). In general, the danger that people might opt out can provide a useful competitive pressure on the public service, helping to lever up the quantity and quality of the service provided.

But, more fundamentally, it does not seem a bad thing if people do become aware of the losses and gains to them associated with public services. Indeed, as we have argued above, this contributes to transparency and thereby goes some way towards turning pawns into queens. If a consequence of this is that some people prefer to opt out from the services concerned, then this has to be accepted. Advocates of increasing individuals' power and sense of control over their lives cannot complain if on occasion that power is exercised in ways of which they might not approve.

Overall, therefore, when the arguments are viewed from the perspective of this book, hypothecation has many merits. But can it work in practice? The remainder of this chapter considers two practical examples: one, national insurance, an illustration of how not to hypothecate, and the other, a health tax, an illustration of how it might be done better.

## HOW NOT TO HYPOTHECATE: BRITISH NATIONAL INSURANCE

We noted above that the British system of national insurance was a kind of hypothecated tax; indeed, it is the most prominent example of hypothecation in the British system. Unfortunately it is a poor example; but, as so often with

---

[6] A 'collective' or 'public' good is usually defined in economics as one whose consumption is non-rival and non-excludable. Neither of these characteristics is affected by its system of funding.

poor examples, it is useful to examine them to see what lessons can be learned from their relative failure.

National insurance in Britain is a system of cash benefits paid out of an account that is financed by compulsory contributions by employers and employees. The account is not a fund that is cumulative; today's benefits are financed by today's contributions (sometimes known as pay-as-you-go). The benefits are designed to meet various contingencies all associated with loss of income: sickness, disability, unemployment, and old age. With the exception of the (now much reduced) state earnings-related pension scheme (SERPS), all the benefits are flat rate. The contributions are levied on earnings between a lower earnings limit (LEL), now aligned with the starting point of income tax, and an upper earnings limit (UEL).

The first problem with the national insurance system is that its aims are neither clear nor consistent. There is no clear statement of purpose; no articulated view of its aims and objectives. Most observers actually see it as trying to do two things at once: to provide insurance against loss of income due to sickness, unemployment, or old age, and to redistribute from rich to poor. Having two aims is in itself not intrinsically a bad thing; many policy tools have more than one function without necessarily losing their effectiveness in consequence. However, multiple purposes are tolerable only if the pursuit of one of the purposes does not militate against the achievement of the others. But this condition is not fulfilled for national insurance. If it were the proper insurance system that its name implies, it should ensure that those who encountered the misfortunes against which it is providing insurance would not suffer major losses of income, as continental European social insurance systems do. Thus it would levy earnings-related contributions and provide earnings-related benefits. However, as indeed the experience of continental social insurance systems demonstrates, it would not be redistributive; for, although those on higher incomes would pay more by way of contributions, they would also receive more by way of benefits. If on the other hand the system were designed to be an effective instrument for redistribution, its benefits should be concentrated on the poor while more contributions were paid by the better-off. But this would vitiate its insurance function for the middle classes, whose incomes would fall very sharply as soon as they were on benefits.

In the impossible attempt to resolve this dilemma, the British national insurance system unsurprisingly performs neither function properly. Since, except for SERPS, benefits are not earnings-related, they do not provide adequate insurance against the drop in living standards caused by the misfortunes they are supposedly protecting people against. In fact in most cases they do not even provide a decent floor to the drop in living standards. So, for instance, since its inception in 1948 those reliant upon the national insurance basic pension have had to have their income topped up by mean-tested benefits—a situation exacerbated (but not created) by the removal of the link between state pensions and earnings in the early 1980s.

Moreover, recent policy changes by both Labour and Conservative governments have eroded the insurance function in other ways. The Conservative government not only ended the link between rises in earnings and the value of retirement pension and other long-term benefits, and abolished earnings-related supplements for short-term benefits, but also introduced the Jobseeker's Allowance, which cut contributory benefits during unemployment from twelve to six months and aligned contributory and means-tested benefits more closely. The process of attrition has continued under the Labour government. In particular, incapacity benefit is to be partially offset against any private pension received, and its eligibility rules are being tightened; and state pensions above the basic pension are to become flat-rate rather than earnings-related, virtually ending earnings relation of benefits altogether.

Whilst some benefits have been cut, national insurance contributions have been increased, especially during the 1980s. More recently, the structure of contributions has been partially aligned to that of income tax. The 'entry fee'—effectively a flat fee for entrance to the system, payable once earnings reached a lower earnings limit—has been abolished for both employees and employers. For employers, the upper earnings limit on contributions has been abolished. The lower earnings limit for employees has already been aligned with the personal tax threshold; this alignment took place for employees in April 2001, but with benefit entitlement preserved on the slice of earnings then exempt from contributions. Although there is currently no move to abolish the UEL for employees or the ceiling on contributions for self-employed people, the UEL is being increased by more than prices.

So the current system of national insurance is far from a proper insurance system. Unfortunately, it is not a very effective instrument for redistribution either. It is a proportional tax on a particular slice of earned income (between the lower earnings limit and the upper earnings limit). It is not levied on income from savings or on other forms of unearned income. As well as thereby being much less effective in redistributive terms than the regular income tax, this creates oddities and anomalies in the system; for instance, the effect of the UEL is to make marginal tax rates actually fall for incomes over a certain range.

Nor are the benefits that national insurance finances an effective instrument for redistribution. The prime function of national insurance contributions is to finance the state pension, which takes up about three-quarters of the revenue raised. But this is a flat-rate benefit and one whose value relative to other forms of income is steadily declining. Hence it does little to dent the inequality in the income distribution, especially when the latter is considered from a lifetime perspective. Indeed, since the rich live significantly longer than the poor, it is only slightly caricaturing the system to describe it as one in which working-class contributions are used to finance middle-class benefits.

So the current National Insurance system has neither clarity nor consistency of purpose—a failing that means that it does not perform any function that it might have very well. Partly as a consequence it does not meet another mark of good hypothecation: consistency. Taxpayers do in fact perceive it as a kind of insurance system and are puzzled (and often angry) when it fails to deliver. Public opinion research shows diminishing confidence in the benefits which will be paid out in future, especially the basic retirement pension—although generalised (if fairly uninformed) support for the contributory principle remains.

Many commentators predict that, if nothing changes, this sense of disillusion will get worse. Nicholas Timmins (1999), noting that the national insurance system has become complex, confused in its purpose, and progressively undermined, has argued 'if the penny drops with the electorate that they are progressively paying more for less, a political rather than merely a structural crisis over NI may yet arise'. As awareness of the difference between the system's ostensible aims and its actual performance increases, it is likely that the erosion of confidence and credibility that it generates is in danger of affecting other parts of the tax system, undermining faith in the fiscal system and in government more generally—and thus exacerbating the problem of 'disconnection'.

Finally, the current system for national insurance fails to meet the criterion of strong hypothecation. Over the years since its inception, the national insurance fund has often had to be supplemented by revenues from general taxation. Currently, with the decline in the relative value of national insurance benefits and the rise in national insurance contributions, this problem has become less acute, and indeed the fund is currently in surplus. Although under current rules any surplus is in fact carried over to the following year, given the likelihood of continuing and ever-growing surpluses it is difficult to imagine future chancellors denying themselves the opportunity to exploit the fund for other purposes.

What lesson can be learned from the experience of national insurance regarding successful hypothecation? First, if the aim is to promote greater knowledge of public spending generally, the purpose for which the hypothecated revenue is to be used must be clear. A mishmash of confused policy aims associated in a vague way with a particular tax or set of taxes will do nothing to further the cause of citizenship. Both clarity and consistency would be best served by having just one overarching aim or purpose. This may not always be possible; but, if the tax is intended to serve more than one aim, then it is important that the several aims are not only clear but also compatible with one another.

Further, however many there are, the nature of the purpose or purposes of the tax should be apparent to the people who pay it. Clarity is obviously a necessary condition for this, but not a sufficient one. A set of goals that are clear and consistent but are known only to policy-makers or policy analysts will do little to motivate citizen taxpayers to comply with the requirements of the tax; indeed, if they have any suspicion that there is some kind of hidden agenda they are more likely to engage in revolt than compliance. Also, the route for channelling the revenue raised towards the service for which it is earmarked must be clear to taxpayers; there should be no misconceptions about the nature and role of the hypothecated fund and the way the revenue is used.

## A HYPOTHECATED HEALTH TAX

As we have seen, there are good arguments for hypothecated taxes in general. But there are two special reasons why hypothecation is particularly appropriate for health services. One of these derives from a concern with citizenship. Many countries take pride in their health services. In particular, the National Health Service occupies a unique place in Britain and in the identity of Britons. When British citizens are asked what they are most proud of about being British, one of the elements to which the overwhelming majority refer is the NHS.[7] They persist in their pride despite their perception of the service's ongoing difficulties. The collectivity of the NHS is part of the national collectivity.

Hence linking hypothecation to health services would link taxation to an intrinsic part of identity and citizenship—especially in Britain. Although they would probably not express it precisely this way, most Britons are proud that health care is available to everyone largely free of charge; that access to medical treatment does not depend on ability to pay; that the country has made a collective decision to help those with the misfortune to be struck by down by illness or disability in the most direct way possible: by providing health care paid for out of taxation.

The second reason why health services are *sui generis* at least as far as hypothecation is concerned concerns the relationship between the demand for the service and the volume of resources devoted to it. The demand for health care is widely regarded as income-elastic (that is, it rises more than proportionately with income) and in most countries spending has been steadily increasing as a proportion of GNP over the longer term. That being the case, governments of countries with publicly funded health systems are faced with an uncomfortable choice. Either they continue to increase the volume of resources going into publicly funded health care relatively slowly, with all the damaging political consequences that this would entail, or they engage in some dramatic increase in expenditure—which in turn would either involve some sharp falls in other areas of public spending or a large increase in general taxation. As we saw earlier, health spending can be a cuckoo in the nest. A hypothecated non-general tax earmarked for health care would seem to be the obvious way around this dilemma.

What tax? It is often assumed that hypothecated taxes must be taxes on income. But this is not necessarily the case. Other taxes could equally well serve the purpose of raising revenues for the NHS, such as VAT, taxes on

---

[7] Witness two recent media reports: 'What exemplifies Britishness? In a recent survey 91% said the NHS', *BBC News*, 10 December 2001. And Patrick Wintour wrote in the *Guardian* on 28 March 2000, under the heading 'Labour tries to reclaim the flag', that '[Gordon] Brown's group had gone so far as to commission qualitative and quantitative polling to find out what values and institutions had come to represent Britishness in the public mind. They discovered that the NHS was the single most cherished and unifying institution in Britain and even emblematic of British values'.

tobacco, and alcohol (the so-called sin taxes), or environmental taxes. In fact, for some of these a positive case could be made for hypothecating them to expenditure on health care. In the British case VAT currently raises almost exactly as much as is spent on the NHS. Sin and environmental taxes are levied on activities that actually damage health; so there is a logic in tying their revenues to funding activities that promote health.

However, there are compelling arguments against using these taxes for this purpose. It is only coincidence that the sums raised by VAT currently match desired levels of spending on the NHS. If the latter changed, as it undoubtedly will, then either the rates or the base of a hypothecated VAT would have to change as well; and this raises much bigger issues, not least with respect to the requirements of the European Union. Each of the sin taxes raises less than a quarter of the revenue required; and the one existing environmental tax (on hydrocarbon oils) raises much less than half. Moreover, none of them is as progressive as the income tax; indeed, the tax on tobacco is actually regressive.

The only realistic alternative to the income tax would be some form of social insurance. However, social insurance is an unsatisfactory form of hypothecation for health care. This is for a number of reasons. First, the tax base for social insurance—earned income—is smaller than that of the full income tax. Second, the burden falls disproportionately on employees and employers. Third, social insurance systems tend to be much less progressive than those financed out of more general forms of taxation (van Doorslaer, Wagstaff, and Rutten 1993). For all these reasons, many countries that have previously relied upon social insurance as a means of financing health care have moved away from it. Italy and Spain have both largely replaced the funding of health care out of social insurance by funding from general taxation; France, under strong pressure from employers, is doing the same. In short, if we are to hypothecate tax for health care spending, the most suitable candidate seems to be the income tax.

## CONCLUSION

The systems of taxation and expenditure current in the Western world are classic examples of treating individuals as pawns, not queens. This arises not only because of taxation's nature as a legal obligation (unavoidable if revenue is to be raised in this fashion) but because of the way in which tax revenues are used. The revenues are paid into a central pool. Decisions on the use of that pool are taken by government, with only the threat of a potential electoral defeat acting as a check to governmental power. Hypothecation can act as a restriction on government's freedom of action, thus shifting the balance of power back towards individuals. The gains could be considerable: more accountable government, more autonomous individuals, and a restoration of trust between government and its citizens. For such ends, the price of less government flexibility would be worth paying.

# Epilogue: *Doux Commerce Publique*

> Act in such a way that you always treat humanity, whether in your own person or in the person of any other, never simply as a means, but always at the same time as an end.
>
> (Immanuel Kant, *Groundwork of the Metaphysics of Morals*)

> Organise policy until self-interest does what justice requires.
>
> (Anon.)

Let me conclude on a more reflective note. It will not have escaped the attentive reader of this book that I believe that public policy should be designed so as to empower individuals: to turn pawns into queens. As I hope to have shown in the last three chapters, innovative fiscal measures that would further this end include demogrants, matching grants to encourage savings, and the hypothecation of certain taxes. Obviously, these do not cover the full range of fiscal measures that a society could adopt to empower its citizens; but they are ones currently on the policy agenda and that could be readily implemented without excessive political or economic upheaval.

Earlier chapters concentrated on reforms to public services: specifically, the use of competitive quasi-market mechanisms of one kind or another to deliver those services. Again the argument was that, suitably designed, these were a good way to turn pawns into queens: that they empowered service users. Motivation issues were also important; the incentives in such markets would have to be appropriately structured so that they were robust, appealing to both the knight and the knave.

Now some readers, including those sympathetic to the general aim of turning pawns into queens, may find the part of the argument involving quasi-markets unacceptable. The essence of a public service, they might feel, is that it is not provided through markets of any kind. Markets rely upon the pursuit of knavish self-interest by service providers; and the pursuit of self-interest in the context of public services can only be destructive both to service users themselves and to the wider society. Better to rely upon ways of service delivery that rely upon different forms of motivation for providers: specifically, ones that utilise providers' knightly or altruistic feelings or, more generally, rely upon trust and the 'public service ethos'. This would not only produce superior service outcomes but would also be morally preferable. A society that regards those engaged in public service as knights is better than one that treats every one involved in the public sector as a knave.

This book has considered these arguments and demonstrated, using both theoretical arguments and empirical evidence, that these doubts are misplaced. In terms of outcomes, services delivered by appropriately designed quasi-market mechanisms can be empowering, efficient, and equitable. Moreover, they can even be moral: market-type reward structures can reinforce altruistic motivations and reduce exploitation. But there is a further, even more fundamental argument in favour of quasi-markets, and this I want to develop here.

As Albert Hirschman (1977; 1986) has pointed out, in the seventeenth and eighteenth centuries many philosophers saw the pursuit of financial interests in a market context as having a positive merit in and of itself. This was because financial interest acted as a countervailing power against other, more destructive 'passions', such as pride, envy, and the lust for power and glory. The process of market exchange was itself viewed as a largely innocuous activity, especially when contrasted with the activities of the marauding armies and pirates of the time. Hence Dr Johnson's famous assertion that 'there are few ways in which a man can be more innocently employed than making money'.[1]

This view in turn led to the idea of 'doux commerce', whereby commercial activity acted as an instrument of civilisation. As Montesquieu put it, 'commerce . . . polishes and softens barbarian ways' (quoted in Hirschman 1977: 60). William Robertson and Condorcet both endorsed this view, as did Thomas Paine in the *Rights of Man.* So Hirschman (1986: 108) quotes Paine:

[Commerce] is a pacific system, operating to cordialise mankind, by rendering Nations, as well as individuals, useful to each other . . . the invention of commerce . . . is the greatest approach towards universal civilisation that has yet been made by any means not immediately flowing from moral principles.

These ideas are not unique to the eighteenth century. They were taken up by much later writers such as John Maynard Keynes in the 1930s and Francis Fukuyama in our own time. As Keynes (1935/1964: 374) put it:

Dangerous human proclivities can be canalized into comparatively harmless channels by the existence of opportunity for money-making and private wealth, which, if they cannot be satisfied in this way may find their outlet in cruelty, the reckless pursuit of personal power and authority, and other forms of self-aggrandizement.

And Fukuyama (1992: 316):

It would seem not entirely a bad thing . . . that economic activity can preoccupy [the most talented and ambitious] natures for an entire lifetime. This is not simply because such people create wealth which migrates through the economy as a whole, but because such people are kept out of politics and the military. In those latter occupations, their

---

[1] Boswell (1934: 323). Letter to William Strahan, 27 March 1775.

restlessness would lead them to propose innovations at home or adventures abroad, with potentially disastrous consequences for the polity.

Few would argue for a return of marauding armies to Europe (or indeed anywhere else); and, if the pursuit of financial interest acts as a bulwark against that return, then it has to be applauded. However, that is not quite the dilemma that faces us here. Rather, it is the question as to whether there is any positive moral virtue attached to market or quasi-market processes as they are applied in public services, especially when they are compared to other forms of delivery that apparently place less reliance upon financial interests as a motivating force. In this context, it is not cruelty or the lust for glory but knightly motivations that eschew financial considerations and concern themselves only with the public welfare that are to be set against financial interest.

Yet this historical debate is not irrelevant to the public versus financial interest issue. For the earlier contributions led directly to a defence of market exchange by later philosophers and economists such as James Steuart, Adam Smith, Immanuel Kant, and G. W. F. Hegel that does abut directly on our question.[2]

As Rupert Gordon (1999) has pointed out, both Steuart and, to a greater degree, Smith argued that a key feature of market exchange was that it led to a respect for other people. To offer something in exchange is to make an effort to understand the needs and wants of the other party to the potential exchange and to persuade them that what is on offer will meet those needs or wants. This is unlike forcible acquisition through robbery or war, where no effort is made to understand and no attempt is made to persuade. Efforts to understand and persuade are both a cause and a consequence of respect for others; hence, since respect for others is morally desirable, so are understanding and persuasion, and so is the mechanism that brings them about: market exchange.

As we can see in the epigraph to this chapter, Kant agreed about the importance of respect. He argued that, in the ideal society, individuals must treat others as ends, not only as means. This incorporated his fundamental belief that individuals must respect others. This belief in turn formed part of his 'categorical imperative': something that was necessary in and of itself apart from its relationship to a further end.

Hegel shared with Kant the view that individuals must respect each other. However, he argued that the route to ensuring this lay not in an appeal to some metaphysical categorical imperative but through the educative processes of the free market. As with Smith and Steuart, he argued that market relationships foster mutual respect and counter human impulses to dominate others. A merchant must respect the dignity of his or her customers, or they will turn

---

[2] See Gordon (1999), on which much of the following three paragraphs is based. I am grateful to Jeremy Kendall for drawing my attention to this article and to the arguments it contains.

elsewhere. Similarly, customers must respect the dignity of the merchants from whom they purchase or the merchants will not sell to them.

The proposition that market systems can encourage mutuality of respect and indeed even other virtues such as equity or altruism is supported by some recent behavioural experiments concerning the so-called ultimatum game. In these experiments, one person is given a fixed cash sum, say, £10, and told to split it in some way with another individual. If the other person accepts the proposed division, they both get the share of the money proposed. If he or she rejects it, both get nothing. If both pursued only their knavish self-interest, the outcome would be quite unequivocal: the first person would offer one penny and the second would accept it. However, the experiments consistently yield quite different outcomes. Even when played on a one-off basis, the acceptors reject what they consider to be unfair offers; whereas the proposers, either because they suspect that this may happen or because they themselves have an innate sense of fairness, tend to make fair offers.[3]

The particularly interesting thing about these experiments is that the results are *not* replicated when they are tried out in non-market societies. Anthropologists have experimented with these games with Peruvian Amazon tribes, Orma tribes in east Africa, and Quichua communities in Ecuador. They found that the less market-oriented the society was, the less likely were the experiments' participants to make more generous (or more egalitarian) offers. Thus, out of $100, the Orma, used to trading cattle and work for wages, would offer $44 on average, whereas the subsistence slash-and-burn farmers, who engage in little trade of any kind, would offer $25 on average (Henrich 2001). Overall, the anthropologists suggest, experience of market transactions may make people fairer or less exploitative when dealing with strangers.

Now to some eyes, especially to those versed in Marxist and other critiques of capitalism, these assertions might seem incredible. Surely market exchange encourages exploitation, particularly of strangers? The operations of capitalist markets, far from conferring respect on individuals, actually robs them of dignity through their monopolistic exploitation of labour. Also, the poverty that all too frequently accompanies unfettered capitalism is itself demeaning and disrespectful, quite apart from the misery it creates through deprivation.

But, whatever their force as part of a more general critique of capitalism, these criticisms would not apply to the quasi-market mechanisms for delivering public services that are under review here. The quasi-market experiences we have reviewed did not seem to result in exploitation of users. Perhaps this was because of the impact of 'doux commerce', as the anthropologist experiments would suggest; or perhaps it was because the quasi-markets concerned had competitive purchasers and providers, and hence the monopolistic exploitation of either labour or consumers was not an issue. Indeed, arguably the state is potentially more exploitative when it acts as a monopoly provider

---

[3] For a detailed discussion of these experiments, see Rabin (1997).

of services or a monopsony purchaser of labour.[4] And individuals do not come to the quasi-market with their own, unequal resources (the source of poverty and deprivation); the state provides the funding on an egalitarian basis for all.

And the positive arguments from Smith, Steuart, and Hegel can be transferred directly over to the case for competitive quasi-markets in public services. It is often remarked that the problem with state monopolistic systems of public service delivery is the degree of power that they give to providers of services. Arrogant doctors, insensitive teachers, uncaring social workers, overweening bureaucrats: these are the stuff of the standard critique of state-provided services. There often seems to be little mutuality of respect; instead there is deference and resignation on one side, and arrogance, indifference, or condescension on the other.

This insensitivity may arise among providers because the providers are in fact knaves, not knights. However, it could arise even if the providers were altruists imbued with the public service ethos. For, although to undertake an altruistic act requires a compassionate interest for the welfare of the beneficiary of that act, this does not necessarily imply a respect for the person concerned. Indeed, rather the reverse; the altruist at least in his or her own perception often feels he or she is in a superior position to the beneficiary. Feelings of superiority are difficult to reconcile with mutuality of respect. Some knights need pawns if their knightly impulses are to be properly satisfied.

An interesting illustration of this is provided by Hartley Dean (forthcoming), who explored the attitudes of social workers and benefit administrators to the idea that their clients might have rights. He found that, although they were more committed to the public service ethos than the public they served, they felt their clients should be good: that is, cooperative or compliant. Demands based on rights were viewed as threatening.

So a positive case can be made that, appropriately structured, competitive quasi-markets for the delivery of public services have the moral virtue of encouraging respect for users in a way that other systems do not. Users operate as queens, not pawns. Further, such quasi-markets do not suffer from the corrosive effects on mutual respect of the poverty and exploitation that accompany pure markets.

Moreover, the use of quasi-markets does not have to rely upon knavish motivations. For the quasi-market to work effectively, the agents concerned do have to be interested in the financial health of the institution that is providing the service. However, this interest need not be entirely or even partly knavish. Providers of the service may have a genuine commitment to the welfare of users, and feel that they themselves and the institution in which they work are contributing materially to that welfare. In that case it would be rational for them to fear that that welfare would be seriously damaged if their own

---

[4] 'Monopsony' is a technical term describing a situation where there is only one purchaser—as distinct from the term 'monopoly', used where there is only one seller.

financial health or that of the institution suffered, or to expect improvements in user welfare if finances improved. Quasi-market pressures would then operate as effectively as if the providers were knaves and purely self-interested. And the spirit of caring for others, which writers from Richard Titmuss to Richard Sennett have claimed is an essential part of the decent society, would be retained.

Indeed, if it is to work in the true interests of users, the quasi-market system has to have this kind of knightly concern. For, as we have seen in earlier chapters, providers of public services often (though not always) have superior information to users, especially about the quality and the costs of the service they are providing. They are therefore in a position to exploit that information for their own ends at the expense of the user, if they are so motivated. This can be overcome to some extent by the use of informed purchasers to act on behalf of the user and/or by systems of contracting. But often even expert purchasers cannot be fully informed; and contracts, however detailed, can never be complete. New developments in incentive contracting may help here in the long run, but there is still a long way to go before the models that have been developed are operationally useful. Hence we must rely upon some degree of knightliness among providers so that they will not set out to exploit their informational advantage to the detriment of the user.

However, the danger of introducing financial incentives where previously they did not exist is that, as Richard Titmuss and others have argued, they will turn the knight into a knave—or at least allow self-interested motivations to dominate or even suppress altruistic ones. However, as we saw in Chapter Four, this is not an automatic consequence of introducing market reward systems, provided these are properly designed. At the least, they must not be arranged so that knightly and knavish incentives do not operate to motivate actions in different directions. More positively, they should be designed in such a way as to be *robust*: that is, so that the same action appeals to both the knight and the knave. This can be achieved by systems that offer personal (or institutional) rewards for activities that are perceived to benefit users, but for which the rewards are not so great as to eliminate any sense of personal sacrifice that is associated with the activity concerned.

In short, it is not necessary to turn knights into knaves for pawns to become queens. What is needed is well-designed public policies, ones that employ market-type mechanisms but that do not allow unfettered self-interest to dominate altruistic motivations: a form of 'doux commerce publique'.

# POSTSCRIPT

This postscript contains three reprinted review articles. Each addresses the book specifically or deals with topics contained within the book. The articles are followed by an Afterword in which Julian Le Grand reflects on the points raised in each of the articles and addresses various critiques of the book.

The original publication details of the articles are as follows:

Rudolf Klein (2005). 'The Great Transformation' *Health Economics, Policy and Law,* 1(1): 91–98.

Mathias Risse (2005). 'Should Citizens of a Welfare State be Transformed into Queens? A Critical Notice of Julian Le Grand, Motivation, Agency, and Public Policy: Of Knights and Knaves, Pawns and Queens', *Economics and Philosophy*, 21(2): 291–303.

Robert Pinker (2006). 'Firm Gift Relationships to Quasi-Markets: an Odyssey Along the Policy Paths of Altruism and Egoism', *Social Policy and Administration*, 40(1): 10–25.

Julian Le Grand (2005). 'Should Citizens of a Welfare State be Transformed into "Queens"? A Response to Risse', *Economics and Philosophy*, 21(2): 305–308.

# The Great Transformation

*Rudolf Klein*

Over the past quarter century or so there has been, in Peter Hall's formulation (Hall 1993) a paradigm shift in macro-economic policy making: a movement from a Keynesian mode of policy making towards one based on monetary theory. The latter was open to a variety of interpretations and has been modified in practice. However, there was clearly a transformation in the way we think about economic policy making. Is the same true of social policy? Has there been an equivalent paradigm shift in the way we think about social policy?

A recent edited selection of Richard Titmuss's papers on the National Health Service (NHS) illustrates what might be called the conventional wisdom—or operating paradigm—of the social policy community as forged in the post-war decades (Oakley and Barker 2004). Titmuss himself was largely responsible for articulating that paradigm: an enormously revered figure during his lifetime, his disciples at the London School of Economics and Political Science (LSE) dominated social policy studies after his death in 1973 and his views still have much resonance in the social policy community today. In this book, Julian Le Grand, the Richard Titmuss Professor of Social Policy at LSE, challenges many of the ideas of his predecessor and provides an alternative way of thinking not only about the NHS but also about social policy more generally. The contrast between these two books provides an opportunity to examine the transformation in the intellectual foundations of social policy that has taken place over the past decades.

Both Titmuss and Le Grand reflect the intellectual and policy environment of their time. Just as Titmuss provided an intellectual and moral justification for the post-war Welfare State, so Le Grand provides a rationale for the new social policy model that has emerged over the last 20 years or so. And just as LSE social policy staff of the Titmuss era were in and out of Whitehall during the Labour Governments of the 1960s and 1970s, so Le Grand served as policy adviser to Tony Blair. To state the obvious, intellectual development does not take place in a vacuum: ideas reflect the policy world—the success or otherwise of policy experiments (be it the creation of the NHS in 1948 or the invention of quasi-markets in the 1980s)—as well as influencing policy. Policy and ideas fertilise each other: there is no such thing as intellectual virginity when it comes to social policy discourse.

One important difference between Titmuss and Le Grand must be noted before addressing the specifics of their arguments. This is the difference in their styles of argument, reflecting partly their personal histories and partly changes in the academic environment in the 30 plus years that separate their writings. Titmuss was a self-made academic who had no university degree and eclectically drew on a variety of disciplines in the study of social policy. His publications ranged from rigorous statistical analysis to more general, speculative essays, the latter of which make up the bulk of the book under review. But I suspect that the quality that made him such an appealing figure was that he was a moralist, a sort of latter-day prophet. That, and the fact that he could write clearly and without technical jargon, made him appealing to his readers emotionally as well intellectually. Le Grand, in contrast, is a modern academic: a card-carrying economist with a Ph.D. to prove it. He is a more disciplined writer than Titmuss, building up his arguments step by step and acknowledging the strengths and weaknesses of any case that he is making. In contrast, as we shall see, Titmuss sometimes seems to avoid the logic of his own arguments and seldom acknowledges that there might be something to be said against them. If Titmuss is the master of persuasive rhetoric, very much in the mould of Tawney and others writing at the same time, Le Grand follows the rules of the academic game: he writes clearly, but avoids arm waving gestures. Both are advocates—making a case for particular policies—but their ways of addressing the jury are very different.

Le Grand's book is an expanded and elaborated version of his influential article, 'Knights, knaves or pawns? Human behaviour and social policy' (Le Grand 1997b). His starting point was the observation that in Britain—and elsewhere—there had been a significant shift in social policy: notably the introduction of competition in the delivery in social services—as epitomised by the invention of quasi markets—and the design of social security programmes. In turn, this implied a largely implicit shift 'in the assumptions concerning motivation that underlay older models of welfare systems'. The assumption of the founders of the post-1945 model Welfare State was that those providing the services or deciding on benefits—be they doctors, teachers or council house managers—were altruistic paternalists: they were considered to be, in Le Grand's terminology, knights. In contrast, the assumption of the quasi-market and other reforms of the 1980s and 1990s was that service providers pursued their own self interest but would respond to incentives: they were considered to be (in Le Grand's phrase, borrowed from Hume) knaves. Finally, sticking to his chess analogy, Le Grand argued that recipients of services and benefits were seen as pawns—essentially passive—in the 1945 model, while later policy discourse challenged this assumption: a theme which he did not develop in his 1997 article, but which he greatly amplifies in this book (see below). These assumptions shaping policy needed to be made explicit, Le Grand argued, so that their validity and their implications could be tested.

This is precisely what Le Grand's book does, as it develops 'a theory of public service motivation'. We start with a definition: 'In our terminology, knaves can be defined as self-interested individuals who are motivated to help others only if by so doing they will serve their private interests; whereas knights are individuals who are motivated to help others for no private reward, and indeed who may undertake such activities to the detriment of their own private interests'. In the former case it cannot be assumed that, for example, a doctor's decisions about treating his or her patients is not contaminated by self-interest. In the latter case, it is assumed that the doctor's decisions will be driven exclusively by what is best for the patient. Which assumption is empirically correct? Le Grand trawls the available evidence and concludes that the picture is mixed. The point is not that all doctors, teachers and other public service providers are knaves or knights, but that there is evidence of both knightly and knavish behaviour (often in the same person). So the policy trick is how to devise systems of rewards that provide incentives to knaves to behave in a more knightly fashion without turning knights into knaves by devaluing their dedication. The evidence for informing policy is, however, thin and mixed. On the one hand, there is evidence that incentives can change, or at least promote certain kinds of, behaviour: the experience of fundholding in the NHS is a case in point. On the other hand, it also suggests that there is a 'threshold effect'; that if knights are not going to be turned into knaves, incentives have to be set at a level which suggests public recognition for their dedication without being so high as to imply that they are being bribed to do worthy things. So designing incentives requires a fine balancing act.

The strength of Le Grand's analysis lies in its recognition that self-interest is a problematic concept and is defined by context (Wildavsky 1994). Taking his arguments one step further, even altruistic, selfless behaviour can be seen as a form of self-interest if it is pursued in search of non-material rewards, whether in this world or the next (the honours system can be seen as part of the public sector reward structure, shoring up the much-invoked public service ethos, a system which has the merit of being extremely cheap). But subtle and sophisticated as the exposition of his case is, it seems to me that he does not give sufficient weight to two considerations.

The first, which reinforces Le Grand's thesis, is the overwhelming evidence from the organisational literature that service deliverers make their own rules and policies (for example, Lipsky 1980), which is why policies may be subverted or even perverted in the process of implementation. Hence the proliferation of targets, indicators and so on as governments try to control public services. The point is mentioned by Le Grand but not much elaborated, although the current interest in incentives largely reflects frustration with the shortcomings of a hierarchic, bureaucratic system of control.

The second, which complicates Le Grand's argument, is that knaves from the perspective of governments (inasmuch as they subvert policy) may be knights from the perspective of patients and other clients (inasmuch as they bend rules in the latter's favour). Again, Le Grand touches on this, but does not explore the full implications, which is that both types of motivation may have undesirable consequences. From the perspective of public policy, I am inclined to argue, knightly behaviour may often be the problem rather than the solution. And, from the perspective of users, knights may be authoritarian paternalists acting in the sure faith that they are altruists who know best. If the pursuit of self interest at the expense of the public interest is the pathology of knavery, self-righteous rectitude is the pathology of knighthood.

From the theory of public service motivation, Le Grand moves on to addressing the problem of agency: the capacity of individuals for action and choice. Should power lie with the users of services or with the professionals and others providing them? Le Grand tends to argue the normative case for consumer power—though carefully qualifying the scope of that power—by building on his analysis of public sector motivation. The case for paternalism (what Le Grand calls 'the welfarist case') rests on the assertion that professionals like doctors and teachers can, because of their expertise, do better than the users themselves. But this assumes, Le Grand argues, that professionals 'face no conflict between their own interest and those of the users'. They must be 'something close to knights or perfect altruists'. Failing that, 'there is no guarantee that professionals will use their decision-making power in the interests of users'. As indicated above, I tend to think that the same problem arises in the case of knights who may well see themselves as acting in the interests of consumers but who take it upon themselves to define what those interests are.

Le Grand's line of reasoning seems to flow from his desire to link the case for agency—the active participation of users in decisions affecting them—to his analysis of motivations. But, taking another tack, there is an even stronger normative case to be made by building on the principle of equal autonomy (Klein and Miller 1995). As classically put by Weale (1983: 42): 'This principle of autonomy asserts that all persons are entitled to respect as deliberative and purposive agents capable of formulating their own projects, and that as part of this respect there is a governmental obligation to bring into being or preserve the conditions in which this autonomy can be realized.' This formulation has the merit of linking the case for individual decision making to the general case for redistributive social policies: for what is the argument for redistributing income, if it is not to allow individuals to make the kind of autonomous decisions that society take for granted. If lack of resources is one constraint on people's autonomy, paternalist public services are another.

So my main reservation about Le Grand's conclusion—that users should be queens rather than pawns—is that it could be strengthened by widening its conceptual base. Given this conclusion, what follows for policy? Here Le Grand is conspicuously—and rightly—cautious. There is no call for unlimited choice or unfettered competition. The existence of publicly funded services— like the NHS and the school system—is taken for granted. So, in the case of the NHS, he argues for something like the existing quasi-market, plus an incentive system combining a salary element and fee-for-service payments for consultants. In the case of schools, he argues for a positively discriminating voucher, where the value of the voucher would increase in areas with a high proportion of poor families. He also throws in proposals for demogrants and (most unconvincingly, to my mind) hypothecated taxes. These are proposals that Le Grand has put forward at one time or another and there is inevitably a sense of pet ideas being recycled. In any case these policy specifics are of less interest for the purposes of this review—which is to ask whether there has been a paradigmatic change in the way we think about social policy—than the arguments leading up to them. To what extent does the new language of social policy, as articulated by Le Grand, challenge the traditional social policy paradigm as expounded by Titmuss?

Le Grand (like the present reviewer) would probably not quibble very much with Titmuss's vision of what social policy should seek to achieve—a more egalitarian, communitarian society, integrating all its citizens—though he might well demand tighter definitions of what these phrases actually mean and might even mutter something about utopian ambitions being an inadequate guide to policy making. The real difference lies in their assumptions of how to achieve these goals: the theories underlying the mechanics of policy (just as the monetarist challenge to Keynesian theories was about the mechanics of economic management). To exaggerate only a little, Titmuss saw economics as the enemy, rejecting the discipline's central assumption that the real world could be modelled on the basis of individuals pursuing their self-interest. Social policy started where economics left off: its role was to deal with the disbenefits of economic growth and to develop 'those social institutions that foster integration and discourage alienation' (quoted in Reisman 1977: 10).

The selection of Titmuss's writings in the book under review (Oakley and Barker 2004) demonstrate the range, scope and depth of his work on the organization and delivery of health care, and the humane spirit in which he writes. They range from his early work on rheumatic heart disease to an extract from his last, perhaps bestknown book on the gift of blood, as well as essays on the origins and structure of the NHS. They show his ability to identify issues which still have much resonance and relevance today: notably inequalities in health. In what follows, however, I shall concentrate on those aspects of his writings challenged by Le Grand's revisionist analysis.

Titmuss never developed a theory of public sector motivation, and it would be anachronistic to expect him to have done so. In trying to fillet out what his ideas were, there is a real problem: his failure to follow up the logic of his own insights. Despite his general thesis that the NHS owes its birth to the spirit of wartime solidarity, and should thus be seen and cherished as a symbol of social solidarity, he wrote (accurately) 'The present structure of the Health Service owes more to the opinion of doctors than to political and public opinion.' Despite his celebration of the fact that the NHS enlarged professional freedom, allowing doctors 'to serve their patients according to their medical needs', he was far from uncritical about the way in which they actually treated patients. He wrote scathingly about hospital inertia and the survival of 'primitive customs', citing a study which showed *(plus ca change)* that 'hardly any of the measures to prevent cross-infection recommended by the Medical Research Council were in operation in the 24 wards of the eight hospitals studied'. 'One of the new problems', he observed, 'is the danger that hospitals may tend increasingly to be run in the interests of those working in and for them, rather than in the interests of the patients'.

So would he have subscribed to the view that professionals might be knaves? The answer must be a firm 'no'. Having described some of the perverse (from a patient's point of view) hospital routines, Titmuss makes a crucial caveat: 'I do not want to leave an impression that hospital staffs are deliberately callous to their patients. These things are done . . . unthinkingly by people who are devoted to their calling, working unselfishly and for long hours in the interests of the sick.' So they should be seen as knights in Le Grand's terminology. The fact that this was not enough to ensure good care Titmuss attributes to a variety of factors: fragmentation of services, the absence of critical self-examination, administrative preoccupation with detail and so on. Behaviour, in short, depends on context. But how is that context to be changed in order to ensure that unselfish altruist can live up to the knightly ideal? Here Titmuss offered few clues. Some asides might suggest that he saw research as a tool for prompting reform—and this was indeed the route followed by his LSE social policy disciples—but he offered no coherent theory of the dynamics of organisational or policy change.

Was altruism the joker in the pack? Certainly Titmuss saw altruism as not only desirable in itself but as the cement of social policy. Hence his celebration of voluntary blood donation in *The Gift Relationship* (Titmuss 1970/1997) from which there is a short extract in the book. Here the problem is not so much doubt about whether voluntary giving is more efficient or effective than buying blood—although developments since the publication of his study suggest that the evidence is less clear-cut than he suggested—but about how generalisable this particular example of altruism is. As Collard (1978: 148) has commented: 'Generalising from the blood example, the relatively small band of Kantian altruists would find themselves bearing the whole cost of the welfare state'. Given that voluntary contributions cannot be expected to generate sufficient funds for building hospitals or motorways, 'The relevant gift relationship then becomes that implied in altruistic voting behaviour'. One weakness of the Titmussian social policy tradition—whose effects are still observable today—has been the assumption that tax payers are indeed altruists and that Labour Governments are to be castigated for not committing political suicide by raising taxes more in order to redistribute income. There is an interesting study waiting to be done to investigate whether blood donors are readier to pay higher taxes than the rest of the population: whether altruism in one sphere breeds or reinforces altruism in another.

When it comes to the question of agency, the participation of users in decisions affecting them, there is once again some ambiguity about Titmuss's position. On the one hand, he saw the enlargement of freedom for patients as one of the achievements of the NHS, as indeed it was in the sense that it gave many the ability to opt for medical treatment when previously they had been unable to do so. So a commitment to positive freedom, the ability to make one's own decisions, was certainly one of his values: indeed it provides (as we have seen) the foundations of the case for income redistribution. On the other hand, he was emphatic in his rejection of consumer choice in health care, producing a list of 13 factors (citing Kenneth Arrow) which distinguish medical care from other goods. Most of the 13 factors implied that the doctor knew best. While Titmuss recognized that there was 'a tendency for more people to adopt a questioning and critical attitude to medical care', and that this implied a somewhat different doctor-patient relationship than the submissive one of the past, he did not pursue the logic of his insight any further.

Titmuss's apparent rejection of choice in health care has to be put into context. It was made in the course of his battle with the Institute of Economic Affairs (IEA), which in the 1960s was the lonely flag-carrier for private markets in health care and other social services. For Titmuss this raised the spectre of American-style health care—and he devoted much energy to expounding the inadequacies of the US system. Similarly, the theme of money corrupting and contaminating other, higher motives in the provision of social services was illustrated in *The Gift Relationship* by counterpointing British and American experience. It was, in a sense, too easy: it encouraged a certain degree of chauvinistic complacency about Britain's NHS which might have been dispelled by comparing the UK with, say, Sweden or France. More important, perhaps, by using the United States case as a stick to beat the IEA and others, Titmuss left a legacy of suspicion in the social policy community towards anything which might be described (often wrongly) as the adoption of American-style ideas or policies. To use a vocabulary of competition, choice and markets was for long guaranteed to produce a knee-jerk reaction of indignation, as distinct from consideration of what these words might mean in a different context.

The knee-jerks are rarer these days, though there are still occasional twitches. Here the credit must, I think, go largely to the Conservative policies of the 1980s: an example, as argued at the beginning of this review, of the two-way traffic between policies and ideas. In effect, the experiments with quasi-markets in publicly funded services—in education as well as health care—undermined the view that introducing competition and choice could be equated with privatization and the path to the perdition of an unbridled capitalist economy (though some still confuse the two). Further, one of the weaknesses of the Titmuss social policy tradition, as I have argued, is that his prescriptions were not based on any analysis of politics and power, or of the relationship between social policy, labour markets and economic performance. It is one of the strengths of the revisionism represented by Le Grand and others that they are attempting to fill this gap. Writing a decade ago my then colleague Jane Millar and I (Klein and Millar, 1995) entitled our review of the changing world of social policy—'Searching for a New Paradigm?'. I suspect that the question mark can now be removed.

Reproduced with permission

# Should Citizens of a Welfare State be Transformed into 'Queens'?

*Mathias Risse*[1]

Julian Le Grand offers an account of public policy that arranges views along two axes: a motivational axis, along which individuals can be knights or knaves, and an agency axis, along which they can be pawns or queens. Knaves are concerned to further their self-interest, understood broadly in terms of whatever people may care about. Following Hume, Le Grand calls such characters 'knaves,' but this has no automatic connotations with illegal activities. Knights, on the other hand, are motivated to help others for no private reward, even to the detriment of their interests. Pawns, like the pieces on the chess board, are passive victims of circumstances, unable to make responsible choices. Queens do make such choices: they are empowered agents responsible for their fates.

Taken literally, these characterizations are a caricature, but they are useful to sketch political standpoints. For instance, social democrats take individuals to be largely products of circumstances and thus treat them as pawns *qua* targets of policy. At the same time, they have an optimistic view of human nature, thinking of those empowered to execute policy as knights. So they design policy in such a way that service recipients are left with rather limited choices, whereas providers (doctors, teachers, etc.) are taken to want the best for their clients. Neo-liberals take a pessimistic view of human nature, treating policy makers and providers as knaves. At the same time they believe targets of policy should be transformed into queens. Since Le Grand introduces the two distinctions independently, other combinations are possible, as well as more or less strong views on the extent to which individuals are to be transformed into pawns or queens and to be considered knaves or knights. Hobbes, for instance, can be read as taking individuals to be knaves and as arguing that in virtue of being knaves, they would found a state in which all are left to be pawns—except for one all-powerful queen, known as the Leviathan.

So: should policy makers regard public servants as knights or knaves, and should they aim to transform recipients into pawns or queens? These are the two main questions Le Grand sets out to answer. In Part I, he argues on empirical grounds that individuals are moved by a mixture of knightly and knavish

[1] Thanks to Richard Bradley and a referee for helpful comments.

motivations, and that therefore policies should be 'robust' in speaking to both knights and knaves. The success of a policy, that is, should not depend on whether those it affects or those who execute it are knights or knaves. In Part II, he argues on normative grounds that policies should be adopted that transform individuals into queens. His arguments for that claim form the philosophical core of his book. In Part III, then, he applies the responses to his two questions to a range of policy questions: he explores what his views entail for the organization of (universal state-funded) health-care and the organization of the educational sector; he argues in support of a 'demogrant' (a grant to young people for investment purposes), and proposes that a matching system of 'partnership savings' should replace mandatory retirement schemes; and finally he writes in support hypothecating ('earmarking') taxes for specific purposes, rather than raising taxes for purposes to be determined by the state independently of the tax.

Le Grand's main advice for policy makers is that measures should be taken to transform service users into queens. (Le Grand was appointed an adviser to Tony Blair in October 2003, which put him in a position to act on this advice himself.) While I will argue in due course that his arguments for this recommendation are unsatisfactory in a way that is troublesome for various bits of the book, Le Grand is right that academics often make grand claims about politics without transforming them into policy, and he must be congratulated on his effort to proceed differently. The book is highly readable and offers a wealth of thought-provoking claims and insights; studying Le Grand's ideas will be rewarding for anybody interested in public policy in a manner that takes seriously the intellectual foundations of policy advice, and this will be true even for non-British readers although most of Le Grand's discussion focuses on questions that have shaped the agenda of British domestic politics over the last 25 years. Le Grand has rendered us a great service by contributing so much to this urgently needed form of policy discourse. Still, Le Grand leaves unexplored the philosophical underpinnings of arguments that require such underpinnings, and once we do explore them, we encounter some difficulties in completing the arguments Le Grand needs to support his views. More specifically, the challenge will be for him to say more about theories that underwrite *both* the view that individuals should be citizens of a welfare state *and* the view that they should be transformed into queens in their capacity as service users. I will argue that there is some tension between these two views, and that the fact that he leaves this tension unaddressed haunts some of his discussions.

But first of all, let me dwell some more on the terminology that figures in the title of this book. Again, Le Grand is aware that his distinctions are rough, that individuals can be both knights and knaves to some extent or in some of their actions, as well as both pawns and queens with regard to different parts of their lives. Note three more points on this terminology. First, the broad notion of self-interest that is needed to make the conception of knaves interesting in the first place raises the question of whether there can be non-selfish motivation and hence a distinction between knaves and knights at all. Those who care about others find benefiting them to be in their interest, but they no more act against their own self-interest than villains who do not. But we need not worry about this issue: all that matters for Le Grand is that individuals' actions can be more or less focused on themselves, and that much is clear enough.

Second, one can ask whether individuals simply happen to be knights or knaves (or maybe both to some extent), and queens or pawns (or maybe both in some parts of their lives), or whether, instead, policy itself has an impact on these matters. Obviously, different views on the political spectrum can take different stances on these questions. As I will shortly explain in more detail, Le Grand thinks the knave-knight distinction is to some extent endogenous to policy: policy design can influence whether knavish or knightly motivations carry the day. As far as the pawn-queen distinction is concerned, Le Grand argues that policy should be designed so as to transform individuals into queens. That is, he does not take it for granted that this is what individuals are, but argues on normative grounds that it should be a goal of politics to make them into queens.

Third, note that knights come in two sorts: act-relevant and act-irrelevant knights. Act-irrelevant knights want good states of affairs to obtain. They may want that nobody in their town is hungry. Being knights, they are willing to support that goal, but if somebody beats them to it, they feel no need to do anything themselves. Act-relevant knights need to do good themselves: they derive benefits from behaving in a knightly fashion. If most knights are of the act-irrelevant sort, we will observe that private donations to charity decrease as welfare programs improve. Such knights, after all, only need to know that the problems are solved while gaining no particular benefit from having done it themselves. Yet if most knights are of the act-relevant sort, we will not observe such behavior: such knights still feel the need to do good deeds. According to Le Grand, empirical studies support the view that knightly behavior exists, especially among public servants (though it interacts in complex ways with knavish behavior); but also that such studies suggest that much knightly behavior is act-relevant. In fact, Le Grand thinks most people are act-relevant knights. Nevertheless, the presence of knaves makes it unwise to rely on such behaviour for policy design.

The background to Le Grand's discussion is that in the 1980/90s governments such as the British (his main subject), while retaining control of finance, stopped providing a range of welfare services. Provision became competitive, with independent providers competing in markets or quasi-markets. There is a *quasi-market*, say, in the educational sector if the state finances schools and education, but provides vouchers for students or parents to give to schools of their choice. In quasi-markets the state finances the services, and often the competitors for service are publicly owned or non-profit organizations. Before Margaret Thatcher became Prime Minister in 1979, providers were assumed to be knights while recipients were assumed to be pawns. After Thatcher, providers were assumed to be knaves and recipients were supposed to be transformed into queens; services (e.g., education, health care) were reorganized accordingly. But quasi-markets were the most Thatcher could do: privatization was politically undoable in Britain. Blair's Labour government, in power since 1997, has kept most of the changes—changes reflected also in the policies adopted by other countries over the last two decades in response to fiscal crises and disenchantment with large bureaucracies.

Le Grand offers a wealth of empirical material on motivation and on how different views on agency work out when built into policies. For instance, many economists and policy makers assume that behavior is exogenous: individuals display knightly or knavish behavior to this extent or that, and policy must respond to it. As opposed to that, and as I already mentioned above, Le Grand argues that behavior is endogenous: the extent to which individuals act knightly or knavishly is influenced by policies. He claims that

[i]n cases of knightly activity that involve large sacrifices, people do value some form of payment both as a form of recognition and as partial compensation for the costs involved. However, that payment should not be so great as to compensate fully for the sacrifice, for if it did there would be no satisfaction from making the sacrifice in the first place. In fact, if people were paid an amount that fully compensated them—or more than fully compensated them—the effect might be perverse, reducing rather the increasing the supply of the activity concerned.

People are not attracted to making deals by receiving compensation for sacrifices: they like to feel public-spirited, and take that sentiment to be a large part of their reward. Modest payments for activities (where previously there were none) may leave the supply constant or increase it. As payments increase, the supply may drop, because now the sacrifice is viewed as a commodity that neither comes with a feeling of public-spiritedness nor is worth it for the payment offered. As payments increase further, the supply gradually increases again because the activities now come to be seen as commodities demanded at a good price, no longer as sacrifices for recognition or for the sake of feeling public-spirited. No matter what delivery model is used (command and control, quasi-markets, etc.), it influences how individuals behave.

Let me now begin the critical part of my discussion. I will raise some problems that focus on chapters 5 and 6 of Le Grand's book, those chapters that argue that individuals should be transformed into queens. Le Grand distinguishes three approaches to the question of whether users should be transformed into pawns or queens: the liberal approach, the welfarist approach, and the communitarian approach. Liberals answer that individuals should be turned into pawns or queens depending on which more increases their liberty; welfarists think the answer turns on which best increases individual well-being, and communitarians make it turn on which stance has a better impact on society. Liberals find little in support of transforming individuals into pawns, says Le Grand; at most they may be willing to transform individuals into pawns in some parts of their lives for the sake of overall greater empowerment. For welfarists there is a presumption for empowering individuals. Following John Stuart Mill's discussion in *On Liberty*, Le Grand submits that individuals are the best judges of their own welfare. Still, there are exceptions: individuals may decide to defer to experts; have insufficient information; or display 'individual failure' (may be incompetent to complete mental tasks, display weakness of will, be too emotional, or lack experience). Communitarians hold welfarist views for or against empowering individuals, but at stake is communal, not individual welfare. Yet Le Grand thinks no welfarist reason against empowering individuals, seen at the communal level, speaks against transforming individuals as queens.

After discussing these views, Le Grand concludes that 'it does seem as though there is a convincing case for the user to have a measure of power, possibly considerable, over public service provision' (p 81). He acknowledges restrictions on this argument, to 'avoid the overuse or over-provision of the service concerned, or the uses of the service in such a way that damages either the user himself or herself or the wider society' (p 84). He does, however, assume a very strong presumption for transforming users into queens. Again, the essential recommendation of his book is for policy makers to act on this advice. Still (and this is my main point), his case for transforming users into queens is much weaker than Le Grand asserts, and I will argue this now by going through his three argumentative strategies for supporting the claim that they should be so transformed. Consider first the liberal view. Note that Le Grand leaves unquestioned basic constraints on the British context. Universal health care or the responsibility of the state to provide for education is not questioned: the welfare state is assumed. Distinguish now libertarians and liberal egalitarians. Libertarians, such as Robert Nozick, support a minimal (decidedly non-welfare) state; liberal egalitarians, such as John Rawls, support a state that suitably combines equality and liberty and thus register strong affinities with the welfare state, or at any rate with a state that includes strongly redistributive measures.[2]

---

[2] A referee expressed scepticism about my claim that the Rawlsisan view shows affinities with the welfare state, since both in the 1999 second edition of the *Theory of Justice* (Cambridge: Harvard University Press), and in his 2001 *Justice as Fairness: A Restatement* (edited by Erin Kelly, Cambridge: Harvard University Press) Rawls seems to reject the welfare state. Indeed, in section 41 of the *Restatement* Rawls does reject welfare-state capitalism, and does so in favor of a property-owning democracy or a liberal socialism. For both it is true that they 'set up a constitutional framework for democratic politics, guarantee the basic liberties with the fair value of the political liberties and fair equality of opportunity, and regulate economic

Le Grand's argument does not speak to libertarians: rejecting the welfare state, they part from him long before he calls on them to cheer for transforming service users into queens. Nor does his argument entice liberal egalitarians. While they find a welfare state plausible (or at any rate a state that shares strongly redistributive policies with a welfare state), they do so because they value equality, which in turn they do (if they are of the Rawlsian kind) because they believe coercive institutions must be justifiable to everybody, an endeavor that can succeed only if society is a fair system of cooperation among free and equal citizens. Liberal egalitarians support redistribution required for universal health care and state funded education. They think of individual fates as tied together, and of benefits of social cooperation as to be shared out among participants. Crucially, they therefore take individuals (and argue that those would want to be seen) as pawns in some aspects: individuals are not empowered to opt out of the redistributive system, and hence the extent to which they are to be transformed into queens must be limited. Individuals are indeed to be empowered, but only within the confines of a redistributive system from which to withdraw is not at their discretion. Rawls himself is explicit that his view of justice

includes what we may call a *social division of responsibility*: society, the citizens as a collective body, accepts the responsibility for maintaining the equal basic liberties and fair equality of opportunity, and for providing a fair share of the other primary goods for everyone within this framework, while citizens (as individuals) and associations accept the responsibility for revising and adjusting their ends and aspirations in view of the all-purpose means they can expect, given their present and foreseeable situation.[3]

Despite the Rawlsian jargon in this passage the connection to Le Grand should be clear: as much as they (being liberals) champion responsible agency, liberal egalitarians take individuals as pawns in some ways and as queens in others; in fact, it is *so that all can be queens to some extent that all must be pawns to some extent too*. To push this point a bit more, in a way that is not meant to be unfair to Le Grand but to highlight what is at issue here: to suggest that liberal egalitarians, in virtue of their basic political stances, must be committed to the desire to transform service users into queens is a bit like suggesting that

and social inequalities by a principle of mutuality, if not by the difference principle' (p 138). However, both in the *Restatement* and the preface to the 1999 edition of *Theory* Rawls rejects a welfare state only in the sense of rejecting a state that is merely concerned with making sure that individuals do not fall below a basic income level while ignoring further-reaching distributional issues. Rawls, that is, rejects the welfare state because it does not go far enough by way of controlling inequalities. There is in particular no sense in which Rawls rejects the welfare state because he wants individuals to be Le Grandian queens. At any rate, all that matters to my discussion is that a liberal-egalitarian view of the Rawlsian sort favors strongly redistributive measures.

[3] This quote is from Rawls, 'Social Unity and Primary Goods,' reprinted in Samuel Freeman (ed.), *Collected Papers*, Cambridge: Harvard University Press, p 371.

Rawls in particular would have to be committed to solving all distributional problems within society by appeal to the difference principle only because socio-economic inequalities that remain after the principle of liberty and the principle of fair equality of opportunity have been implemented are to be governed by the difference principle.

So liberal egalitarians would not automatically endorse Le Grand's anti-pawn stance and thus not without qualification endorse his goal of transforming individuals into queens. Therefore Le Grand's 'liberals' can be neither Nozickian libertarians nor Rawlsian liberal egalitarians. Note that nothing in this argument turns on tying anything to Nozick or Rawls. The central issue is whether we take liberals to endorse views that support the kind of redistributive measure needed for a welfare state. If so, they will not support Le Grand's strong stance in favor of transforming service users into queens. If not, Le Grand's argument entirely ignores them. For neither libertarians nor liberal egalitarians is it a matter of their political identity to want to have service users transformed into queens.

The crucial point is that questions about user empowerment arise at a conceptually rather late stage of reflecting about how a state should be organized, a stage at which views about scope and limits of state responsibility must already be in place. Le Grand, however, gives such views no consideration. Therefore, too much political philosophy is ignored for him to be in a position to deliver satisfactory arguments in support of his views. Since liberal egalitarians (like all those endorsing a welfare state, or at any rate strongly redistributive systems) must regard individuals as pawns in some aspects, they share no presumption to regard individuals *qua* service users as queens. Liberal egalitarian would agree that, since individuals are pawns for the sake of funding welfare services, the design, say, of health care institutions must be *justifiable* to all. Such justifiability entails that resources should be used efficiently (being everybody's resources); that users be treated respectfully and their views consulted in a manner that is not merely superficial (users both fund and are affected by services). Yet to the question of whether users should actually be transformed into queens liberal egalitarians would take a pragmatic, or at any rate context-dependent attitude: if, for instance, regarding users as queens means that health care resources are used most efficiently, that stance will be more easily justifiable than considering them pawns. I suppose Le Grand would in fact want to argue that such efficiency speaks in favour of transforming users into queens: but if so, then what really drives his argument in support of such a transformation is *efficiency*, not the independent plausibility of the aim to make users queens. By the same token, if it is more efficient to administer such services by transforming individuals *qua service users* into pawns, liberal egalitarians should have no qualms endorsing that view (within the constraints mentioned above).

Next I discuss Le Grand's welfarist and communitarian approach. The welfarist approach should strike Le Grand as unattractive per se. Again, he accepts that a welfare state exists. Therefore, services must be administered in a manner justifiable to all. Recall that the welfarist strategy inquires about what is best for each individual. Yet given that Le Grand already assumes a shared commitment to a welfare state, he must think of individuals as co-financers of the welfare state. Therefore it is not open to him any longer to argue for the claim that service users should be transformed into queens simply by asking how each individual should want public resources to be applied to herself—that is, without any consideration for others, as if she were alone, rather than in the presence of others who are co-financers of the welfare state. Instead, he would have to ask how each individual should want such resources to be applied *given* that she is only one among many such co-financers a good number of whom will have similar medical needs. To put the point differently: the welfarist strategy focuses on one individual at a time, and asks how this person would want public funds to be applied to her situation. Whatever the upshot of this person-by-person question is, it is the answer to the wrong question. The right question is: how should *jointly* provided resources be distributed among people with certain medical needs, *given* that others will have similar needs? Yet the welfarist strategy does not speak to *that* question at all, and thus cannot justify Le Grand's claim that users should be transformed into queens. Crucially, even if it is best for *any* *given* person if *she* were transformed into a queen *qua* service user, that does not mean it would be best for *everybody* if policies were adopted with the goal of transforming *everybody* into queens. Perhaps, of course, transforming individuals into queens leads to the most efficient distribution of resources. Yet such a result, again, would show that individuals should be treated as queens because that makes for the most efficient distribution of resources; but it would not show that individuals should be treated as queens because there is a justificatory strategy (the welfarist one) rendering it compelling or plausible to treat individuals as queens *independently* of efficiency considerations.

As far as the communitarian approach is concerned, consider first that Le Grand assumes that the 'impact on the wider society' (p 74) must be assessed along welfarist (utilitarian) lines. It makes a philosopher's heart bleed that a thinker at the intersection of academia and policy is unaware that the last 30 years of philosophical reflection on politics have done much to explore non-welfarist approaches to assessing this impact (an effort to which British philosophers have contributed considerably). But setting this aside, Le Grand's reasoning itself is also problematic. He argues that, even if we consider the impact of, say, health care decisions on society as a whole along utilitarian lines, it is unclear that doctors are better positioned to pass verdicts than patients:

In health care, the doctor has to have knowledge of thousands of potential ailments, whereas the patient has to know only about those potentially or actually affecting himself or herself. Medical handbooks can aid self-diagnosis; and, once their illness is diagnosed, especially in these days of the Internet, patients can—and indeed often do—'train' themselves in their own disease. Similarly with respect to teaching: teachers have to be able to assess the educational requirements of thousands of pupils, whereas parents have only to do so for their own offspring, about whom they have considerable knowledge. (p 79)

This is unsatisfactory. Sometimes a patient may know a condition better than a doctor. But such reasoning fails more often than it succeeds. Diagnoses often require machinery and more expertise than found on the Internet. This applies even more to treatment than to diagnosis. Moreover, when it comes to resource distribution, each patient has an interest in her health and is thus a poor judge of how to distribute resources also needed by others. The reason why patients should be consulted about distributive questions, and why decisions must be justifiable to them, is also the reason why they should not actually *make* such decisions.

What Le Grand's reasoning supports is the need for designing resource distribution mechanisms that speak to both knaves and knights among providers, a conclusion he reaches earlier in his book; but it does not show that users should be queens—not if the existence of a welfare state is assumed, which again presupposes that individuals are to some extent pawns to each of whom, in turn, use of jointly contributed resources must be justifiable. Similar points apply to the other arguments in Le Grand's discussion of the communitarian approach: in each case he seeks to show that, even as far as general welfare is concerned, affected individuals are better judges of decisions for their cases than the professionals. Each time this remains implausible as long as there are strategies speaking both to knaves and knights among providers so that their better judgment is not undermined by knavish motivations. Le Grand's plea for such strategies makes it hard for him to support the communitarian approach to the queen/pawn issue. Expertise, after all, is worth a lot once providers' knavish motivations are neutralized.

The upshot is that Le Grand's case for treating users as queens is weaker than he thinks. He does qualify the argument, acknowledging limits to the extent users should be queens. But he also takes his arguments to deliver a presumption in favor of his view. Yet his case is a lot weaker than even that. The welfarist and communitarian approaches fail completely, and the liberal approach, while not speaking against regarding users as queens, certainly delivers no strong presumption in favor of doing so. By way of concluding, let me explore implications of this result for other parts of the book. But before doing so, I would like to draw attention to one other way of putting the point that my distinction between the libertarian and the liberal-egalitarian stance on Le Grand's reasoning was meant to make, this time cast in terms of differences in the political cultures in the United States and Western European countries. The political culture in the US is much more shaped by libertarian intuitions than by liberal-egalitarian sentiments, and vice versa for Western Europe. A reader thinking from an American point of view about what political positions most urgently require justification (because of their degree of deviation from what is considered a default in society) will find it peculiar that Le Grand pushes so strongly for transforming users into queens and *still* seems to see no reason to question the welfare state as such. As opposed to that, a reader thinking about politics from a Western European standpoint (including a British one) will find it peculiar that Le Grand takes the welfare state and its redistributive system for granted and *still* so strongly champions the view that service users should be transformed into queens. It is hard to have it both ways.

On to the conclusion, then. Following the chapter discussing the three strategies in support of the claim that users be transformed into queens, Chapter 6 asks: If there is a presumption in favor of taking individuals as queens, why can the state force individuals to save for old age or to buy long-term care insurance? Le Grand's answer draws on Derek Parfit's stance on personal identity. In a nutshell, the connection between younger individuals and their older selves is so tenuous that it is rational for the former to disregard the needs of their future selves. This justifies state interference on behalf of future selves. But there are three difficulties with the solution and this way of asking the question in the first place.

First, given that we grant for the moment that the question arises in the manner in which Le Grand asks it, his answer is unsatisfactory. Consider the following dilemma. Either it is rational for younger selves to disregard their future selves, or it is not. If it is, then it is hard to see why the state should have any concern for older selves. For the only plausible reason why the state would worry about them in ways in which it does not about people living elsewhere or *their* future selves is that there is a strong connection between those future selves and somebody presently living in the state (their younger selves being the only plausible candidates). Yet by assumption, that connection is so weak as to not prompt such concern. So in this case, no argument in support of forcing people to save for old age is forthcoming. If, on the other hand, it is not rational for individuals to neglect their future selves, then those who think individuals should be transformed into queens should find it implausible that the state would interfere on behalf of future selves. For such interference would mean to force individuals who are supposed to be transformed into queens to save for old age although those queens themselves have rational grounds for doing so (in virtue of having no rational grounds to neglect their future selves). Exerting such force then would be entirely unnecessary paternalism. Thus any laws to such an effect would have to strike those as absurd who, like Le Grand, support the view that individuals should be transformed into queens. So once again, no argument in favor of forcing individuals to save for old age is forthcoming.

Second, the problem is ill-posed given that Le Grand assumes at this stage of his argument that users should be transformed into queens. If we must ask why the state can intervene to benefit the queens themselves, we must also ask why those queens can in turn be forced to support the welfare state at all. Once we do so, as I argue above, Le Grand's reasoning on behalf of his thesis unravels. Third, neither this question about justifiability of forcing individuals to save for old age nor these problems would arise if Le Grand had not overstated his case on behalf of treating users as queens. Since no view supporting the welfare state endorses this stance at the strength at which Le Grand defends it, there is not as much of a problem about forcing individuals to save for old age as he thinks there is. For instance, on the liberal egalitarian view, again, individuals must be taken to be pawns to some extent anyway so that all can be queens to some extent as well. Mandatory retirement savings are not terribly problematic on such an account. So the discussion of Chapter 6 is an artifact of Le Grand's overstatement of his case: the problem it raises would not really arise without this overstatement.

Let us consider, finally, implications of my argument for Le Grand's policy recommendations. The two case studies most explicitly present throughout the book are health care and education. But in both cases in Le Grand's proposals (to a large extent implemented in Britain) the thrust of the argument is efficiency: the question is in each case how to optimize delivery of a service. Le Grand's terminology plays a role only because it helps pinpoint non-optimal delivery: the argument itself can be stated without reference to knights, knaves, queens, or pawns. This is unsurprising, given what I have argued before. For liberal egalitarians, in particular, the philosophically interesting battles are won once it is established that the state has a duty to finance equal and universal basic education in the first place. Within limits, how to organize it is plausibly left to efficiency considerations. That is, the political identity of liberal egalitarians is at stake at the conceptually earlier stage of arguing about the provision of funding for universal basic education, not at the later stage of organizing the service delivery.

The goal of transforming users into queens really comes into its own in Le Grand's three remaining proposals: to give demogrants to young adults (an amount of money to invest); to replace mandatory retirement schemes with a matching-system of partnership savings; and to hypothecate ('earmark') taxes for certain purposes. I think demogrants are a fine idea, but I am not attracted to them because they transform individuals into queens. However, in societies in which life chances are increasingly shaped by inheritance this is arguably a good redistributive measure, where such redistribution is appropriate because benefits of social cooperation exist only because most individuals do indeed cooperate. I have no view on hypothecation and partnership-savings: but it should come as no surprise now that I do not find myself persuaded of them only because they help transform users into queens, which is what Le Grand considers their greatest virtue. Again, anybody who thinks a welfare state is justified (as I do) should feel less attracted to transforming users into queens than Le Grand does. Theories requiring everybody to be pawns in some aspects cannot also push for service users to be regarded as queens as much as he does.

Reproduced with permission

# From Gift Relationships to Quasi-markets—an Odyssey Along the Policy Paths of Altruism and Egoism

*Robert Pinker*

## INTRODUCTION

Way back in the 1950s and 1960s the discipline of social policy and adminis-tration was dominated by a rather complacent collectivist consensus about the best way of running a welfare state. Reading Julian Le Grand's Motivation, Agency and Public Policy reminded me how much more challenging and interesting the subject has become since then. The intellectual transformation started nearly forty years ago. The publication of Michael Cooper's and A J Culyer's *The Price of Blood* in 1968 and Richard Titmuss's *The Gift Relationship* in 1970 added a new dimension of ideological conflict to the debate about the salient points of reference, values, ends and means of social policy. The questions that Richard Titmuss posed in The Gift Relationship are still discussed in current debates about the respective merits of unitary and pluralist models of welfare, the egoistic and altruistic motives that underpin them and the rights and responsibilities, intrinsic to the status of citizenship.

In this essay I will review the ways in which the content and focus of these debates have changed over the past forty years, taking Titmuss's *The Gift Relationship*, my own contributions in *Social Theory and Social Policy* (1971) and *The Idea of Welfare* (1979) and Julian Le Grand's *Motivation, Agency and Public Policy* (2003) as the temporal and salient points of reference.[1]

## RE-APPRAISING THE GIFT RELATIONSHIP

In *The Price of Blood*, Cooper and Culyer reviewed the arguments for and against paying blood donors and developing a role for competitive markets in the sale and purchase of blood products. They concluded that there was a positive case to be made and that it should be tested further, by setting up

[1] A slightly longer version of this article first appeared in Social Policy and Administration, Volume 40, February 2006, No 1, Blackwell Publishing Ltd, Oxford, UK.

an experimental market-based scheme for a trial period. Their monograph was edited by Arthur Seldon and it appeared under the imprint of the Institute of Economic Affairs.

*The Price of Blood* has long been out of print but its publication was swiftly followed by a rejoinder from the doyen of British social policy and one of the principal architects of its postwar welfare state, Richard Titmuss. This was *The Gift Relationship*, which subsequently became an established classic in the literature of social policy. It gave rise to a debate which, in its intensity, had as much to do with the drawing of blood as with its donation by members of the general public. The subject of the book is the role of altruism in modern society, taking the example of voluntary blood donorship as one of the ultimate tests of where the 'social' begins and the 'economic' ends in order to demonstrate the potential scope for 'providing and extending opportunities for altruism in opposition to the possessive egoism of the market place' (Titmuss 1970/1997: 59). It is also a passionate indictment of the corrupting influence of competitive markets across the whole field of social policy.

The empirical sections of *The Gift Relationship* consist of a detailed and illuminating survey of blood transfusion services and donors in England and Wales, the USSR, the USA, South Africa, Japan and other countries. From this data, Titmuss constructs an eight-point typology of blood donors, in which he explores the causal relationships between their personal motivations to give and the dominant political and moral values of the societies in which they live.

On the basis of this comparative study, he concludes that blood supply systems based on an altruistic ethic of voluntary donorship are administratively more efficient, clinically safer and morally superior to those based on the egoistic values of competitive markets. From this conclusion, he proceeds to a sweeping moral indictment of all forms of private sector service provision. Market forces coerce the poor, corrupt the rich and exacerbate class conflict. By contrast, collectively provided social services foster the values of altruism, social integration and fellowship.

There are a number of reasons why I found Titmuss's analysis of the moral qualities that underpin exchange relationships deeply unconvincing. In the first instance, as I wrote at the time, he uses the terms 'altruism' and 'egoism' in such as a way as to describe a polarity of antipathetic sentiments and motives which, in the real world, are more likely to be interactive and conditional. In their extreme forms, altruism and egoism are marginal phenomena.

As I suggested in *The Idea of Welfare*, 'for the egoist social life is meaningless, and for the altruist it is impossible. The egoist could be likened to a black hole in the social universe, devouring everything which comes within its range, while the altruist may be compared to a brightly burning star, ineffectually striving to illuminate and warm a dark and limitless universe' (1979: 10).

As for the welfare claims of Titmuss's 'universal stranger', I can think of no reason why we should treat them as being self-evidently more morally deserving of our attention than those of our closest relatives and friends.

There is no master principle by which the claims of one social group may be measured against the claims of others, once we abandon the crude utilitarian principle of seeking the greatest good for the greatest number. This is not to deny that the claims of Titmuss's universal stranger merit our consideration but only to point out that they are a part of a highly complex network of claims and obligations.

Even if we were to make unconditional altruism the crowning glory of our moral sentiments, it would still be as well to remember that crowns are reserved for special occasions, and that most good deeds are done in the fustian of a more homespun philosophy. Titmuss invests his concepts of the 'unnamed' stranger, the 'universal' stranger and 'stranger' relationships with immense moral significance. Giving to strangers and, in particular, the 'universal' stranger is his ultimate touchstone of altruism and the good society. It is as if the virtue intrinsic to the act of giving grows exponentially as the recipients become more anonymous, more scattered and more distant from the giver. Yet it remains the case that none of the donors interviewed in his survey were 'purely altruistic' in their actions because they were well aware that they might also, at some time, need a blood transfusion and, therefore, stood to benefit from the altruism of future unknown strangers.

Secondly, the example of blood donorship fails to bring out the full complexity of the phenomenon of altruism. The fact that blood is a gift which costs the donor nothing is more important than the fact that giving blood can be profitable. A more searching test of the scope and limits of altruism would be the giving of bodily organs, the loss of which will place the donor's life or health in jeopardy. Most adults would unhesitatingly donate a kidney to a needful spouse or child. Nevertheless, such prospective donors would have to consider very carefully the extent to which they are morally justified in placing at risk the future welfare and security of their own families in order to save the life of a total stranger. Blood donorship poses no such dilemma and it is, therefore, by no means self-evident that other kinds of altruistic acts on behalf of strangers are morally superior to altruistic acts on behalf of one's immediate kin.

Thirdly, Titmuss's concepts of altruism and egoism so elevate the institutions of the social market and debase those of the economic market as to give the impression that the main effects of competition and entrepreneurial activity have been the infliction on humanity of diseconomies, diswelfares, social disintegration and alienation. Much of Titmuss's published work can be read as a continuous indictment of the values of private enterprise and the profit motive. It is, therefore, easier for us to form an impression of the kind of economic system which he would have eschewed than the one he would have preferred.

We are, however, left in ignorance about the system of values and means by which wealth is to be created and goods and services are to be produced.

Competitive markets are demonstrably more effective in the continuous creation of wealth than any other known system of economic organization. Globalization may well have inflicted 'diseconomies' on the poorest nations of the Third World but these failures are open to remedy. It remains the case that without the wealth creating capability of competitive markets, the whole structure of international aid, both statutory and voluntary, would swiftly collapse and the needs of countless 'universal strangers' would go unmet (Pinker, 1977, vii–xvi).

Fourthly, we come to the philosophical implications of Titmuss's views on the respective roles of freedom and compulsion in public policy making. He categorically rejected Cooper and Culyer's modest proposal that, for a limited trial period, the voluntary system of blood donorship should be supplemented by a fee-paid market scheme so that their respective performances could be evaluated. Titmuss dismissed this proposal because its authors were doing nothing less than 'making an economic case *against* a monopoly of altruism in blood and other human tissues. They wish to set people free from the conscience of obligation' (1970/1997: 220).

It is difficult to understand why a social scientist would reject outright a proposal for a limited control study of this kind on moral grounds. Part of the explanation lies in Titmuss's highly determinist account of the inter-relationships between types of society, human nature and the respective opportunities for altruism and egoism that these societies provide. Titmuss was convinced that the statutory social services, in general, and the voluntary giving of blood, in particular, fostered social integration and encouraged the growth of altruism more effectively than any other system of welfare provision. Having compared the different blood transfusion services of six very different countries, he concluded that a free service was not only morally superior but administratively and economically more efficient than its private market alternatives. The quality of freely given blood was also safer because it was less likely to carry dangerous infective diseases. The offer of payment attracted donors who tended to be very poor and, therefore, more prone to such diseases. (With the benefit of hindsight, of course, we now know that statutory services relying exclusively on voluntary donors can also inadvertently collect and provide contaminated blood to patients with tragic consequences for them.)

Titmuss, however, was adamantly opposed to the suggestion that patients, as consumers, should have any choice in the matter. In the interests of freedom, altruism and public safety, he thought that the buying and selling of blood should be prohibited by law and that the resolution of this matter 'has to be a policy decision; in other words it is a moral and political decision for society as a whole' (1970/1997: 310). He justifies this conclusion on the grounds that, 'In a positive sense . . . policy and processes should enable men to be free to choose to give to unnamed strangers. They should not be coerced or constrained by the market. In the interests of the freedom of all men they should not, however, be free to sell their blood or decide on the specific destination of the gift' (1970/1997: 310).

It would, therefore, seem that Titmuss wanted to prohibit people from making the 'wrong' choices so that they could be 'free' to make the right choices. The alternative was to leave them at the mercy of the 'atomistic private market' which 'freed' men from 'any sense of obligation to or for other men regardless of the consequences to others . . .' (1970/1997: 307). People's opportunities for altruism are ultimately determined by the type of society in which they live. They become more altruistic only in societies where needs are met primarily by reference to the collectivist values of the social market. They inevitably become more egoistic in societies where the individualist values of the economic market prevail.

Rather than leaving people to make their own decisions as to where the path of duty lies, Titmuss wanted to compel them to be moral. He does not seem to recognise that acts of duty are only moral acts if they are voluntarily undertaken. Throughout *The Gift Relationship* he frequently refers to the problem of alienation in capitalist societies. Marx's remedy for this state of mind was the abolition of private property, social classes and the division of labour. Titmuss's remedy appears to be the creation of a unitary welfare state and a drastic reduction in the range of consumer choice in the use of social services. All these considerations led me to the conclusion that the philosophy of *The Gift Relationship* is based on a double oxymoron— namely, that, in policy terms, we are 'free' to choose between compulsory altruism in the social market and compulsory egoism in the economic market.

## REAPPRAISING SOCIAL THEORY AND SOCIAL POLICY AND THE IDEA OF WELFARE

In 1973, shortly after Titmuss's death, T H Marshall published 'An Appreciation' of his achievements in the British Journal of Sociology. He generously acknowledges Titmuss's masterly skills as an assembler and classifier of factual data and his idealistic commitment to social reform. He also suggests that whenever he stepped outside 'the confines of his official subject of social administration into regions where sociologists fear to tread . . . a gap appeared between his factual evidence and the conclusions he helped to derive from them, a gap which could not be effectively bridged without the help of a more elaborate conceptual and theoretical apparatus than he had needed hitherto' (1973: 138–139). On the theory underpinning *The Gift Relationship*, Marshall concludes that 'the facts illuminated an arresting concept, that of the free, altruistic gift to the stranger . . . But they were too specialized and a-typical to provide a basis for generalizations about the possible role of altruism as a cohesive force in a whole society. For this one must re-examine the concept of altruism' (1973: 139).

This was exactly what I set out to do in the 1970s when I wrote *Social Theory and Social Policy* (1971) and *The Idea of Welfare* (1979). It was largely thanks to the encouragement of Marshall that I did so. In *Social Theory and Social Policy*, I set out a model of social welfare as a system of exchange relationships between providers and recipients of social services. Shortly after the book appeared, Marshall advised me to develop my model of exchange relationships in a second book, giving greater attention to the value systems that underpinned them. The moral dynamics of welfare institutions and the respective roles of egoism and altruism became the two main themes of enquiry that I explored in *The Idea of Welfare*.

At the time when I wrote *Social Theory and Social Policy*, I was becoming increasingly disenchanted with Titmuss's unitary model of social welfare or, to use his own terminology, 'the institutional Redistributive model of Social Policy'. In this model, Titmuss conceptualised social welfare 'as a major integrated institution in society, providing universalist services outside the market on the principle of need' (Titmuss 1974: 31). It is important to note that concepts like 'unitary' and 'pluralist' models of welfare were not generally used by social administrators in the 1970s. In terms of his ideology and interests, however, Titmuss was undoubtedly a unitarist. He wrote very little about the voluntary sector and it is scarcely mentioned in his benchmark essay on 'The Social Division of Welfare'. The occupational and fiscal welfare sectors are, however, subjected to much closer scrutiny but they are conceptualised in largely negative terms—as institutional obstacles to the creation of a more unified and egalitarian welfare state (Titmuss 1958: 34–55).

In *Social Theory and Social Policy*, I paid particular attention to the impact of universalist and selectivist modes of social service on the status of citizenship and the implications for that status of being dependent on different kinds of service provision. On reflection, I think that I ought to have given more prominence to the two main forms of social service organization—unitarism and pluralism—in developing my model of social welfare. If I were to undertake a revision of *Social Theory and Social Policy*, I would reformulate my thesis on the following pluralist lines in order to make their intellectual continuities more explicit.

The problem with the unitary model of social welfare is that it cannot respond with sufficient sensitivity to the diversity of human aspirations and needs and this will be the case, irrespective of whether the sole providers of services are statutory, voluntary or private sector agencies. Most significantly, the risks of total dependency are maximised when there is only one provider of social services and support.

By contrast, a pluralist system of welfare is less likely to generate stigma and undermine the authenticity of citizenship than a unitary system—irrespective of the relationship that holds between universality and selectivity. Not all universalist services enhance the status of citizenship. Not all selectivist services debase it. Too much universality can leave the residual means tested minority profoundly stigmatised. Too much selectivity can residualise the welfare state altogether. The ideal compromise is a pluralist model in which the state is both a direct provider and purchaser of non-statutory social services and selectivity operates within a broadly universalist structure. At times, dependency is an inescapable fact of life but partial dependency is preferable to total dependency. For most people complete independence is an unattainable and unattractive condition. The same may be said of complete dependency.

Good social policies ought, therefore, to be designed to complement and reinforce the qualities of interdependence and reciprocity. These are the ideals by which most people try to order their social relationships. Welfare pluralism optimises opportunities for interdependence and reduces the risks of total dependency. The greatest risks of stigma arise when the dependency is total and only one set of welfare agencies—public or private, formal or informal— has a monopoly or near monopoly of service provision. In a pluralist mixed economy of welfare there is a diversity of service providers which greatly reduces the risk of total dependency and, of course, the risk of total system failure.

Given the diversity of human values and aspirations it is, therefore, essential that the component rights and duties that make up the concept of citizenship are grounded in a similar diversity of social institutions and personal experiences and sentiments. Unitary models of welfare, whether they are ideologically driven by individualist market values or collectivist welfare values, ignore this diversity, increase the risks of total dependency and thereby impoverish the status of citizenship.

The theoretical models outlined in The Idea of Welfare were developed within this pluralist tradition of social policy analysis. It was my interest in the relationship between modes of service delivery, dependence and the status of citizenship that led me on to explore the moral dynamics of welfare institutions and, more specifically, the respective roles of egoism and altruism in shaping our notions of entitlement and obligation. All of our normative models of welfare ends and means rest on certain assumptions about the moral qualities of human nature. On the basis of the relevant empirical evidence, I rejected those models which drew sharp distinctions between our propensities for egoism and altruism. I argued that if people were predominantly altruistic, compulsory forms of social services would not be necessary. Conversely, if people were exclusively self-regarding, such compulsion would be impossible.

Egoism is often equated with self-interest but it is also associated with the positive qualities of self-help and a willingness to accept restraints on our more selfish dispositions and show consideration for other people. Familial altruism is the first and most natural way in which we express our concern for other people's welfare.

Familial altruism may be a limited form of altruism, restricted to those we know and love, but it is the mainspring from which all our other moral concerns for other people's welfare flow. As we mature and become citizens of a wider community, our notions of obligation and entitlement also grow more extensive and take on the formal character of social rights and duties. As I extended my institutional field of enquiry in *The Idea of Welfare*, I subsumed the concept of familial altruism under the broader category of conditional altruism (1979: 39).

Once again, this extension in the range of our awareness is driven by a combination of egoistic and altruistic motives. We learn from personal experience that familial altruism alone cannot guarantee our welfare in an uncertain world. We learn that collective forms of social provision—statutory and voluntary—are sensible ways of pooling risks and helping each other in times of need. The compassion we feel for those less fortunate than ourselves is also an important factor but, as I suggested in *Social Theory and Social Policy*, the welfare institutions of a society can best be understood in terms of 'an unstable compromise between compassion and indifference, between altruism and self-interest' (1971: 211).

The continuities of familial altruism both complement and conflict with the formal redistributive ends of statutory social policies. Through acts of voluntary saving, we give substance to the hope of leaving wealth to those we know and love. Through the processes of redistributive taxation, we make provision for the welfare of total strangers who lack the means to help themselves. All governments have to live with the difficult task of striking the right balance between the conflicting claims of familial and collective altruism.

Although conflicts of interest frequently arise between these institutional elements, they are, in the last analysis, dependent upon each other. The welfare of many individuals are families would be jeopardised if statutory social services were to disappear. Conversely, the statutory social services could not compensate or provide adequate substitutes if the structures of familial altruism ceased functioning.

In summary, I rejected the idea of a unitary model of welfare on the grounds that it took insufficient account of the diversity of human preferences and needs and increased rather than reduced the risks of people experiencing conditions of stigmatizing dependency. I also concluded that a model of human motivation based on a sharply drawn distinction between the qualities of egoism and altruism bore little or no relationship to what we know about human nature and the realities of the world in which we live. By contrast, pluralist approaches which conceptualised social policies in terms of a mixed economy of welfare are more likely to generate useful explanatory theories and the provision of better quality social services.

## APPRAISING MOTIVATION, AGENCY AND PUBLIC POLICY

I now recognize—with the benefit of hindsight—that, in my preoccupation with the issues of citizenship, status, stigma and dependency, I failed to give sufficient attention to those of motivation and agency which Le Grand explores with such insight and authority in this book. Had I been familiar with Le Grand's illuminating variations on the game of chess, I would have described users of non-statutory social services as 'queens' endowed with independence and freedom of choice, in contrast with the 'pawns' dependent on the statutory services. 'As we grow up', I suggested, 'the most authentic rights we acquire and exercise are those we use in the roles of buyers and sellers in the market-place. We do not have to be persuaded that we have rights to what we buy.' By contrast, 'the idea of paying through taxes or holding authentic claims by virtue of citizenship remains largely an intellectual conceit of the social scientist and the socialist . . . Consequently most applicants for [statutory] social services remain paupers at heart' (Pinker 1971: 141–142).

Le Grand convincingly demonstrates how, in the pluralist mixed economy of quasi-markets, the likelihood of more social service users becoming 'queens' rather than 'pawns' (or paupers) can be greatly enhanced. As for the service providers, Titmuss would have categorically rejected his suggestion that public administrators could ever behave like 'knaves', or that private sector managers could ever be motivated by 'knightly' sentiments. Least of all, would he have accepted the possibility that by providing the right kinds of incentive at the agency levels of service provision their qualities of altruism and egoism could both be directed towards enhancing public welfare.

Like Titmuss, Le Grand recognises that the ways in which social policies are designed and implemented have a profound influence on people's disposition to behave altruistically or egoistically in their roles as service providers and users. Unlike Titmuss, he argues that the most effective social polices are those which complement and encourage the positive qualities of both of these moral dispositions. Drawing on a wide range of empirical evidence, he argues that altruism and egoism are not diametrically opposed forms of human motivation and that the values of the social and the economic markets do not have to be in permanent and irreconcilable conflict with each other.

Le Grand starts by exploring the ways in which the growth of quasi-markets have beneficially influenced 'the balance of knightly and knavish behaviour in the individuals affected' (p. 50). Most public service providers, he argues, derive great personal satisfaction from helping other people. In this respect, they behave like 'act-relevant' knights who are directly involved in helping needful people. At the same time, their motivation to act altruistically 'also seems to depend positively upon the degree of personal sacrifice associated with the act'.

Le Grand describes personal sacrifice in terms of its 'opportunity cost', that is, 'the cost to the individual concerned of other opportunities for personal benefit that have had to be forgone because he or she has chosen to undertake that act' (p. 51). If, however, the personal (or opportunity) costs involved are too great or too little, the motivation of the service provider to act altruistically will be weakened.

Intelligently designed incentive structures can, however, be used to achieve more effective 'trade-offs' between the altruistic and egoistic motivations of service providers. Le Grand argues that such outcomes may 'lead to the provision of more public services, which, other things being equal, would be morally desirable' and also less exploitative of the altruism of service providers 'which again would be desirable on moral grounds' (p. 66). Le Grand's theory of public service motivation rests on the premise that *both* altruism and egoism have positive moral properties and he goes on to conclude that, 'it is impossible to say that, in all circumstances, the morality of altruism should always be in the ascendant over that of positive service outcomes' (pp. 66–7).

We can summarize the essential difference between Le Grand's and Titmuss's approach to this issue in the following terms. Le Grand believes that positive service outcomes are more likely to be optimised when social policies work with the grain of human nature and take account of the duality of our moral sentiments. Titmuss believed that social policies should be directed towards changing human nature and should give unequivocal priority to the moral claims of statutory altruism.

Le Grand's theory of public service motivation is complemented by a second theory about the role of welfare agencies and the status of social service users in the public sector. He describe this approach as a 'theory of pawns and queens' and he starts by asking what 'a successful system for delivering a public service would look like'. His answer is that, 'It would be one that treats the users of the service as queens not pawns: that is, it would have user power at its base'. Such a system would have to be able to prevent the overusage or overprovision of the service concerned, or the 'use of the service in such a way that damages either the user himself or herself or the wider society'. It would have to include appropriate incentives for service providers which took account of both their altruism and egoism. It would also have 'to do all this in as efficient a manner as possible, and in a way that did not violate equity or other social objectives that society might have with respect to the service (p. 84).

Le Grand goes on to illustrate the various ways in which some of these objectives have already been partially achieved in the policy fields of health care and education by providing 'robust incentives' to medical and other professional workers, more choice for patients, more autonomy for primary care budget-holders, hospital consultants and head-teachers, and more choice and information for the parents of school children.

Throughout his review of these policy trends, Le Grand contends that we cannot 'rely solely upon purely knightly motivations—upon the public service ethos—to deliver public services to the level of quality and quantity that we require'. What matters most is that 'knavish and knightly incentive structures' should complement each other and 'be aligned in a "robust" fashion'. As for the service users, they are most likely to behave like 'queens' rather than 'pawns' when social services are provided through 'a system of quasi-market competition with independent providers run by public sector professionals and with users or their agents having fixed budgets' (p. 118).

From this retrospective review, Le Grand proceeds to set out his own policy proposals for further change. His most radical proposal is for the provision of a universal capital grant of £10,000 to all young people on reaching the age of eighteen. Such a scheme would be financed from the proceeds of a reformed inheritance tax. Le Grand describes the scheme as a policy of 'asset-based egalitarianism'. It is asset-based insofar as the capital grants would be invested and managed by public trustees. Withdrawals of cash would be subject to trustees' approval and might be restricted to such purposes as payment of educational fees, down payments on house purchases, the start-up costs of small businesses or investment in a personal or stakeholder pension. It is egalitarian insofar as the scheme would redistribute from rich to poor and enable more people to become asset-owners in their own right.

Le Grand suggests that such a scheme would have widespread appeal across the political spectrum. From the perspective of the right, it extends the ownership of assets and encourages self-help. From the left, it reduces inequality and increases equality of opportunity and outcome (p. 124). More than anything else, it gives people more power, more independence and more choice in making their own welfare decisions (p. 125).

What would Titmuss have made of such a proposal? In terms of its redistributive implications, the whole idea of a universal capital grant can be seen as a revamped version of *The Gift Relationship*, designed to function on a much broader institutional scale than the voluntary giving of blood. Nevertheless, it seems likely that Titmuss would have rejected such a scheme on both political and moral grounds.

On all matters relating to the political ends and means of social policy, as had been noted, Titmuss was an uncompromising unitarist. The idea of a universal capital grant could only be effectively implemented within the pluralist framework of a mixed economy of welfare and quasi-markets providing more scope for competition and consumer choice. On all matters relating to choice in welfare, Titmuss believed that it was more important that people should make the right choice than they should be free to choose for themselves. Most importantly, he argued, 'for the vast majority of workers covered by . . . private schemes, there is no choice' (1968: 144). And he would have found the whole idea of providing opportunities and incentives for both altruism and egoism a morally objectionable proposition. For similar reasons, Titmuss would probably have rejected Le Grand's other proposals regarding the hypothecation of health taxes, partnership saving schemes and long term care provision.

Nevertheless, Le Grand's pluralist model of welfare still leaves a substantial role for the statutory social services. While making provision for the extension of personal choice, it also leaves ample scope for compulsion, notably with regard to peoples' obligations to plan and pay for their long term needs. In particular, he accepts that governments and welfare agencies must retain sufficient powers to prevent service users from acting in ways that damage 'either the user himself or herself or the wider society' (p. 84).

Among the various reasons why people should not be left entirely free to choose for themselves, Le Grand cites those cases in which individuals lack the willpower to make the right choices. They include people who damage their own health through overeating, smoking and other forms of self-damaging personal behaviour. In these respects, it is worth noting that governments are becoming increasingly active in seeking to change peoples' personal behaviour by exhortation, education and regulating what they may or may not do in public places. In these respects, private insurance companies are able to be more actively interventive and regulatory than governments. Their policies include both incentives to adopt healthy styles of living and penalties for not doing so. So far, governments have not found it possible to adopt similar policies without infringing more general social and political rights to welfare. They cannot exclude or penalise people who make themselves 'bad risks' because of their self-indulgent life styles.

## CONCLUSION

*The Gift Relationship* and *Motivation, Agency and Public Policy* are both benchmark texts in the literature of social policy. *Social Theory and Social Policy* and *The Idea of Welfare* are both out of print, although *Social Theory* is still cited as a 'key text' in Blackwell's Student's Companion (Alcock et al 2003: 468). Taken together they illustrate the ways in which the normative debate about the ends and means of social policy has changed, as has its entire institutional framework. Titmuss's approach is charged throughout with the intensity of his moral commitment to a vision of collectivist social progress. As I wrote nearly two decades ago, it is really a book about the possibility for human redemption and its message, like that of John Bunyan's Pilgrim's Progress, is advanced in the form of an allegory.

Apart from both being Bedfordshire men, Bunyan and Titmuss shared the same unmistakably English quality of moral earnestness in the pursuit of self-improvement. Bunyan was driven by religious and Titmuss by secular convictions, but both were sustained by a distinctive vision of salvation. Bunyan's pilgrim, Christian, confronts the 'foul fiend, Apollyon' and scorns the material temptations of Vanity Fair (Bunyan 1965: 90 and 124). Titmuss confronts the menace of predatory competitive markets and exposes the falsity of the promises that they can deliver greater freedom of choice. Christian sets out for a heavenly Celestial City. Titmuss tells us what kind of social institutions we must establish in order to build a more just and compassionate society here on earth. And it this visionary quality that explains why *The Gift Relationship* is still read while better works of scholarship have slipped into obscurity (Pinker 1987: 60).

Both *Social Theory and Social Policy* and *The Idea of Welfare* were written largely as critiques of Titmuss's analysis of the moral dynamics of welfare institutions, the uncompromising distinction he drew between egoism and altruism, and the unitary model of social policy on which his analysis was based. I thought that his ideal of social welfare as 'a major integrated institution'—were it ever to be realised—would impose nothing less than an intellectual and normative straightjacket on the diversity of policy ends and means that ought to characterize a free society. I preferred the idea of a pluralist mixed economy of welfare which took more account of the necessities of human nature and gave more opportunities for us all to pursue what The Book of Common Prayer describes as 'the devices and desires of our own hearts'. Titmuss, in his preoccupation with 'opportunities for altruism', would undoubtedly have endorsed the whole of this quotation which penitentially confesses that 'we have followed too much the devices and desires of our own hearts'.

Like *The Gift Relationship*, *Motivation, Agency and Public Policy* also conveys its message in the form of an allegory but its similes are drawn from the chessboard where games are won, not by passionate commitment, but by the cunning of reason and the insights of imaginative calculation about other people's intentions. Nevertheless, Le Grand does succeed in demonstrating that 'market systems can encourage mutuality of respect and indeed even other virtues such as equity or altruism'. At the same time, the fact that public service providers are often driven by altruistic motives 'does not necessarily imply a respect' for the people whom they are serving. Some providers will always feel they are 'in a superior position to the beneficiary' and 'feelings of superiority are difficult to reconcile with mutuality of respect' (pp. 166–7). As Le Grand concludes, '. . . it is not necessary to turn knights into knaves for pawns to become queens. What is needed is well-designed public policies, ones that employ market-type mechanisms but that do not allow unfettered self-interest to dominate altruistic motivations' (p. 168).

Reading these texts, separated as they are by forty years of continuous policy changes, we are left with a choice between two very different normative models of welfare, service providers and service users. We can opt for Titmuss's dichotomous and confrontational model of chivalrous public sector knights and self-interested private sector knaves. Alternatively, we can settle for Le Grand's more equivocal portrayal of knightly knaves and knavish knights whose motivations are as complex as those of the people they serve and as diverse as the pluralist economies of welfare in which they work.

I agree with Le Grand's conclusion that, in the real world, it is preferable that the relationship between knights and knaves should be symbiotic rather than confrontational. They need each other in the same way that those two great archetypal figures of chivalric romance, Don Quixote and Sancho Panza, needed each other. At one level, Cervantes often seems to be juxtaposing the visionary idealism of the knightly Don Quixote and the pragmatic realism of his squire, the knavish Sancho Panza. But as the story unfolds, it becomes clear that these companions survive the vicissitudes of their perilous expeditions because, in their differences, they complement each other so perfectly. And that, in essence, is what Le Grand seems to be telling us about the conjunction of moral attributes that are most likely to bring success in the more prosaic enterprises of social policy.

Reproduced with permission

# Afterword

*Julian Le Grand*

The three distinguished authors whose contributions are included here have each provided thoughtful critiques of the book, raising serious issues about some of its arguments. I am glad to have the opportunity to reflect further on them.

Rudolf Klein makes several important points. The first is that, in large organisations, service deliverers make their own rules and policies and that these may subvert or even pervert government policies in their implementation. I would agree with this. Indeed, I think it strengthens the argument for quasi-market systems of delivery. For in such systems the relationship between government and provider is one involving specified contract rather than one relying upon what is often a more permeable hierarchical management structure. Although the full specification of contracts has its own difficulties, the process of contract formulation and agreement has a key role in clarifying what it is that governments or purchasers more generally actually want from providers; and the subsequent monitoring of the contract has an equally important role in ensuring that they get it.

A second point made by Klein is that providers may be knaves from the point of view of government (in that they subvert policy) but knights from the point of view of users in that they bend rules in the latter's favour. The second part of this could be viewed as part of a wider point: knights may be favoured by users because they act as user advocates in the face of a possibly uncaring bureaucracy. Again I would agree with this, and again would point out that it strengthens the argument for quasi-markets over bureaucratic systems—or more generally, for exit over voice. For the reason why users might feel that they need knightly advocates from within a bureaucratic system is because they doubt their own ability to manipulate that system to serve their ends—or, in other words doubt their ability to exercise their voice. Users only need advocates to bend rules if there are rules to be bent. If users have the power of exit, as in quasi-markets, then they have no need of experts in bending the bureaucracy to get what they want or need; for they can go elsewhere.

Against this it might be argued that knightly advocates operating within a bureaucratic system might do a better job of getting users what they want or need than users making their own choices between alternative providers. But here a third point by Klein has relevance. 'Knightly behaviour may be the problem rather than the solution. (F)rom the perspective of users, knights may be authoritarian paternalists acting in the sure faith that they are altruists who know best. If the pursuit of self-interest at the expense of the public interest is the pathology of knavery, self-righteous rectitude is the pathology of knighthood'. Put another way, knightly advocates operating within bureaucratic systems may get users what the knights think users' need, but not necessarily what users think they need.

In the Epilogue, I do refer the possibility that public service knights may not have as full a quota of respect for users that would be desirable. That is fine for a system that relies on knightly behaviour to provide services to pawns, but more problematic for one that aims to turn pawn into queens. And the problem is exacerbated if the knights are actually knaves: for then they may use their ability to manipulate the bureaucracy to serve their own ends rather than those of users.

But should pawns be turned into queens? This brings us to Mathias Risse's contribution. He seems happy with the book's arguments concerning the essentially empirical propositions relating to knights and knaves, and indeed supports many of the policy ideas. He reserves his principal criticisms for the philosophical justifications that I put forward for the normative position that I take in Chapter 5: that service users ought to be turned from pawns to queens. In that chapter I contend that the case for turning pawns to queens can be made from any of three perspectives: liberal, welfarist, and communitarian. Risse argues that from each of these perspectives the argument is 'weaker than [Le Grand] thinks.'

First, the liberals. Risse divides these into two—libertarians of a Nozickian kind and liberal egalitarians of a Rawlsian kind—and claims that neither would support my position. Libertarians would agree with the general proposition that in our liberal society citizens should be queens not pawns. In fact they would endorse the principle of equal autonomy that Rudolf Klein argues for in his article, in turn quoting Albert Weale 'This principle of autonomy asserts that all persons are entitled to respect as deliberative and purposive agents capable of formulating their own projects, and that as part of this respect there is a governmental obligation to bring into being or preserve the conditions in which this autonomy can be realised' (Weale 1983: 42. See also Klein and Miller 1995).

This principle, that governments have an obligation to respect autonomy or establish it where it does not exist, Risse would claim conflicts with my position because I set my arguments for transforming service users from pawns into queens within the context of a universalist welfare state. That is, I assume that the service whose users are to be empowered—the service whose pawns are to be transformed into queens—is financed from some form of redistributive taxation, and that the purchasing power for the service concerned is equalized before the market or quasi-market is allowed to let rip.

Risse argues a true libertarian would stop well before this, on the grounds that redistributive taxation has no place in any scheme really designed to promote people's freedom of action. Taxation is coercive by definition and thus automatically restricts liberty. Far better from this perspective to allow users to keep their own money and let them make their own decision about how much health care or education to buy.

In contrast, a liberal egalitarian would accept the need for redistributive taxation, but, in doing so, would acknowledge that the coercive element essential to such taxation must imply that people are being treated to some extent as pawns. Hence she too would not advocate pawns being turned completely into queens.

At a later stage in his review, Risse returns to this libertarian/liberal egalitarian divide, arguing that an American reader, likely to be more subject to libertarian intuitions, would find it odd that I push for the empowerment of users but do not question the redistributive welfare state; while a European one would find it peculiar that, while both she and I would accept the legitimacy of limiting individuals' freedoms through redistributive taxation, I can still argue for users to be queens. Risse says that 'it is hard to have it both ways.'

I would not presume to argue with a philosopher as to the way that different schools of thought might react to my arguments, and I accept the implied rebuke that my ascription of the label 'liberal' to what are actually two very different positions was simplistic. But I do not agree that my own position is in some way inconsistent. For my argument simply represents a trade-off between different values, none of which has automatic priority over another in all circumstances. I am not a pure libertarian, in the sense that I consider policies designed to promote liberty or freedom of action always and in every context dominate other concerns, such as equity or social justice. Redistributive taxation and its use to promote the equalization of people's ability to obtain health care and education is thus perfectly acceptable—and indeed desirable. In that case the requirements of equity or social justice trump those of liberty.

On the other hand, I am not a pure egalitarian (or, perhaps more accurately, equitarian) in the sense that I consider concerns of equity or social justice should always dominate every other consideration. So a complete curb on everyone's freedom of action in the name of equity is not acceptable. Since to achieve 'full' equity and 'complete' liberty simultaneously is probably impossible, the aim is to find a policy solution that achieves an acceptable measure of both equity and liberty, while accepting that neither objective is likely to be completely satisfied. And using the revenue from redistributive taxation to move towards greater equality of capital ownership (as with the demogrant), or to equalize purchasing power in health care and education (as with quasi-market systems of service delivery) seems to be an illustration of just such an acceptable balance.

Of course, the problem with that position for political philosophy is that it does not really explain why this balance is acceptable but another is not. Ideally there would be an even more fundamental principle that would determine the point of an acceptable trade-off between liberty and equity; but the search for such a principle is well beyond my scope here. However, I do have other reasons why I believe that policy proposals that incorporate the balance concerned are attractive. And this is where the welfare and what I call the communitarian arguments come in (Risse points out—correctly—that I only consider a welfarist interpretation of communitarianism). Essentially I argue that both the welfare of each individual, and the welfare of others in the wider community, will be better served by these policies than by alternative ways of providing services such as education and health care—especially those that give professionals control over the allocation of children to schools or patients to hospitals, effectively reducing the users of these services to pawns.

This is not because I believe that the policies that turn pawns into queens do not have their problems with respect to individual and community welfare; indeed, I refer to several of these difficulties in the chapter concerned. It is just that I consider them superior in these respects to the alternatives. Risse does not buy all my arguments, and I would accept some of his points (for instance, that we might place a greater faith in the professionals making decisions on behalf of users, if, as I advocate elsewhere in the book, we could successfully line up knightly and knavish incentives). But ultimately this is more of an empirical question than a philosophical one, and we probably need more evidence of the impact of different systems on welfare before we can arrive at a definitive assessment.

To take up one specific point in this context. Discussing the proposal that patients should have more control over their treatment, Risse argues that 'when it comes to resource distribution, each patient has an interest in her health and thus is a poor judge of how to distribute resources also needed by others.' I agree with this in so far it refers to choice of treatment, and indeed use similar arguments elsewhere in the book to justify GP fund-holding: the system where family practitioners hold the budget for purchasing secondary care for their patients. But, so long as there is available capacity in the relevant hospitals, the argument does not apply to choice of hospital, once the diagnosis has been made and the appropriate treatment specified; for one person's choice of where to be treated does not displace another's treatment. So the desirability of patient choice can depend on the type of decision being made; and again a trade-off between patient and professional power may be necessary in certain circumstances.

Finally, a specific point in a different context. Risse takes issue with my argument for state intervention in decisions concerning savings for old age. The argument is that state intervention to encourage savings is justified even in a world of queens, because there is a form of market failure here: that individuals have only a tenuous connection with their future selves and hence impose external costs on those future selves by their current savings (or lack of savings) decisions. Risse's argument against this is that either it is rational for current individuals to neglect their future selves, in which case the state should similarly neglect them, or it is not rational, in which case the state would have no need to encourage savings over and above that which rational individuals are doing already. Here Risse is assuming that the state only has a responsibility to its current citizens. But I think it is reasonable to assume that it also has a responsibility to other people who suffer external costs as a by-product of the actions of those citizens, including those who live in other states, and, of more relevance to my argument, including those who live in the same state in the future. The correction of external costs has always been seen as a proper role for the state, and, in encouraging current individuals to save more and hence benefit future individuals, the state is legitimately exercising that role.

Until I read Robert Pinker's essay, I had not realised the extent to which his two seminal works—*Social Theory and Social Policy* (1971) and *The Idea of Welfare* (1979)—had prefigured mine, and I am glad to have the opportunity to acknowledge this. He criticised simplistic notions of altruism and egoism, pointing out that most people are driven by a combination of altruistic and egoistic motives and that this fact must be taken into account in any development of social policy. He emphasised that the extent of the sacrifice involved in an altruistic act as an important test of the scope and limits of altruism as a moral motivator. He was an early advocate of pluralistic systems of welfare—at a time when it was deeply unfashionable to do so. He argued that the most authentic rights that we have are those of the market place, and, in a phrase that has echoes of the pawn/queen analogy but that has a quality all of its own, points out that in unitary or state monopoly systems welfare users of social services are 'paupers at heart'.

Pinker also makes two points that I do not, but that I am happy to appropriate. First, familial altruism is a key element in overall welfare provision, driving as it does arguably the most important element of that provision, viz family support for those in need. This has just a strong a moral claim as Titmuss's altruism to strangers, and, moreover, has an essential practical value—probably more than does the kind of altruism that involves gifts to strangers. Second, monopolies, or unitary systems in Pinker's terminology, are poor at meeting the diversity of human needs and aspirations. Even more importantly, all systems of welfare provision create dependency, but that dependency is total when the provider is a monopoly. This is bad psychologically for users, but also carries major risks for them in the case of provider failure. Pluralism of providers (quasi-markets in my terminology) reduces the risk both of total dependency and of the distress created by total system failure.

Finally, it is worth noting that none of the authors included here—nor, I might add, any other of the book's many reviewers—have challenged one of the central arguments of the book: that the structure of motivation of those working in public services is complex, that it includes knavish as well as knightly motives, and that 'robust' incentive structures that appeal to both are needed. Indeed, if anything the subsequent debate seems to have re-inforced the argument. The case that users should be pawns not queens has been more contentious, but I think remains strong. The conclusion that the best—or least worst—way of achieving both of these ends is through quasi-market systems of provision is being tested within the public services of the United Kingdom and other countries as I write. The jury on that will soon be in.

Reproduced with permission

# References

6, Perri (2003). 'Giving Consumers of British Public Services More Choice: What Can Be Learned from Recent History?'. *Journal of Social Policy*, 32: 239–70.

Abel-Smith, Brian and Titmuss, Richard (1956). *The Cost of the National Health Service in England and Wales*. Cambridge: Cambridge University Press.

Abrams, Burton A. and Schmitz, Mark A. (1978). 'The Crowding-out Effect of Government Transfers on Private Charitable Contributions'. *Public Choice*, 33: 29–39. Reprinted in Digby Anderson (ed.) (1992). *Loss of Virtue: Moral Confusion and Social Disorder in Britain and America*. London: Social Affairs Unit.

Ackerman, Bruce and Alstott, Anne (1999). *The Stakeholding Society*. New Haven: Yale University Press.

———— (forthcoming). 'Why Stakeholding?', in Erik Olin Wright (ed.), *Rethinking Redistribution*. London: Verso.

Agulnik, Philip and Le Grand, Julian (1998*a*). 'Partnership Pensions versus Compulsory Pensions'. *New Economy*, 5: 147–52.

———— (1998*b*). 'Tax Relief and Partnership Pensions'. *Fiscal Studies*, 19: 403–28.

Alcock, Pete, Erskine, Angus and May, Margaret (2003). *The Student's Companion to Social Policy*. Oxford: Blackwell.

Allen, Isobel (1997). *Committed but Critical: An Examination of Young Doctors' Views of their Core Values*. London: British Medical Association.

Altmann, Ros (2003). 'Beyond Tax Relief: A New Savings Incentive Framework', in Will Paxton (ed.), *A Wealthy Society? Progressive and Coherent Asset Based Welfare*. London: Institute for Public Policy Research.

Andreoni, James (1990). 'Impure Altruism and Donations to Public Goods: A Theory of Warm-Glow Giving'. *Economic Journal*, 100: 464–77.

—— (1993). 'An Experimental Test of the Public-Goods Crowding-Out Hypothesis'. *American Economic Review*, 83: 1317–27.

—— and Miller, John (2002). 'Giving According to GARP: An Experimental Test of the Consistency of Preferences for Altruism'. *Econometrica*, 70: 737–53.

—— and Vesterlund, Lise (2001). 'Which Is the Fair Sex? Gender Differences in Altruism'. *Quarterly Journal of Economics*, 16: 293–312.

Antonazzo, Emanuela, Scott, Anthony, Skatun, Diane, and Elliott, Bob (2000). *The Labour Market for Nursing: A Review of the Labour Supply Literature* (HERU Discussion Paper 01/00). Aberdeen: Health Economics Research Unit, University of Aberdeen.

Arrow, Kenneth (1963). 'Uncertainty and the Welfare Economics of Medical Care'. *American Economic Review*, 53: 941–73.

Atkinson, Anthony B. (1972). *Unequal Shares: Wealth in Britain*. London: Allen Lane.

Bacon, Francis (1870). 'Of Seditions and Troubles', in *Works of Francis Bacon, Vol VI*. London: Longmans.

Baldwin, Peter (1990). *The Politics of Social Solidarity: Class Bases of the European Welfare State 1875–1975*. Cambridge: Cambridge University Press.

Banks, James, Dilnot, Andrew, and Tanner, Sarah (1997). *Taxing Household Saving: What Role for the New Individuals' Savings Account?* London: Institute for Fiscal Studies.

Banks, James, Dilnot, Andrew and Tanner, Sarah (1999). *Household Saving in the UK*. London: Institute for Fiscal Studies.

Barkema, H. (1995). 'Do Job Executives Work Harder When they are Monitored?' *Kyklos*, 48: 19–42.

Barnett, Corelli (1986). *The Audit of War*. London: Macmillan.

Barr, Nicholas (2001). *The Welfare State as Piggy Bank*. Oxford: Oxford University Press.

Barrow, Michael (1998). 'Financing of Schools: A National or Local Quasi-Market?', in Will Bartlett, Jenny Roberts, and Julian Le Grand (eds.), *A Revolution in Social Policy*. Bristol: Policy Press.

Barry, Brian (1965). *Political Argument*. London: Routledge & Kegan Paul.

Bartlett, Will, Roberts, Jenny, and Le Grand, Julian (eds.) (1998). *A Revolution in Social Policy*. Bristol: Policy Press.

——, Propper, Carol, Wilson, Deborah, and Le Grand, Julian (eds.) (1994). *Quasi-Markets and the Welfare State*. Bristol: School for Advanced Urban Studies.

Batson, C. Daniel (1991). *The Altruism Question*. Hillsdale, NJ: Lawrence Erlbaum Associates.

Beardow, Rosemary, Cheung, Kathy, and Styles, W. McN. (1993). 'Factors Affecting the Career Choices of General Practitioner Trainees in North West Thames Regional Health Authority'. *British Journal of General Practice*, 43: 449–52.

Becker, Gary (1976). *The Economic Approach to Human Behavior*. Chicago: Chicago University Press.

—— (1981). *A Treatise on the Family*. Cambridge, MA: Harvard University Press.

Beeferman, Larry (2001). *Asset Development Policy: The New Opportunity*. Asset Development Institute. Waltham, MA: Center for Hunger and Poverty, Brandeis University.

Bernheim, Douglas B. (1986). 'On the Voluntary and Involuntary Provision of Public Goods'. *American Economic Review*, 76: 789–93.

Berridge, V. (1997). 'AIDS and the Gift Relationship in the UK', in Anne Oakley and J. Ashton (eds), *Richard Titmuss's The Gift Relationship*. London: Allen and Unwin.

BMA (British Medical Association) (1994). *Hypothecated Tax Funding for the NHS*. London: BMA Health Policy and Economic Research Unit.

—— (1995a). *Cohort Study of 1995 Medical Graduates: Parts I and II*. London: BMA.

—— (1995b). *Core Values for the Medical Profession in the 21st Century: Conference Report*. London: BMA.

—— (1995c). *Core Values for the Medical Profession in the 21st Century: Survey Report*. London: BMA.

Bosanquet, Nick and Leese, Brenda (1989). *Family Doctors and Economic Incentives*. Aldershot: Dartmouth.

Boshara, Ray (ed.) (2001). *Building Assets: A Report on the Asset Development and IDA Field*. Washington, DC: Corporation for Enterprise Development.

Boswell, James (1934). *The Life of Dr Johnson*. Oxford: Clarendon Press.

Bowles, Samuel and Gintis, Herbert (1998). 'Efficient Redistribution: New Rules for Markets, States and Communities', in Erik Olin Wright (ed.), *Recasting Egalitarianism: New Rules for Communities, States and Markets*. London: Verso.

Bracewell-Milnes, Barry (1991). 'Earmarking in Britain: Theory and Practice', in Ranjit S. Teja and Barry Bracewell-Milnes (ed.), *The Case for Earmarked Taxes: Government Spending and Public Choice*. London: Institute of Economic Affairs.

Bradley, Stephen, Johnes, Geraint, and Millington, Jim (2001). 'School Choice, Competition and the Efficiency of Secondary Schools in England'. *European Journal of Operational Research*, 135: 545–68.

—— and Taylor, Jim (2000). *The Effect of the Quasi-Market on the Efficiency-Equity Trade-off in the Secondary School Sector* (Centre for Research in the Economics of Education Discussion Paper EC9/00). Lancaster University: Department of Economics.

Brecher, Charles (2002). *The Public Interest Company as a Mechanism to Improve Public Service Delivery*. London: Public Management Foundation.

Brennan, Geoffrey and Buchanan, James (1985). *The Reason of Rules: Constitutional Political Economy*. Cambridge: Cambridge University Press.

—— and Hamlin, Alan (1995). 'Economising on Virtue'. *Constitutional Political Economy*, 6: 35–56.

—— —— (2000). *Democratic Devices and Desires*. Cambridge: Cambridge University Press.

Brewer, Gene, Selden, Sally, and Facer II, Rex (2000). 'Individual Conceptions of Public Service Motivation'. *Public Administration Review*, 60: 254–64.

Brighouse, Harry (1998). 'School Choice: Theoretical Considerations', in Eric Olin Wright (ed.), *Recasting Egalitarianism: New Rules for Communities, States and Markets*. London: Verso.

Brittan, Samuel (1998). *Essays Moral, Political, Economic*. Edinburgh: Edinburgh University Press.

—— (2000). 'In Defence of Earmarked Taxes'. *Financial Times*, 7 December.

Brook, L., Hall, J., and Preston, I. (1996). 'Public Spending and Taxation', in Roger Jowell (ed.), *British Social Attitudes: The 13th Report*. Aldershot: Dartmouth.

Broome, J. (1985). 'The Welfare Economics of the Future: A Review of *Reasons and Persons* by Derek Parfit'. *Social Change and Welfare*, 2: 221–34.

Bryan, J. H. and Test, M. A. (1967). 'Models and Helping: Naturalistic Studies in Aiding Behaviour'. *Journal of Personality and Social Psychology*, 6: 400–7.

Bryson, Alex and Jacobs, John (1992). *Policing the Workshy*. Aldershot: Avebury.

Buchanan, James (1963). 'The Economics of Earmarked Taxes'. *Journal of Political Economy*, 71: 457–69.

—— (1987). 'Constitutional Economics', in John Eatwell, Murray Milgate, and Peter Newman (eds.), *The New Palgrave Dictionary of Economics, Volume 1*. Basingstoke: Palgrave. Reproduced in James Buchanan (1989), *Explorations into Constitutional Economics*. College Station: Texas A&M University Press.

Bunyan, John (1965). *The Pilgrim's Progress*. Harmondsworth: Penguin Books.

Burgess, Simon, Propper, Carol, and Wilson, Deborah (2002). *Does Performance Monitoring Work? A Review of the Evidence from the UK Public Sector Excluding Health Care*. Discussion Paper 02/049. Bristol: Centre for Market and Public Organisation, University of Bristol.

Butler, Eamonn and Pirie, Madsen (1995). *The Fortune Account*. London: Adam Smith Institute.

Butler, Joseph (1997). 'On the Relationship between Self-love and Particular Affections', in Kelly Rogers (ed.), *Self-Interest: An Anthology of Philosophical Perspectives*. London: Routledge.

Bynner, John and Despotidou, S. (2001). *Effects of Assets on Life Chances*. London: Centre for Longitudinal Studies, Institute of Education.

—— and Paxton, Will (2001). *The Asset Effect*. London: Institute of Public Policy Research.

Calcott, Paul (2000). 'New on Paternalism'. *Economics and Philosophy*, 16: 315–21.

Chaix-Couturier, Carine, Durand-Zaleski, Isabelle, Jolly, Dominique, and Durieux, Pierre (2000). 'Effects of Financial Incentives on Medical Practice: Results from a Systematic Review of the Literature and Methodological Issues'. *International Journal for Quality in Health Care*, 12: 133–42.

Chalkley, Martin and Malcolmson, James (1998). 'Contracting for Health Services When Patient Demand Does Not Reflect Quality'. *Journal of Health Economics*, 17: 1–19.

Chevalier, Arnaud, Dolton, Peter, and Mcintosh, Steven (2002). *Recruiting and Retaining Teachers in the UK: An Analysis of Graduate Training Occupation Choice from 1960s to the 1990s*. London: Centre for the Economics of Education.

Chitty, Clyde (1988). 'Central Control over the School Curriculum 1944–1987'. *History of Education*, 17: 321–34.

Clemence, Lynne (1998). 'To Whom Do You Refer?' *Health Service Journal*, 108: 26–7.

Clotfelder, Charles T. (1985). *Federal Tax Policy and Charitable Giving*. Chicago: University of Chicago Press.

Cnaan, Ram and Amrofell, Laura (1994). 'Mapping Volunteer Activity'. *Nonprofit and Voluntary Sector Quarterly*, 23: 335–51.

——, Handy, Fermida, and Wadsworth, Margaret (1996). 'Defining Who is a Volunteer: Conceptual and Empirical Considerations'. *Nonprofit and Voluntary Sector Quarterly*, 25: 364–83.

Coleman, James (1990). *Foundations of Social Theory*. Cambridge, MA: Harvard University Press.

Collard, D. (1978). *Altruism and Economy*. Oxford: Martin Robertson.

Collard, David (1978). *Altruism and Economy: A Study in Non-selfish Economics*. London: Martin Robertson.

—— (1983). 'Economics of Philanthropy: A Comment'. *Economic Journal*, 93: 637–8.

Collini, Stefan (1985). 'The Idea of "Character" in Victorian Political Thought'. *Transactions of the Royal Historical Society* (5th Series), 35: 29–50.

Cooper, Michael and Culyer, Anthony (1968). *The Price of Blood* (Hobart Paper No. 41). London: Institute of Economic Affairs.

Corrigan, Paul, Steele, Jane, and Parston, Greg (2001). *The Case for the Public Interest Company: A New Form of Enterprise for Public Service Delivery*. London: Public Management Foundation.

Coulter, Angela (2002). *The Autonomous Patient: Ending Paternalism in Medical Care*. London: Nuffield Trust.

——, Noone, Ahilya, and Goldacre, Michael (1989). 'General Practitioners Referrals to Specialist Outpatient Clinics: 1. Why General Practitioners Refer Patients to Specialist Outpatient Clinics'. *British Medical Journal*, 299: 304–6.

Crilly, Tessa and Le Grand, Julian (2004). 'The Motivation and Behaviour of Hospital Trusts'. *Social Science and Medicine*, 58: 1809–1823.

Croxson, Bronwyn, Propper, Carol, and Perkins, Andy (2001). 'Do Doctors Respond to Financial Incentives? UK Family Doctors and the GP Fund Holder Scheme'. *Journal of Public Health Economics*, 79: 375–98.

Dawkins, Richard (1989). *The Selfish Gene* (2nd edn). Oxford: Oxford University Press.

Deacon, Alan (1976). *In Search of the Scrounger: The Administration of Unemployment Insurance in Britain, 1920–1931* (Occasional Papers in Social Administration No. 60). London: Bell and Sons.

—— (1993). 'Richard Titmuss: 20 Years On'. *Journal of Social Policy*, 22: 235–42.

—— and Mann, Kirk (1999). 'Agency, Modernity and Social Policy'. *Journal of Social Policy*, 23: 413–35.

Dean, Hartley (forthcoming). 'Reconceptualising Dependency, Responsibility and Rights', in Hartley Dean (ed.), *Dependency, Responsibility and Rights*. Bristol: The Policy Press.

Deci, Edward L. and Ryan, Richard M. (1985). *Intrinsic Motivation and Self-determination in Human Behavior*. New York: Plenum Press.

Disney, Richard, Emmerson, Carl, and Wakefield, Matthew (2001). 'Pension Reform and Saving in Britain'. *Oxford Review of Economic Policy*, 17: 70–94.

Dixit, Avinash (2001). *Incentive Contracts for Faith-Based Organizations to Deliver Social Services* (Working Paper). Princeton: Department of Economics, Princeton University.

—— (2002). 'Incentives and Organizations in the Public Sector: An Interpretative Review'. *Journal of Human Resources*, 37: 696–727.

Dolton, Peter, McIntosh, Steve, and Chevalier, Arnaud (2002). *Teacher Pay and Performance* (Bedford Way Papers). London: Institute of Education.

Donnison, David V. (1982). *The Politics of Poverty*. Oxford: Martin Robertson.

Dowie, Robin (1983). *General Practitioners and Consultants*. London: Kings Fund.

Dowling, Bernard (1997). 'Effect of Fundholding on Waiting Times: Database Study'. *British Medical Journal*, 315: 290–2.

—— (2000). *GPs and Purchasing in the NHS: the Internal Market and Beyond*. Brookfield, VT: Ashgate.

Dunleavy, Patrick (1981). *The Politics of Mass Housing in Britain 1945–1975*. Oxford: Clarendon Press.

Dusheiko, Mark, Gravelle, Hugh, Jacobs, Rowena, and Smith, Peter (2003). *The Effect of Budgets on Doctor Behaviour: Evidence from a Natural Experiment* (Centre for Health Economics Technical Paper No. 26). York: University of York.

Eliot, George (1866/1995). *Felix Holt: The Radical*. London: Penguin Classics.

Elster, Jon (1989). *Solomonic Judgements*. Cambridge: Cambridge University Press.

Emmerson, Carl and Wakefield, Matthew (2001). *A Savings Gateway and a Child Trust Fund: Is Asset-based Welfare 'Well Fair'?* London: Institute for Fiscal Studies.

England, Paula (1992). *Comparable Worth: Theories and Evidence*. New York: Aldine de Gruyter.

——, Budig, Michelle, and Folbre, Nancy (2001). 'Wages of Virtue: The Relative Pay of Care Work'. Chicago: Department of Sociology, Northwestern University. Available on www.olin.wustl.edu/macarthur/papers/englandfolbre-wagesofvirtue.pdf.

—— and Folbre, Nancy (1999). 'The Cost of Caring'. *The Annals of the American Academy of Political and Social Science*, 561: 39–51.

Ennew, Christine, Feighan, Teresa, and Whynes, David (1998). 'Entrepreneurial Activity in the Public Sector: Evidence From UK Primary Care', in Peter Taylor-Gooby (ed.), *Choice and Public Policy*. Houndmills: Macmillan.

Enthoven, Alain (1999). *In Pursuit of an Improving Health Service*. London: Nuffield Trust.

Estrin, Saul (1989). 'Workers' Co-operatives: Their Merits and Limitations', in Julian Le Grand and Saul Estrin (eds.), *Market Socialism*. Oxford: Clarendon.

Evers, Adalbert (1994). 'Payments for Care: A Small But Significant Part of a Wider Debate', in Adalbert Evers, Maria Pijl, and Claire Ungerson (eds.), *Payments for Care: A Comparative Overview*. Aldershot: Avebury.

——, Pijl, Maria, and Ungerson, Claire (1994). *Payments for Care: A Comparative Overview*. Aldershot: Avebury.

Exworthy, Mark, Powell, Martin, and Mohan, J. (1999). 'The NHS: quasi-market, quasi-hierarchy, and quasi-network?' *Public Money and Management*, 19/October–December: 15–22.

Fabian Society (2000). *Paying for Progress: Report of the Commission on Taxation and Citizenship*. London: Fabian Society.

Falkingham, Jane and Hills, John (eds.) (1995). *The Dynamic of Welfare: The Welfare State and the Life Cycle*. Hemel Hempstead: Harvester Wheatsheaf.

Falkner, Robert (1997). *A Conservative Economist? The Political Liberalism of Adam Smith Revisited*. London: John Stuart Mill Institute.

Falush, Peter (1977). 'Trends in the Finance of British Charities'. *National Westminster Bank Quarterly Review*, May: 32–44.

Field, Frank (1995). *Making Welfare Work: Reconstructing Welfare for the Millennium*. London: Institute of Community Studies.

Finch, Janet (1989). *Family Obligations and Social Change*. Oxford: Blackwell.

Fitzpatrick, Tony (1999). *Freedom and Security: An Introduction to the Basic Income Debate*. New York: St Martin's Press.

Folbre, Nancy and Weisskopf, Thomas (1998). 'Did Father Know Best? Families, Markets and the Supply of Caring Labour', in Avner Ben-Ner and Louis Putterman (eds.), *Economics, Values and Organization*. Cambridge: Cambridge University Press.

Fontaine, Philippe (2002). 'Blood, Politics, and Social Science: Richard Titmuss and the Institute of Economic Affairs, 1957–1973'. *Isis*, 93: 401–34.

Forder, Julien (2000). 'Mental Health: Market Power and Governance'. *Journal of Health Economics*, 19: 877–905.

——, Hardy, Brian, Kendall, Jeremy, and Knapp, Martin (1997). 'Residential Care Provider Study (MEOC)'. Unpublished report to the Department of Health. London: Personal Social Services Research Unit, London School of Economics, and Leeds: Nuffield Institute for Health, University of Leeds.

Fotaki, Marianna (1999). 'The Impact of Market Oriented Reforms on Information and Choice: A Case Study of Cataract Surgery in Outer London and Stockholm'. *Social Science and Medicine*, 48: 1415–32.

Frank, Robert (1988). *Passions Within Reason: The Strategic Role of the Emotions*. New York and London: W.W. Norton.

—— (1996). 'What Price the Moral High Ground?' *Southern Economic Journal*, 63: 1–17.

Frey, Bruno (1997). 'From the Price to the Crowding Out Effect'. *Swiss Journal of Economics and Statistics*, 133: 325–50.

—— (1999). *Economics as a Science of Human Behavior*. Boston: Kluwer Academic Publishers.

—— (2000). 'Motivation and Human Behaviour', in Peter Taylor-Gooby (ed.), *Risk, Trust and Welfare*. Basingstoke: Macmillan.

—— Goette, Lorenz (1999). *Does Pay Motivate Volunteers?* (Working Paper No. 7). Zurich: Institute for Empirical Research in Economics, University of Zurich.

—— —— (forthcoming). 'Comment on Freeman (1997), *Working for Nothing: The Supply of Volunteer Labour'. Journal of Labour Economics*.

—— and Jegen, Reto (2000). *Motivation Crowding Theory: A Survey of Empirical Evidence* (Working Paper No. 49). Zurich: Institute for Empirical Research in Economics, University of Zurich.

—— and Oberholzer-Gee, F. (1997). 'The Cost of Price Incentives: An Empirical Analysis of Motivation Crowding Out'. *American Economic Review*, 87: 746–55.

Fukuyama, Francis (1992). *The End of History and the Last Man*. New York: Free Press.

—— (1995). *Trust*. London: Hamish Hamilton. References are to the Penguin edition (London: Penguin Books, 1996).

Gabris, Gerald and Simo, Gloria (1995). 'Public Sector Motivation as an Independent Variable Affecting Career Decisions'. *Public Personnel Management*, 24: 33–51.

Gewirtz, Sharon, Ball, Stephen, and Bowe, Richard (1995). *Markets, Choice and Equity in Education*. Buckingham: Open University Press.

Gibson, Alex and Asthana, Sheena (2000). 'What's In a Number? Commentary on Gorard and Fitz's "Investigating the Determinants of segregation between schools"'. *Research Papers in Education*, 15: 133–53.

Giddens, Anthony (1998). *The Third Way*. Cambridge: The Polity Press.

Glennerster, Howard (1995). *British Social Policy Since 1945*. Oxford: Blackwell.

—— (1998). 'Education: Reaping the Harvest?', in Howard Glennerster and John Hills (eds.), *The State of Welfare* (2nd edn). Oxford: Oxford University Press.

—— (2002). 'United Kingdom Education 1997–2001'. *Oxford Review of Economic Policy*, 18: 120–36.

—— and Le Grand, Julian (1995). 'The Development of Quasi-markets in Welfare Provision in the United Kingdom'. *International Journal of Health Services*, 25: 203–18.

——, Matsaganis, Manos, and Owens, Pat (1994). *Implementing GP Fundholding: Wild Card or Winning Hand?* London: Open University Press.

Goodin, Robert (1993). 'Moral Atrophy in the Welfare State'. *Policy Sciences*, 26: 63–78.

—— (ed.) (1996). *The Theory of Institutional Design*. Cambridge: Cambridge University Press.

—— and Dryzek, John (1987). 'Risk Sharing and Social Justice: The Motivational Foundations of the Post-War Welfare State', in Robert Goodin and Julian Le Grand (eds.), *Not Only the Poor: The Middle Classes and the Welfare State*. London: Allen and Unwin.

—— and Le Grand, Julian (1987). *Not Only the Poor: The Middle Classes and the Welfare State*. London: Allen and Unwin.

Goodwin, Nicholas (1998). 'General Practitioner Fundholding', in Julian Le Grand, Nicholas Mays, and Jo-Ann Mulligan (eds.), *Learning from the NHS Internal Market*. London: Kings Fund.

Gorard, Stephen (2000). 'Here We Go Again: A Reply to "What's in a Number?" by Gibson and Asthana'. *Research Papers in Education*, 15: 155–62.

—— and Fitz, John (1998a). 'The More Things Change . . . The Missing Impact of Marketisation?' *British Journal of Sociology of Education*, 19: 365–76.

—— (1998b). 'Under Starters' Orders: The Established Market, the Cardiff Study and the Smithfield Project'. *International Studies in Sociology of Education*, 8: 299–314.

—— and Taylor, Chris (2001). 'School Choice Impacts: What Do We Know?' *Educational Researcher*, 30: 18–23.

Gordon, Rupert (1999). 'Kant, Smith and Hegel: The Market and the Categorical Imperative', in Frank Trentmann (ed.), *Paradoxes of Civil Society: New Perspectives on Modern German and British History*. Oxford: Berghahn.

Gosden, Toby, Forland, Frode, Kristiansen, Ivar Sonbo, Sutton, Matthew, Leese, Brenda, Giuffrida, Antonio, Sergison, Michelle, and Pedersen, Lone (2001). 'Impact of Payment Method on Behaviour of Primary Care Physicians: A Systematic Review'. *Journal of Health Services Research and Policy*, 6: 44–55.

Gothill, Matthew (1998). 'What Do Doctors Want? Altruism and Satisfaction in General Practice'. *Family Practice*, 15: S36–9.

Graham, Alison and Steele, Jane (2001). *Optimising Value: The Motivation of Doctors and Managers in the NHS*. London: Public Management Foundation.

Green, David (1993). *Reinventing Civil Society*. London: Institute of Economic Affairs.
—— (1996). *Community without Politics*. London: Institute of Economic Affairs.
Gundlach, Erich, Wossman, Ludger, and Gmelin, Jens (2001). 'The Decline of Schooling Productivity in OECD Countries'. *Economic Journal*, 111: C135–C147.
Hall, P. A. (1993). 'Policy paradigms, social learning, and the state: the case of economic policymaking in Britain', *Comparative Politics*, 25(April): 275–96.
Hamilton, Alexander, Madison, James, and Jay, John (1970). *The Federalist*. London: Dent.
Harris, Conrad and Scrivener, Glen (1996). 'Fundholders' Prescribing Costs: The First Five Years'. *British Medical Journal*, 313: 1531–4.
Harth, Phillip (1989). 'Introduction' to Bernard Mandeville, *The Fable of the Bees*. London: Penguin.
Hausman, Daniel (1998). 'Rationality and Knavery', in Werner Leinfellner and Eckehart Köhler (eds.), *Game Theory, Experience, Rationality; Foundations of Social Sciences; Economics and Ethics: In Honor of John C. Harsanyi*. Dordrecht: Kluwer.
—— and Le Grand, Julian (1999). 'Incentives and Health Policy: Primary and Secondary Care in the British National Health Service.' *Social Science and Medicine*, 49: 1299–1307.
Haveman, Robert (1988). *Starting Even*. New York: Simon and Schuster.
Hennessy, Peter (1992). *Never Again: Britain 1945–51*. London: Jonathan Cape.
Henrich, Joseph (2001). 'In Search of Homo Economicus: Behavioral Experiments in 15 Small-Scale Societies'. *American Economic Review*, 91: 73–8.
Hill, Stephen, Lupton, Mark, Moody, Graham, and Regan, Sue (2002). *A Stake Worth Having? The Potential for Equity Stakes in Social Housing*. London: Chartered Institute of Housing and Institute for Public Policy Research.
Hill, Thomas E., Jr (1993). 'Beneficence and Self-Love: A Kantian Perspective', in Ellen Frankel Paul, Fred D. Miller, and Jeffery Paul (eds.), *Altruism*. Cambridge: Cambridge University Press.
Hills, John (2000). *Reinventing Social Housing Finance*. London: Institute of Public Policy Research.
—— and Burchardt, Tania (1997). *Private Welfare Insurance and Social Security*. York: Rowntree Foundation.
—— and Lelkes, Orsolya (1999). 'Social Security, Selective Universalism and Patchwork Redistribution', in Roger Jowell *et al.* (eds.), *British Social Attitudes: The 16th Report—Who Shares New Labour Values?* Aldershot: Ashgate.
Hirsch, Fred (1977). *Social Limits to Growth*. London: Routledge & Kegan Paul.
Hirschman, Albert (1970). *Exit, Voice and Loyalty: Responses to Decline in Firms, Organizations and States*. Cambridge, MA: Cambridge University Press.
—— (1977). *The Passions and the Interests*. Princeton: Princeton University Press.
—— (1986). *Rival Views of Market Society and Other Recent Essays*. New York: Viking.
Hobbes, Thomas (1651/1985). *Leviathan*. London: Penguin Books.
Hoffmeyer, Ulrich K. and McCarthy, Thomas R. (1994). *Financing Health Care*. Netherlands: Kluwer Academic Publishing.
Hoxby, Caroline M. (2000a). 'Does Competition Among Public Schools Benefit Students and Taxpayers?' *American Economic Review*, 90: 1209–38.
—— (2000b). *Do Private Schools Provide Competition for Public Schools?* (NBER Working Paper No. 4978). Cambridge, MA: National Bureau of Economic Research.
—— (2002). 'How School Choice Affects the Achievement of Public School Students', in Paul Hill (ed.), *Choice with Equity*. Stanford: Hoover Institution.

—— (2003). 'School Choice and School Productivity (Or, Is School Choice a Rising Tide that Lifts All Boats?)', in Caroline M. Hoxby (ed.), *The Economic Analysis of School Choice*. Chicago: University of Chicago Press.

Hume, David (1875). 'On the Independency of Parliament', in *Essays, Moral, Political and Literary*, Vol. 1 (ed. T. H. Green and T. H. Gross). London: Longmans.

Institute of Economic Affairs (1991). *The Case for Earmarked Taxes: Government Spending and Public Choice*. London: Institute of Economic Affairs.

Irwell Valley Housing Association (2001). *Gold Service: Report*. Copies available from www.irwellvalleyha.co.uk.

Jacobs, John (1994). 'The Scroungers Who Never Were: The Effects of the 1989 Social Security Act', in R. Page and J. Baldock (eds.), *Social Policy Review 6*. Canterbury: Social Policy Association, University of Kent.

Jones, Andrew and Duncan, Alan (1995). *Hypothecated Health Taxes: An Analysis of Recent Proposals*. London: Office of Health Economics.

Jones, Philip, Cullis, John, and Lewis, Alan (1998). 'Public versus Private Provision of Altruism: Can Fiscal Policy Make Individuals "Better" People?'. *Kyklos*, 51: 3–24.

Kavka, Gregory (1986). *Hobbesian Moral and Political Theory*. Princeton, NJ: Princeton University Press.

Kelly, Gavin and Lissauer, Rachel (2000). *Ownership for All*. London: Institute for Public Policy Research.

Kempson, Elaine and Whyley, Claire (1999). *Kept Out or Opted Out? Understanding and Combating Financial Exclusion*. Bristol: Policy Press.

Kendall, Jeremy (2000). 'The Mainstreaming of the Third Sector into Public Policy in England in the Late 1990s: Whys and Wherefores'. *Policy and Politics*, 28: 541–62.

—— (2001). 'Of Knights, Knaves and Merchants: The Case of Residential Care for Older People in England in the late 1990s'. *Social Policy and Administration*, 35: 360–75.

——, Matosevic, Tihana, Forder, Jules, Knapp, Martin, Hardy, Brian, and Ware, Patricia (2003). 'The Motivation of Domiciliary Care Providers in England: New Concepts, New Findings'. *Journal of Social Policy*, 32: 489–511.

Keynes, John Maynard (1935/1964). *The General Theory of Employment, Interest and Money*. New York: Harcourt Brace.

Khanna, Jyoti, Posnett, John, and Sandler, Todd (1995). 'Charity Donations in the UK—New Evidence Based on Panel Data'. *Journal of Public Economics*, 56: 257–72.

Kingma, Bruce (1989). 'An Accurate Measure of the Crowd-Out Effect, Income Effect and Price Effect for Charitable Contributions'. *Journal of Political Economy*, 97: 1197–203.

Klein, Rudolf (1995). *The New Politics of the NHS* (3rd edn). London: Longman.

Klein, Rudolf and Millar, Jane (1995) 'Do-it-yourself social policy: searching for a new paradigm' *Social Policy and Administration*, 29(4): 303–316.

Klein, Rudolf (2005). 'The Great Transformation'. *Health Economics, Policy, and Law*, 1(1): 91–98.

Krebs, Dennis (1970). 'Altruism—An Examination of the Concept and a Review of the Literature'. *Psychological Bulletin*, 73: 258–302.

Kvist, Jon and Sinfield, Adrian (1996). *Comparing Tax Routes to Welfare in Denmark and the United Kingdom*. Copenhagen: The Danish National Institute of Research.

La Rochefoucauld, Duc de (1678/1964). 'Maximes', in *Oeuvres Complètes*. Paris: Gallimard.

Ladd, Helen F. and Fiske, Edward B. (1999). 'The Uneven Playing Field of School Choice: Evidence from New Zealand'. Paper presented to the annual meeting of the Association of Public Policy Analysis and Management, Washington DC, 5 November.

Land, Hilary and Rose, Hilary (1985). 'Compulsory Altruism for Some or an Altruistic Society for All?', in Philip Bean, John Ferris, and David Whynes (eds.), *In Defence of Welfare*. London: Tavistock.

Lane, Robert E. (1991). *The Market Experience*. New York: Cambridge University Press.

Lauder, Hugh and Hughes, David (1999). *Trading in Futures: Why Markets in Education Don't Work*. Buckingham: Open University Press.

Lawson, Nigel (1992). *The View from No. 11: Memoirs of a Tory Radical*. London: Bantam Press.

Leat, Diana and Gay, Pat (1987). *Paying for Care: A Study of Policy and Practice in Paid Care Schemes*. London: Policy Studies Institute.

Le Grand, Julian (1982). *The Strategy of Equality*. London: Allen and Unwin.

—— (1989). 'Markets, Equality and Welfare', in Julian Le Grand and Saul Estrin (eds.), *Market Socialism*. Oxford: Clarendon.

—— (1991). *Equity and Choice: An Essay in Economics and Applied Philosophy*. London: Harper Collins.

—— (1995). 'The Market, the State and the Distribution of Life Cycle Income', in Jane Falkingham and John Hills (eds.), *The Dynamic of Welfare: The Welfare State and the Life Cycle*. Hemel Hempstead: Harvester Wheatsheaf.

—— (1997a). 'Afterword', in Anne Oakley and J. Ashton (eds.), *Richard Titmuss's The Gift Relationship*. London: Allen and Unwin.

—— (1997b). 'Knights, Knaves or Pawns? Human Behaviour and Social Policy'. *Journal of Social Policy*, 26: 149–69.

—— (1998). 'The Third Way Begins with CORA'. *New Statesman*, 6 March.

—— (1999a). 'New Approaches to the Welfare State', in Andrew Gamble and Tony Wright (eds.), *The New Social Democracy*. Malden, MA: Blackwells.

—— (1999b). 'Tales from the British National Health Service: Competition, Cooperation or Control?' *Health Affairs*, 18: 27–37.

—— (2000). 'From Knight to Knave? Public policy and Market Incentives', in Peter Taylor-Gooby (ed.), *Risk, Trust and Welfare*. Basingstoke: Macmillan.

—— (2002). 'The Labour Government and the National Health Service' *Oxford Review of Economic Policy* 18: 137–53.

—— and Bartlett, Will (eds.) (1993). *Quasi-Markets and Social Policy* Houndmills: Macmillan.

—— and Estrin, Saul (eds.) (1989). *Market Socialism*. Oxford: Clarendon.

——, Mays, Nicholas, and Mulligan, Jo-Ann (eds.) (1998). *Learning from the NHS Internal Market*. London: Kings Fund.

—— and Winter, David (1987). 'The Middle Classes and the Welfare State under Labour and Conservative Governments'. *Journal of Public Policy*, 6: 399–430.

Leat, Diana (1990). *For Love and Money: the Role of Payment in Encouraging the Provision of Care*. York: Joseph Rowntree Foundation.

—— and Gay, Pat (1987). *Paying for Care: A Study of Policy and Practice in Paid Care Schemes* (Research Report No. 661). London: Policy Studies Institute.

Lepper, Mark and Greene, David (1978). *The Hidden Costs of Reward: New Perspectives on the Psychology of Human Motivation*. Hillsdale: Wiley/Erlbaum.

Lewis, Richard (2002). 'Uh . . . Haven't We Been Here Before?'. *Health Matters*, 49/Autumn: 5–7.

Lipsey, David (forthcoming). *Big Tent Welfare* (Health and Social Care Discussion Paper). London: London School of Economics.

Lipsky, M. (1980). *Street-Level Bureaucracy*. New York: Russell Sage Foundation.

Lowe, Rodney (1993). *The Welfare State in Britain Since 1945*. London: Macmillan.

Mandeville, Bernard (1714/1989). *The Fable of the Bees*. London: Penguin Books, 1989.

—— (1731). *Free Thoughts on Religion, the Church and National Happiness* (3rd edn). London.

Margolis, H. (1982). *Selfishness, Altruism and Rationality*. New York: Cambridge University Press.

Marshall, T. H. (1973). 'Richard Titmuss—An Appreciation', *The British Journal of Sociology*, XXIV(2): 138–39.

Mayo, Ed and Moore, Henrietta (2001). *The Mutual State: How Local Communities Can Run Public Services*. London: New Economics Foundation.

Mays, Nicholas, Goodwin, N., Killoran, Amanda, and Malbon, G. (1998). *Total Purchasing: A Step towards Primary Care Groups*. London: Kings Fund.

Mead, Lawrence (1992). *The New Politics of Poverty*. New York: Basic Books.

Mill, John Stuart (1859/1982). *On Liberty*. Harmondsworth: Penguin.

Miller, David (1988). 'Altruism and the Welfare State', in J. Donald Moon (ed.), *Responsibility, Rights and Welfare*. Boulder, CO: Westview.

Monroe, Kristen Renwick (1994). 'A Fat Lady in a Corset: Altruism and Social Theory'. *American Journal of Political Science*, 38: 861–93.

Mueller, D. (1989). *Public Choice II*. Cambridge: Cambridge University Press.

Nagel, Thomas and Murphy, Liam (2002). *The Myth of Ownership: Taxes and Justice*. New York: Oxford University Press.

New, Bill (1999). 'Paternalism and Public Policy'. *Economics and Philosophy*, 15: 63–83.

Nissan, David and Le Grand, Julian (2000). *A Capital Idea: Start Up Grants For Young People*. London: Fabian Society.

Noden, Philip (2000). 'Rediscovering the Impact of Marketisation: Dimensions of Social Segregation in England's Secondary Schools, 1994–99'. *British Journal of Sociology of Education*, 21: 371–90.

—— (forthcoming). 'Education Markets and Social Polarisation: Back to Square One?'. *Research Papers in Education*.

Oakley, Anne and Ashton, J. (eds.) (1997). *Richard Titmuss's The Gift Relationship*. London: Allen and Unwin. London: LSE Books.

Oakley, A. and Barker J. (eds) (2004). *Private Complaints and Public Health: Richard Titmuss on the National Health Service*. Bristol: The Policy Press.

OD Partnerships Network (2002). *Networks, Hierarchies and Markets: Good, Bad and Ugly?* www.odpnetwork.co.uk.

O'Neill, Onora (2002). *A Question of Trust*. Cambridge: Cambridge University Press.

Ouchi, W. (1980). 'Markets, Bureaucracies and Clans'. *Administrative Science Quarterly*, 25:129–41.

Page, Robert M. (1996). *Altruism and the Welfare State*. Aldershot: Avebury.

Pampel, Fred and Williamson, John (1989). *Age, Class, Politics and the Welfare State*. Cambridge: Cambridge University Press.

Parfit, Derek (1984). *Reasons and Persons*. Oxford: Oxford University Press.

Paul, Ellen Frankel, Miller, Fred D., and Paul, Jeffery (eds) (1993). *Altruism*. Cambridge: Cambridge University Press. Also published as a special issue of *Social Philosophy and Policy*, 10/1 (1993).

Pauly, Mark (1990). 'The Rational Non-Purchase of Long-Term Care Insurance'. *Journal of Political Economy*, 98: 153–68.

Peltzman, S. (1980). 'The Growth of Government'. *Journal of Law and Economics*, 23: 209–88.

Pettipher, C. and Halfpenny, P. (1993). 'The 1990–1991 Individual Giving Survey', in S. E. C. Saxon-Harrod and J. Kendall (eds.), *Researching the Voluntary Sector*. Tonbridge: Charities Aid Foundation.

Pettit, Philip (1996). 'Institutional Design And Rational Choice', in Robert Goodin (ed.), *The Theory of Institutional Design*. Cambridge: Cambridge University Press.

Phelps, Edmund S. (ed.) (1975). *Altruism, Morality and Economic Theory*. New York: Russell Sage.

Piachaud, David (1993). *What's Wrong with Fabianism?* (Fabian Pamphlet No. 558). London: Fabian Society.

Piliavin, Jane Allyn and Charng, Hang-Wen (1990). 'Altruism: A Review of Recent Theory and Research'. *American Review of Sociology*, 16: 27–65.

Pinker, Robert (1971). *Social Theory and Social Policy*. London: Heinemann.

—— (1977). 'Preface' in Reisman (1997), vii–xv.

—— (1979). *The Idea of Welfare*. London: Heinemann.

—— (1987). 'Opportunities for Altruism' in Philpot, Terry (Ed) *On Second Thoughts: Reassessments of the Literature of Social Work*, Wallington: Reed Business Publishing.

—— (2003). 'The Conservative Tradition in Social Welfare' in Alcock, Peter, Erskine, Angus and May, Margaret (Eds) *The Student's Companion to Social Policy*, 78–84, Oxford: Blackwell / Social Policy Association.

—— (2006). 'From Gift Relationships to Quasi-markets: An Odyssey along the Policy Paths of Altruism and Egoism'. *Social Policy & Administration*, 40(1): 10–25.

Plant, Raymond (2001). *A Public Service Ethic?* London: Social Market Foundation.

Powell, Enoch J. (1976). *Medicine and Politics: 1975 and After*. Tunbridge Wells: Pitman Medical.

Power, Anne (1993). *Hovels to High Rise: State Housing in Europe until 1850*. London: Routledge.

Power, Michael (1999). *The Audit Society*. Oxford: Oxford University Press.

Propper, Carol, Croxson, Bronwyn, and Shearer, Arran (2002). 'Waiting Times for Hospital Admissions: The Impact of GP Fundholding'. *Journal of Health Economics*, 21: 227–52.

——, Wilson, Deborah, and Soderland, Neil (1998).'The Effects of Regulation and Competition in the NHS Internal Market: The Case of GP Fund-Holder Prices'. *Journal of Health Economics*, 4: 333–56.

Rabin, Matthew (1997). *Psychology and Economics* (Berkeley Department of Economics Working Paper No. 97-251). Berkeley: University of California. Shorter version published in *Journal of Economic Literature*, 36 (1998): 11–46.

Rawnsley, Andrew (2001). *Servants of the People: The Inside Story of New Labour* (revised edn). London: Penguin.

Reisman, D. (1977). *Richard Titmuss: Welfare and Society*. London: Heinemann.

Ridley, Matt (1996). *The Origins of Virtue*. London: Viking.

Risse, Mathias (2005). 'Should Citizens of a Welfare State be Transformed into "Queens"? *Economics and Philosophy* 21: 291–303.

Roberts, Russell D. (1984). 'A Positive Model of Private Charity and Public Transfer'. *Journal of Political Economy*, 92: 136–48.

Rodwin, Mark (1993). *Medicine, Money and Morals; Physicians' Conflict of Interest.* Oxford: Oxford University Press.

Roemer, John (1988). *Free to Lose.* London: Radius.

Rogers, Kelly (1997). *Self-Interest: An Anthology of Philosophical Perspectives.* London: Routledge.

Rose-Ackerman, Susan (1996). 'Altruism, Nonprofits and Economic Theory'. *Journal of Economic Literature,* 34: 701–28.

Sandford, Cedric (1971). *Taxing Personal Wealth.* London: Allen and Unwin.

Scheffler, Richard (1989). 'Adverse Selection: The Achilles Heel of the NHS Reforms'. *The Lancet,* i: 950–2.

Scott, Anthony (1997). *Designing Incentives for GPs: A Review of the Literature on their Preferences for Pecuniary and Non-pecuniary Job Characteristics* (Discussion Paper 01/97). Aberdeen: Health Economics Research Unit, University of Aberdeen.

Seldon, Arthur (1968) 'Commitment to Welfare: A Review Article', Social and Economic Administration, Vol 2, No 3, 196–200.

Sen, Amartya (1985). *Commodities and Capabilities.* Amsterdam: North Holland.

Sennett, Richard (1998). *The Corrosion of Character.* New York: W.W. Norton.

Shaw, R, Mitchell, D., and Dawson, S. (1995). 'The Motivation of Consultant Physicians'. *British Journal of Health Care Management,* 1: 648–52.

Sherraden, Michael (1991). *Assets and the Poor.* Armonk, New York: M.E. Sharpe.

Smith, Adam (1759/1976). *The Theory of Moral Sentiments* (ed. D. D. Raphael and A.L. Macfie). Oxford: Clarendon Press.

—— (1776/1964). *The Wealth of Nations.* London: Dent, Everyman's Library.

Steele, Jane (1999). *Wasted Values: Harnessing the Commitment of Public Managers.* London: Public Management Foundation.

Sugden, Robert (1982). 'On the Economics of Philanthropy'. *Economic Journal,* 92: 341–50.

—— (1984). 'Reciprocity: The Supply of Public Goods Through Voluntary Contributions'. *Economic Journal,* 94: 772–87.

—— (1993). 'Thinking as a Team: Towards an Explanation of Non-selfish Behaviour', in Ellen Frankel Paul, Fred D. Miller, and Jeffery Paul (eds.), *Altruism.* Cambridge: Cambridge University Press.

Taylor-Gooby, Peter (ed.) (2000). *Risk, Trust and Welfare.* Basingstoke: Macmillan.

——, Sylvester, Stella, Calnan, Mike, and Manley, Graham (2000). 'Knights, Knaves and Gnashers: Professional Values and Private Dentistry'. *Journal of Social Policy,* 29: 375–95.

Teja, Ranjit S. and Bracewell-Milnes, Barry (1991). *The Case for Earmarked Taxes: Government Spending and Public Choice.* London: Institute of Economic Affairs.

Thompson, G., Levacic, F., and Mitchell, J. (eds.) (1991). *Markets, Hierarchies, and Networks: The Co-ordination of Social Life.* London: Sage.

Thompson, J. A. K. (1976). *The Ethics of Aristotle: The Nichomachean Ethics.* London: Penguin.

Thomson, Sarah, Busse, Reinhard, and Mossialos, Elias (2002). 'The Demand for Substantive Health Insurance in Germany'. *Croatian Medical Journal,* 43/4: 425–32.

Timmins, Nicholas (1995). *The Five Giants.* London: HarperCollins.

—— (1999). 'The Silent Death of National Insurance'. *Financial Times,* 22 November.

Titmuss, Richard (1958). *Essays on 'The Welfare State'.* London: Allen and Unwin.

—— (1968). *Commitment to Welfare.* London: Allen and Unwin.

—— (1974). *Social Policy.* London: Allen and Unwin.

Titmuss, Richard (1970/1997). *The Gift Relationship*. London, Allen and Unwin. Quotations are from new edition; see Anne Oakley and J. Ashton (eds.) (1997), *Richard Titmuss's The Gift Relationship*. London: Allen and Unwin.

Tversky, Amos and Kahneman, Daniel (1982). 'Judgement under Uncertainty: Heuristics and Biases', in Daniel Kahneman, Paul Slovic, and Amos Tversky (eds.), *Judgement under Uncertainty*. Cambridge: Cambridge University Press.

Unger, Roberto and West, Cornel (1998). *The Future of American Progressivism: An Initiative for Political and Economic Reform*. Boston: Beacon Press.

Ungerson, Claire (1987). *Policy is Personal: Sex, Gender and Informal Care*. London: Tavistock.

United Kingdom. Audit Commission (1995). *The Doctors' Tale: the Work of Hospital Doctors in England and Wales*. London: HMSO.

United Kingdom. Department of Health (1998a). *Establishing Primary Care Groups* (HSC 1998/065). London: Department of Health.

—— (1998b). *Developing Primary Care Groups* (HSC 1998/139). London: Department of Health.

—— (2002). *Reforming NHS Financial Flows*. London: Department of Health.

United Kingdom. Royal Commission on Long-term Care (1999). *With Respect to Old Age: Long-Term Care—Rights and Responsibilities* (Cm 4192-I). London: TSO.

United Kingdom. Treasury (2001a). *Savings and Assets for All* (The Modernisation of Britain's Tax and Benefit System Consultation Paper No. 8). London: HM Treasury.

—— (2001b). *Delivering Savings and Assets* (The Modernisation of Britain's Tax and Benefit System Consultation Paper No. 9). London: HM Treasury.

Upton, W. (1973). 'Altruism, Attribution and Intrinsic Motivation in the Recruitment of Blood Donors' (Ph.D. dissertation). Ithaca, NY: Cornell University.

Vandenberghe, Vincent (1998). 'Educational Quasi-markets: The Belgian Experience', in Will Bartlett, Jenny Roberts, and Julian Le Grand (eds.), *A Revolution in Social Policy*. Bristol: Policy Press.

Van Doorslaer, Eddie, Wagstaff, Adam, and Rutten, Franz (1993). *Equity in the Finance and Delivery of Health Care*. Oxford: Oxford University Press.

Van Parijs, Philippe (ed.) (1992). *Arguing for Basic Income: Ethical Foundations for a Radical Reform*. London: Verso.

Van Parijs, Philippe (ed.) (1995). *Real Freedom for All: What (If Anything) can Justify Capitalism?* Oxford: Oxford University Press.

Ware, Alan (1990). 'Meeting Need through Voluntary Action: Does Market Society Corrode Altruism?', in Alan Ware and Robert Goodin (eds.), *Needs and Welfare*. London: Sage.

Warr, Peter G. (1982). 'Pareto Optimal Redistribution and Private Charity'. *Journal of Public Economics*, 19: 131–8.

Weale, Albert (1980). *Political Theory and Social Policy*. London: Macmillan.

Webber, Carolyn and Wildavsky, Aaron (1986). *A History of Taxation and Expenditure in the Western World*. New York: Simon and Schuster.

West, Anne and Pennell, Hazel (1997). 'Educational Reform and School Choice in England and Wales'. *Education Economics*, 5: 285–305.

—— —— (1998). 'School Admissions: Increasing Equity, Accountability and Transparency'. *British Journal of Educational Studies*, 46: 188–200.

—————— (2000). 'Publishing School Examination Results in England: Incentives and Consequences'. *Educational Studies*, 26: 423–36.

————  ——, and Edge, Anne (1997). 'Exploring the Impact of Reform on School-Enrolment Policies in England'. *Education Administration Quarterly*, 33: 170–82.

White, A. H. (1989) 'Patterns of Giving', in R. Magat (ed.), *Philanthropic Giving: Studies in Varieties and Goals*. Oxford: Oxford University Press.

White, Stuart (2001). 'Asset-Based Egalitarianism: Forms Strengths, Limitations', in Sue Regan (ed.), *Assets and Progressive Welfare*. London: Institute of Public Policy Research.

—— (forthcoming). 'The Citizen's Stake and the Alienation Objection', in Erik Olin Wright (ed.), *Rethinking Redistribution*. London: Verso.

Whitty, Geoff, Power, Sally, and Halpin, David (1998). 'Self-Managing Schools in the Market-Place: The Experience of England, the USA and New Zealand', in Will Bartlett, Jenny Roberts, and Julian Le Grand (eds.), *A Revolution in Social Policy*. Bristol: Policy Press.

Wildavsky, A. (1994). 'Why self-interest means less outside of a social context'. *Journal of Theoretical Politics*, 6(2): 131–59.

Williams, Fiona (1999). 'Good-Enough Principles for Welfare'. *Journal of Social Policy*, 28/4: 667–87.

Williamson, Oliver (1983). *Markets and Hierarchies*. New York: Free Press.

Wolpert, Julian (1993). *Patterns of Generosity in America*. New York: Twentieth Century Fund.

Woods, Philip, Bagley, Carl, and Glatter, Ron (1998). *School Choice and Competition: Markets in the Public Interest?* London: Routledge.

Wright, Erik Olin (ed.) (1998). *Recasting Egalitarianism: New Rules for Communities, States and Markets*. London: Verso.

Wright, Karen (2002). *Generosity versus Altruism: Philanthropy and Charity in the US and UK* (Working Paper No. 17). London: Centre for Civil Society, London School of Economics.

Wright, Robert (1994). *The Moral Animal*. New York: Pantheon Books.

# Index

Ackerman, Bruce, and stakeholder grant
   123, 129
adverse selection, and incentive contracts  60
agency:
   asset ownership  125
   definition  2
   extent of  73
   ideology  16–17
   market socialism  15
   neo-liberals  14–15
   public finance  85–91
   public services  73–84
   social democracy  13–14
   tax revenues  147–50
Alstott, Anne, and stakeholder grant
   123, 129
Altmann, Ros, and matching grants  141
altruism  24 n. 1, 26, 169, 190, 196–7, 208
   act-irrelevant  35–7, 47
   act-relevant  35–7
   blood donation system  31, 41, 175, 191–3
   charitable giving  37–8
   collectivism  29
   compulsory  45
   consultant payment scheme  104–5
   corruption of  40, 46–7, 48–50
   cost thresholds  52
   decision-making  80
   doctors  32–3
   existence of  38
   exploitation  65–6, 199
   gender  44–5
   market incentives  40–6, 52, 166
   moral superiority  167, 195
   non-existence of  26–7
   non-profit organisations  63
   opportunity cost of  51–2, 194, 200–2
   public sector managers  31–2
   public services  35
   self-interest and rationality  28–9, 198
   self-sacrifice  45–6, 51–2, 55
   trust  29–30
Andreoni, James  44
   and crowding out  38
Aristotle  47 n. 8

asset ownership:
   agency  125
   asset-based egalitarianism  125–7
   autonomy  125–6
   benefits of  125
   empowerment  121, 122, 127
   inequality  124
   popular capitalism  124
   welfare  125
   youth poverty in  128
   see also demogrant
Atkinson, A. B. and demogrants  121
attainment tests, performance in school  110
autonomy:
   asset ownership  125–6, 173, 199, 205
   compulsion  138

Bagley, Carl, impact of school competition  113
Baldwin, Peter  8
Ball, Stephen, and educational selection  111
Banks, James, youth wealth  128
Barkema, H. G.  49
Barnett, Corelli  4
basic income  123
behaviour:
   distinguished from motivation  25, 172, 198, 201
   financial incentives  35
   physicians and market incentives  105, 175
   policy  2, 171, 173, 180
   residential care providers  34, 204–5
Belgium:
   educational reform  115
   quasi-market  10
benefits, universal  131
Beveridge, William  4
Blair, Tony:
   quasi-market  11
   the third way  15–16, 170, 179
blood donation system  40–2, 175
   altruism  31
   motivation  31
Bowe, Richard, and educational selection  111
Bowles, Samuel, and voucher system  116
Bradley, Stephen:
   educational selection  113–14

Bradley, Stephen (*cont.*)
  impact of school competition 113
  school exam performance 113
Brennan, Geoffrey 54
Brewer, Gene, public service motivation 34
British Medical Association, and doctors'
  motivation 32–3
British Medical Journal, online survey of
  medical professionals 74 n. 1
British Social Attitudes Survey (1995) 152
British Social Attitudes Survey (1999), public
  attitudes towards government spending
  152
Brittan, Samuel 151
  share distribution 123
Broome, John, and personal identity 89–90
Brown, Gordon 156
Brown, John 30
Buchanan, James 12 n. 15
Burgess, Simon 35
Butler, Eamonn, and demogrant 122
Butler, Joseph, and self interest 27
Bynner, John, and youth asset poverty 128

capitalism, popular, and asset ownership 124
care, long-term:
  matching grants 142–3
  partnership scheme 141–6
carers:
  exploitation 65–6
  motivation 43–5
Chalkley, Martin 61
charitable giving:
  crowding out hypothesis 37–8
  patterns of 37–8
  types of altruism 37–8
child trust fund 122
  *see also* demogrant
civilisation, and commerce 164–5
Clinton, Bill, and the third way 15–16
Clotfelter, Charles, and charitable giving 37
collectivism:
  altruism 29
  neo-liberal distrust of 13
  post-war 4
command and control, model of service
  delivery 48–50, 181
commerce, and civilisation 164–5
communitarianism:
  empowerment 74, 78, 82
  professionals' power 81
compassion 36 n. 14, 197

Condorcet, Marie Jean Antoine de Caritat,
  Marquis de 164
consultants, payment of hospital 103–4, 173,
  199
cooperatives, and public interest 63
costly verification problem, and incentive
  contracts 60
Crilly, Tessa, and NHS Trusts 33
Crosland, Anthony 4
  on council housing 7 n. 8
Croxon, Bronwyn, and fund-holding GPs 100

Dawkins, Richard, and selfish genes 28
Deacon, Alan 7, 14
Dean, Hartley 167
decentralisation, fund-holding GPs 98–101,
  116–17
decision-making:
  altruism 80
  communitarian approach 74, 78, 82
  liberal approach 74, 77
  professionals' power 79–81, 173
  welfarist approach 74–7, 79–81, 81–2
  *see also* empowerment
democracy, and use of tax revenues 148
democratic socialism, and origins of welfare
  state 4–5
demogrant:
  abuse of 130–1
  arguments against 126–7, 206
  asset-based egalitarianism 124–7
  conditions on use 128–31
  contemporary interest in 122–3
  contributions to 135–6
  definition 121
  disincentives 136
  empowerment 127
  financial training 131
  financing of 121–3, 133–5, 179
  means-testing 131–2
  origins of idea 121
  pawns and queens 127–8
  size of 129
  timing of 133
  universal application 131–2
  uses for 130
dentists, and motivation 33
Dixit, Avinash, and incentive contracts 59
doctors, motivations of 32–3, 185
Dolton, Peter 35
Dryzek, John 8
Dusheiko, Mark, and fund-holding GPs 100

economic man 25–6
Education Reform Act (1988) 108
education system:
  communitarian approach 78
  decision-making 74–84
  empowerment 82–4, 115, 117
  excess demand 78
  impact of school competition 113–15
  incentive schemes 109
  liberal approach 77
  Local Management of Schools
    initiative 108
  motivation in 109
  network model of service delivery 49
  parental choice 74, 108, 112, 117
  parental powerlessness 108
  parentalism 77, 83
  performance 110, 112, 113
  pre-1980s structure 107
  professionals' power 79–81
  public expenditure 112
  quasi-market system 10, 109–15, 116–17
  selection 110–11, 113–14
  Thatcherite reform of 108–9
  voucher system 108, 116
  welfarist approach 75, 77
egalitarianism, asset-based 121, 124–7, 200
  *see also* demogrant
elections:
  empowerment 82
  tool of accountability 148
  *see also* referendums
empowerment:
  asset based egalitarianism 121, 124–7
  communitarian approach 74, 78, 82
  demogrant 127
  education system 82–4, 115, 117
  elections 82, 148
  exit 82, 83–4, 103–4
  GP fund-holders 117–18
  hypothecation 153
  individual failure 77–8, 79–80
  liberal approach 74, 77, 206
  parental 108–9
  public policy 163
  public services 74
  referendums 153
  savings 86
  user 74
  voice 82, 83–4, 103
  welfarist approach 74–7, 78, 79–81, 182, 184
England, Paula, and exploitation 65–6

equality, and education system 6
exit, and empowerment 82, 83–4, 103–4
exploitation, and altruism 65–6

Fabian Society:
  demogrant 122
  public attitudes to taxation 149–50, 151–2
faith-based organisations, and public
    interest 63
Field, Frank 9
Finch, Janet 44
  altruism 26
Fiske, Edward, and New Zealand education
    reform 115
Fitz, John, impact of education reform 111
Folbre, Nancy 54
  exploitations 65
Forder, Julian, behaviour of residential care
    providers 34
Frank, Robert, and exploitation 65
Frey, Bruno 42–3, 49, 52–4
Fukuyama, Francis, commerce and
    civilisation 164–5
fund-holding, general practitioner 98–101,
    116–17

gender:
  altruism 44–5
  impact of financial incentives on
    motivation 44
general practitioners (GPs):
  effects of fund-holding 100–1
  fund-holding 98–101, 116–17
  incentive structures pre-1991 96–8
  motivations 96, 97–8
  as private contractors 96
  rationing of health care 98
  referral system 97
  role 96
Gewirtz, Sharon, and educational
    selection 110
Giddens, Anthony, and the third way 15–16
Gintis, Herbert, voucher system 116
Glatter, Ron, impact of school
    competition 113
Glennerster, Howard, and educational
    reform 109, 110, 112
Goette, Lorenz 43
Goodin, Robert 8, 26
Gorard, Stephen, impact of education
    reforms 111
Gordon, Rupert, advantages of markets 165

government:
  corruption of altruism 48–50, 197
  distrust of 149
  influence on motivation 46–7
  intervention in individual savings 86–91
  matching grants 139, 140–1
  moral atrophy 46–7
  provision of social services 3
  regulation 57
Graham, Alison, NHS and managers'
    motivation 32
grants, matching 139, 140–1, 142

Hamlin, Alan 54
Haveman, Ralph, and demogrant 122
health care:
  communitarian approach 78, 82
  decision-making 74–84
  empowerment 74, 82–4
  excess demand 78
  hypothecated health tax 161–2
  liberal approach 77
  long-term and partnership scheme 141–6
  primary care trusts 101–4
  professionals' power 79–81
  rationing of 98
  welfarist approach 75, 76, 77, 81–2
  *see also* general practitioners; National
    Health Service
Hegel, G. W. F. 165–6
Hennessy, Peter 4
Hills, John:
  housing ownership 123
  public attitudes towards government
      spending 152
Hirsch, Fred, and corruption of altruism 40
Hirschman, Albert 164
  empowerment 82
  voice and exit 103
Hobbes, Thomas 30, 178
  non-existence of altruism 26–7
*homo economicus* 25–6, 28
housing:
  council 6–7, 7 n. 8
  demogrant and ownership 130
  incentive schemes 118–19
  owner-occupation 8, 123
  quasi-market in 10
Hoxby, Caroline, impact of school
    competition 114
Hughes, David, New Zealand education
    reform 115
Hume, David 2, 12, 25, 27

hypothecation:
  advantages of 153
  arguments for 151–7
  definition 150–1
  extent of 153–4
  financing demogrant 133
  genuineness of 154–5
  impact on other expenditure 156
  national insurance 157–60
  objections to 153–5, 156–7
  origins of idea 150
  proposed health tax 161–2
  referendums 153
  stabilisation funds 154
  strong 155
  tax-resistance 151–2
  types of 155

identity:
  hypothecated taxation 161
  personal 89–90, 187
ideology:
  agency 16–17
  motivation 16–17
  public policy 11–16, 195
incentive contracts:
  adverse selection 60
  costly verification problem 60
  moral hazard 59
  non-profit organisations 64
  robust incentives 64–5
  service delivery 58–61
incentive schemes:
  education system 108–9
  fund-holding GPs 98–101, 116–17
  hospital consultants 104
  housing 118–19
  pre-1991 for general practitioners 96–8
  primary care trusts 102–4
independence, and asset ownership
    125–6, 198, 200
individual failure:
  decision-making 77–8, 79–80
  myopia 89
individualism 14
individuals:
  autonomous beings 14–15, 172
  victims 13–14, 178–9, 180–4
inequality 121
  age-related 124
  asset ownership 124, 200
  inheritance 124–5
  *see also* egalitarianism

inheritance tax 121
   demogrant 121–2, 133–5
   inequality 124–5
insurance 87
   matching grants 142
   moral hazard 87, 201
   social, and long-term care 142, 187
   state intervention 86–91
   *see also* national insurance; social insurance
Irwell Valley Housing Association 118–19

Jegen, Reto 49
Johnson, Samuel 164
Jones, Geraint, impact of school competition 113
Jones, Philip 40
justice, sense of 36 n. 14

Kant, Immanuel 165
Kelly, Gavin, and demogrant 122
Kendall, Jeremy, and residential care
   providers motivations 33–4
Keynes, John Maynard 4
   commerce and civilisation 164
Khanna, Jyoti, and charitable giving 38
Kingma, Bruce, and charitable giving 37–8
Klein, Rudolf 6, 169, 204–5
knaves:
   definition 2, 25, 27, 178
   education system 108, 109
   general practitioners 96–7, 175
   hospital consultants 105
   housing 118–19
   quasi-market 167–8
   rationality 28–9
   service delivery 56, 57–8, 61, 171–2, 181, 198
   trust 29–30, 180, 205
knights:
   act-irrelevant 35–7, 47
   act-relevant 35–7, 51, 61
   collectivism 29
   corrupted by government 46–7
   definition 2, 26–7, 178
   different types of 38
   education system 107–8, 109
   general practitioners 96–7, 98–9, 101, 102
   hospital consultants 104–5
   housing 118–19
   markets influence on 40–6
   motivation 26–30
   public sector workers 36
   quasi-market 168
   rationality 28–9
   self-interest 26–7

self-sacrifice 45–6, 54
service delivery 56–7, 171
trust 29–30

La Rouchefoucauld, François Duc de, and
   self interest 27
Ladd, Helen, and New Zealand education
   reform 115
Lane, Robert, and motivation 53
Lauder, Hugh, New Zealand education
   reform 115
Le Grand, Julian, and demogrant 122
Leat, Diana 43
Lelkes, Orsolya, public attitudes towards
   government spending 152
liberalism:
   empowerment 74, 77
   professionals' power 81
Lissauer, Rachel, and demogrant 122
Local Management of Schools initiative 108
Lowe, Rodney 4

Madison, James 12 n. 15
Major, John 151
Malcolmson, James 61
management, and motivation 31–2, 174, 204
Mandeville, Bernard 12 n. 15, 27, 30
Mann, Kirk 14
market incentives:
   advantages of 164
   altruism 40–6, 52, 166
   impact of 42–3
   motivation 55–6
   physician behaviour 105
   self-sacrifice 52
   service delivery 55–6
market socialism 15
markets:
   civilisation 164–5
   impact on motivation 42–3
   influence on knightly activity 40–6
   limitations 41
   market failures 86–8
   moral justification of 165–7
   neo-liberals 11–12
   public services 9, 163–4, 176
   self-interest 12–13
   social democracy 12, 13
   welfare state 9–10, 180
   *see also* quasi-markets
Marshall, T. H. 4, 194–5
Mayo, Ed 62
Mead, Lawrence 14–15

means testing:
   demogrant 131–2
   long-term care 142, 143
middle class, and welfare state 7–8
Mill, John Stuart 27, 74–5
Millington, Jim, impact of school
      competition 113
Montesquieu, Charles de Secondat 164
Moore, Henrietta 62
moral hazard:
   incentive contracts 59
   insurance 87
   pension provision 138
morality, and motivation 65–7
motivation 23–5, 197
   altruistic 35–7, 198–9, 202
   blood donations 31, 191
   Crowding-Out effect 54–4
   definition 2
   distinguished from behaviour 25
   doctors 32–3
   education system 109, 115, 117
   extrinsic 53
   general practitioners 97–8, 117–18
   government influence on 46–7
   ideology 16–17
   intrinsic 53
   knavish 25–6, 172, 179, 186
   knightly 26–30
   management 31–2
   market incentives 42–3
   market socialism 15
   models of service delivery 48–50
   morality 65–7
   neo-liberals and 12–13
   NHS Trusts 33
   non-profit organisations 62–4
   policy reform 40–50
   public services 31–8, 51–5, 67–70, 171,
      173–4, 202
   regulation 103
   Relative Price Effect 53–4
   residential care providers 33–4
   self interest 25–6, 180
   self-sacrifice 54
   social democracy 13–14
   social housing tenants 118–19
myopia, and savings 88–91

National Health Service:
   managers and motivation 32
   network model of service delivery 48–9
   payment of consultants 104–5
   primary care trusts 101–4

quasi-market 10, 11
   reputation 161
   role of patients 6
   *see also* general practitioners; health care
National Health Service Trusts, and
      motivation 33
national insurance:
   benefits cut 159
   contributions increased 159
   functions of 158
   hypothecation 150, 157–60
   ineffective redistribution instrument 159
   lack of clarity 160
   public disillusion with 160
   shortcomings of 158–9
   weak hypothecation 160
National Lottery 151
neo-liberalism:
   agency 14–15
   collectivism 13
   motivation 12–13
   public policy 11–16
Netherlands:
   educational reform 115
   quasi-markets 10
network model of service delivery 48–50, 61
New Zealand:
   competition amongst schools 114–15
   quasi-markets 10–11
New, Bill, and individual failure 76–7
Nissan, David, and demogrant 122
Noden, Philip, impact of education
      reforms 111
non-profit organisations:
   altruism 63
   service delivery 62–4

Office for Standards in Education (Ofsted) 112
old age:
   provision for 86, 88, 187–8, 207
   *see also* care, long-term; pensions
O'Neill, Onora, and trust 80

Paine, Thomas:
   commerce and civilisation 164
   demogrants 121
parental choice, education system 107, 108,
      112, 117
parentalism, and education 77, 83
Parfit, Derek, personal identity 89–90, 187
partnership schemes:
   long-term care 141–6
   pension 138–41
Pauly, Mark 87

pawns:
  decision-making 74–84, 183
  definition 2, 180
  demogrant 127–8
  education system 107–8, 181
  hypothecation 152–3, 178
  public policy 163, 171, 173, 182, 184, 200
  taxation 147
Pennell, Hazel, impact of educational reform
    109–10
pensions 85
  compulsory contributions 137–8
  matching grants 139, 140–1
  myopia 88–91
  partnership scheme 139–41
Perkins, Andy, and fund-holding GPs 100
Piachaud, David 8–9
Pinker, Robert 7 n. 10, 169, 190–203, 208
Pirie, Madsen, and demogrant 122
policy-makers, assumptions of 2, 181
Posnett, John, and charitable giving 38
power:
  inequalities in 120–1
  users' over public service provision 81–2,
    182
  *see also* decision-making; empowerment
Power, Michael 50
powerlessness, and taxation 148–9
preference 25 n. 2
primary care trusts 101–4
principal-agent theory, and incentive
    contracts 59–61, 64
privatisation 9
professions, and regulation 57
Propper, Carol 35
  fund-holding GPs 100
psychology, evolutionary 28
public choice theory, influence of 8, 10
public finance, and agency 85–91
public interest, and non-profit organisations
    63
public policy:
  affect on motivation 40–50, 172
  empowerment 163
  ideology 11–16, 193
  quasi-market 39, 98, 109–15
public sector:
  financial incentives and behaviour 34–5,
    200
  management motivation 31–2, 173–4
  trust 80–1
public sector workers, knightly and knavish
    behaviour 35
public service ethos 1, 5, 24, 39, 172, 179, 199

public services:
  agency 73–84
  altruistic behaviour 35
  command and control model of delivery
    48–50, 172
  excess demand 78
  financing of 85–91
  market mechanism 9
  motivation 31–8, 51–5, 67–70, 199, 208
  network model of delivery 48–50
  overuse 84
  user empowerment 74, 81–2
  *see also* quasi-markets

quasi-markets 163–4, 169
  education system 10, 109–15, 116–17, 180
  housing 10
  knaves 167–8, 198
  knights 168, 204
  moral justification 165–7
  NHS 10, 11, 170, 176
  public policy 3, 39, 98, 109–15, 181
  welfare state 3, 9–10, 98, 171, 200
queens:
  decision-making 74–84, 178
  demogrants 127–8
  hypothecation 152–3
  public policy 163, 173, 179–80
  savings 85, 185

Rabin, Matthew, and altruism 30
rationality, and self-interest and altruism 28–9
redistribution, resistance to 8–9
referendums, and hypothecation 153
regulation:
  governmental 57
  primary care trusts 103
Risse, Mathias ix, 169, 178–89, 205–7
Robertson, William 164
Roemer, John, and demogrant 123

sacrifice, *see* self-sacrifice
Sandford, Cedric, and demogrants 121
Sandler, Todd, and charitable giving 38
savings 85
  compulsory 137–8
  disempowerment 86
  future self 90–1
  Individual Development Accounts 138–9
  individual failure 89
  individual myopia 88–91
  market failures 86–8
  matching grants 135, 140–1
  partnership pensions 139–41, 179, 188

savings (*cont.*)
  Savings Gateway 139
  state intervention 86
  state partnerships 138–9
  welfare state 87, 207
self-interest 25–6
  definition 26, 196
  knightly motivation 26–7, 178, 180
  neo-liberalism 12–13
  policy 2, 174
  provision of public services 9, 171, 173
  rationality and altruism 28–9, 172, 197, 202
self-sacrifice:
  altruism 51–2, 55
  consultant payment scheme 104–5
  cost thresholds 52
  levels of 45–6
  market incentives 52
  motivation 54
Sen, Amartya 77
Sennett, Richard, and corruption of
    altruism 40
service delivery:
  incentive contracts 58–61, 64
  knaves 56, 57–8, 61
  knights 56–7, 61
  market incentives 55–6
  models of 48–50, 188
  non-profit organisations 62–4
  robust incentives 64–5
  *see also* incentive schemes
Sherraden, Michael, and Individual
    Development Accounts 138–9
Singapore, demogrant 123
Smart, Gavin, and house ownership 130
Smith, Adam 12, 27, 165
social democracy:
  agency 13–14
  markets 12, 13–14
  motivation 13–14
  public policy 11–16
social insurance 162
  hypothecation 150–1
  long-term care 142
  *see also* insurance; national insurance
social investment state 15–16
social policy, quasi-market revolution 3, 98,
    109–15
social security, recipients and choice 7
stakeholder grants, *see* demogrant
state, the:
  corruption of altruism 48–50
  distrust of 149

influence on motivation 46–7
intervention in individual savings 86–91
matching grants 139, 140–1
moral atrophy 46–7
provision of social services 3
Steele, Jane, and management motivation 31–2
Steuart, James 165
Sweden, quasi-market 10, 176

Tanner, Sarah, youth wealth 128
taxation:
  citizen powerlessness 148–9
  hypothecated 133, 150–7, 161–2
  inheritance 121, 133–5
  morality of 147
  pawns 147, 206
  pension provision 137
  public attitudes towards 149–50, 151–2
  resistance to redistributive 8–9, 205
  revenues and agency 147–50
  savings 139, 197
  tax relief 139–40
  tax resistance 151–2
Taylor, Jim, impact of educational reform
    113–14
Taylor-Gooby, Peter, and dentists'
    motivation 33
teachers, and behaviour 35, 172
Thatcher, Margaret 9, 181
third way 15–16
Timmins, Nicholas, crisis with national
    insurance 160
Titmuss, Richard 4, 6, 7, 8, 13, 168, 170–1, 176
  altruistic supply 65, 175, 192
  blood donation 31, 40–2
  individualism 14
  limitations of markets 41
  public service ethos 24, 174
  *The Gift Relationship* 31, 40–2, 175, 190–1
trust:
  altruism 29–30
  network model of service delivery 48–50
  public sector 80–1
  tax policy 148

Unger, Roberto, and demogrant 122–3
United States:
  charitable giving 37–8
  competition amongst schools 114
  demogrant 122–3
  public service motivation 34, 176
  quasi-market 10
universal benefits, and demogrant 131–2

Van Parijs, Philippe, and basic income 123
Vandenberghe, Vincent, and Belgian
    education reform 115
Vesterlund, Lise 44
voice 103, 204
  empowerment 82–3
volunteers:
  impact of financial incentives 43–4
  public perception of 54–5
voucher system:
  education 108, 180
  positively discriminating 116, 174

Ware, Alan, and corruption of altruism 40
Webber, Caroline, and hypothecation 156
Weisskopf, Thomas 54
  exploitation 65
welfare, and asset ownership 125
welfare state:
  assumptions behind 3–11, 171
  democratic socialist influence 4–5
  effects of compulsion 138
  ideological influences 11–16

market mechanisms 9–10
moral atrophy 46–7
post-war origins 4–5, 170, 191
quasi-market revolution 3, 9–10, 98
roles of actors within 5–7, 182
savings 87
standardization challenged 7–8
Wesley, John 30
West, Anne, impact of educational reform
    109–10
West, Cornel, and demogrant 122–3
White, Stuart, financial training 131
Wildavsky, Aaron, and hypothecation 156, 172
Wilson, Deborah 35
Winter, David 8
Wolpert, Julian, and charitable giving 38
women, and altruism 44–5
Woods, Philip, impact of school
    competition 113
Wright, Karen, and character of charitable
    giving 37 n. 18

youth, asset poverty of 128